Trisha

Business Intermediate

GNVQ

Contents

Introduction iii

Unit 1 **Business organisations and employment** 1

Unit 2 **People in business organisations** 51

Unit 3 **Consumers and customers** 99

Unit 4 **Financial and administrative support** 147

Index 196

LONGMAN

This book is part of the Longman Business GNVQ series

Series Editor **Kittie Lambers**

Advisors and Critical Readers	Judy Boyce	*Broad Green Community School. Intermediate and Foundation level series advisor*
	Ian Chambers	*Advisor for Business and Careers Education, Tameside*
	Martin Jephcote	*School of Education, University of Wales, Cardiff*
	Marija Kontic	*Colne Community College*
	Susan Squires	*General Advisor (Economics and Business Studies), Metropolitan Borough of Sefton*
	Yvonne Feagan	*Pendyford High School, Wolverhampton*
	Margaret Hendrick	*South Thames College*
	Howard Pilot	*Hackney Community College*
	Sally Wood	*Harlow College*

LONGMAN GROUP LIMITED
Longman House, Burnt Mill, Harlow, Essex, CM20 2JE,
England and Associated Companies throughout the World.

First published 1995
ISBN 0 582 27427 3

Design: Gecko Ltd, Bicester, Oxon.
Set in Zurich and New Baskerville in QuarkXpress 3.3 on the Apple Macintosh.
Printed in Great Britain by Butler & Tanner Limited, Frome and London.

The publisher's policy is to use paper manufactured from sustainable forests.

Introduction

This book covers the four mandatory vocational units of the Intermediate GNVQ in Business. The four chapters include all the skills, knowledge and understanding outlined in the specifications for these four units.

They are outlined briefly below.

Unit 1: Business organisations and employment
A wide range of different businesses exist to produce goods and services to meet consumers' needs and wants. These provide employment opportunities.

This unit encourages you to investigate different businesses and find out more about their purposes and activities, and to look at current trends in employment.

Unit 2: People in business organisations
Understanding how organisational structures influence the way businesses operate can enable changes in working arrangements which encourage for example increased productivity or better team working.

This unit looks at job roles and activities in organisations, and covers legislation relating to employment, focusing on equal opportunities and health and safety. The unit presents opportunities to plan for employment or self-employment.

Unit 3: Consumers and customers
Without customers and consumers creating demand for particular products, businesses would not exist. Buying habits often change with time, and businesses need to be aware of underlying causes and trends in demand.

This unit considers how businesses communicate with their customers to meet the customers' needs, evaluating the promotional materials produced to market products, and the customer service that businesses provide.

Unit 4: Financial and administrative support
Practical financial and adminstrative skills help business organistions run smoothly and efficiently, and it is essential to have accurate records

of buying and selling transactions to monitor how a business is performing.

This unit covers the documents used in financial transactions, their purpose, accurate completion, and methods of processing and storage.

Format and approach

This book has been prepared in order to promote active, independent learning. The units are based on the NCVQ units which form the award, and are further divided into sections reflecting the elements. Each unit, as well as fully covering the performance criteria, range and evidence indicators in the standards, also contains activities and assignments to encourage you to test out what you know, and to think about applications for what you are learning. The activities are self-contained tasks which might test new knowledge and understanding, involve group or pair discussion, role playing, or looking at or analysing further information. Assignments are larger, research-type activities which require you to investigate a particualr aspect of the topic you are studying. These are usually closely linked to the evidence indicators for each element, providing the opportunity to collect work for assessment.

Core skills

You are encouraged to incorporate core skills into your work for the vocational units. This aim is reflected in the units of this book. Assignments and activities are constructed so that there is adequate opportunity for you to cover core skills. The symbol © indicates that core skills can be covered by doing the work suggested; the type of core skill is indicated by C (Communication), AN (Application of number), or IT (Information technology).

Longman Induction booklets

You may find it helpful to look at the booklet *Introduction to GNVQ Business: Intermediate level* before you start work on the programme. This booklet contains detailed information about GNVQs, their structure, assessment and grading opportunities, as well as case studies and suggestions of how to approach GNVQ work through the *Longman Study Units*. Students and teachers will find it a useful introduction to GNVQs in general, and the Business programme in particular.

Intermediate Level: Unit 1

Business organisations and employment

G N V Q

Contents

Introduction	2
1 **Purposes and types of business organisations**	2
2 **The business environment**	21
3 **Employment**	35
Summary	46
Answers to activities	48
Glossary	49

LONGMAN

Introduction

All businesses exist for a reason – the most usual is to make a profit for the owners. But what is a business? Why is it located in one place and not in another? What are its links with other businesses? This unit will help you to increase your understanding of business purposes, their activities and their links with employment opportunities.

You will see that industry can be described according to sector in the economy and businesses according to ownership and purpose. Changing trends in sizes of sectors and businesses, in employment opportunities as well as in types of employment are explained. You will be asked to research trends in employment and demand for a new product.

1 Purposes and types of business organisations

In this first part of Unit 1 you will look at the two main types of business sector – the private sector and the public sector – and their different purposes. Many different types of business organisation exist in the UK and these can be grouped according to industrial sector or industry. Developments and trends in industrial sectors are described and you will be investigating one business and its links with other businesses.

UK economy

In the UK there are over 2 million business organisations formed to meet the demand for goods (products) and services. Every individual has wants and needs which are satisfied by businesses that provide goods or services – that is, they make things or do things.

Activity

In a small group, discuss some wants and needs. Think of 'needs' as the essentials of life, i.e. at the top of people's shopping lists, and 'wants' as luxuries.

'Needs' usually include food, housing and clothing. You may have argued that items such as education, health care and public transport are also necessities of life. A society's views about what are basic needs alters with changes in standards of living. 'Wants' usually include fashionable clothes, holidays and labour-saving devices.

In the UK products and services are produced by both the public and private sectors. This is called a *mixed economy*. The private or market sector is made up of largely profit-making organisations. The **public sector** is financed and managed by central and local government.

The **private sector** produces a wide range of goods and services in order to satisfy consumer demand. These may range from basic foodstuffs to exotic holidays, from designer clothes to TV game shows.

The public sector is largely concerned with producing essential items that society and the private sector may not produce in the right quantity, the right quality or at the right time. These include education, health services and policing.

A third sector includes charitable and non-profit-making organisations.

Business purposes

It is important to distinguish between the different purposes of these types of business as it helps to explain their activities within the economy.

To make a profit

Profit is the surplus remaining from **sales revenue** after all costs have been deducted.

For the majority of businesses profit making is a number one priority. Generally, the owner wishes to maximise profit which means that every decision is taken to increase profits.

Profit is an important objective or purpose because it:

- ensures the long-term survival of the business
- is the major source of finance for future investment
- rewards shareholders with dividends and employees with higher wages
- provides funds to research into the improvement of the product

While profit may be the main purpose for most businesses, some may have other objectives, particularly in the short term, which are more important.

Virgin Atlantic broke into the trans-Atlantic passenger market by offering cheap, no-frills flights to a limited number of American cities.
Netto and Aldi supermarkets have attempted to win part of the retail market by offering a limited range of cheaper products.

To establish market share

A new business, for example, may see securing a permanent foothold in the **market** as its primary objective. To achieve this the business could offer its products at a price that covers its costs, i.e. it justs breaks even, for example, through limited-period special offers often associated with the opening of a business. The aim is to attract customers away from other firms or products and to build a regular customer base.

In the early 1990s the telecommunications company Mercury tried to win a share of the market from BT by offering lower charges for long-distance and overseas phone calls.

To provide essential services

The purpose of the public sector is to achieve maximum benefit for the general public, not to maximise profit. The government intervenes in the economy in order to:

- guarantee that certain 'public goods' are provided for all, for example defence, street lighting, policing and the judiciary.
- guarantee the provision of goods that the government believes add to the quality of life, for example, education, health care, municipal housing, leisure services – these are called **merit goods**.
- take account of the **social costs** of business.
- redistribute income – some services are provided free or at minimal cost so that lower-income groups share in the wealth of the nation. The services are largely paid for out of general taxation which aims to be progressive, meaning that wealthier groups contribute more. Examples include library services, community centres and swimming pools.
- to provide uneconomic services, such as rural rail services. It is in the wider public interest to provide these so as to reduce road congestion and not to penalise those living in the country.
- to deliver 'value for money'. **Public corporations** are expected to, at least, break even over a number of years and where possible to make enough profit to finance new investment.

British Rail is expected to make a rate of return of 7 per cent on any new investment such as the rail link to the Channel Tunnel. In recent years even government departments have been given service targets which must be met within an authorised budget.

Activity

1 **As a group, list some of the public services provided by:**
  a central government
  b local government.

2 **How many of these are paid for by taxation but provided:**
  a free to all
  b free to some sections of society?

3 **Discuss the merits of providing medical and dental services free of charge to all citizens whatever their age or income.**

You could have identified subsidised services such as prescription charges, entry to local leisure facilities, school meals and the hire of public buildings. You may have argued that wealthier citizens should pay the full cost despite the fact that they have paid taxes on their income.

Did you realise that none of the services are really 'free' as they have to be paid for out of taxation?

In the UK there are over 170,000 charities, controlled by the Charity Commissioners under the 1992 Charities Act. Charitable trusts may be set up for a range of local and national purposes such as poverty relief, education, conservation, medical research and assistance with disabilities. The charity sector accounts for more than £17 billion of funds each year.

To help others

Non-profit-making organisations and charities exist primarily to help their members or specifically defined groups. Charitable organisations exist to raise funds and to provide services for particular causes. For example, the purpose of the Guide Dogs for the Blind Society is to provide and train dogs for people with impaired vision.

Activity

In pairs, design and complete a table that lists at least ten charities. Include the following information:

- the name of the charity
- its purpose
- the type of fund-raising activities associated with the charity
- publicity/marketing methods used by the charity.

Information about charities can be found in the local library, from local authority centres or direct from the charity itself. Newspapers and magazines often carry advertisements appealing for donations or volunteer help.

Non-profit basis

One of the best-known non-profit-making organisations is the **cooperative** movement. Founded in the nineteenth century its purpose is to provide good value for money to the benefit of its members.

Mission statement

The mission statement of Scottish Power
'Our strategy is to optimise our core electricity operations, making them of world-class standard; to expand our existing business; and to look for and develop opportunities in related activities' – Scottish Power annual review, 1994

The purpose of the company must be clearly defined if the business is to focus its resources successfully. The principal objective is normally given in a brief one or two sentence statement called the **mission statement**. This provides a summary of the company's long-term targets.

For large multi-national companies the purpose may be concerned with international growth, expanding market share and development of new foreign markets for their products. For a small corner shop the purpose may be to survive and make a reasonable profit.

Small businesses

Over 96 per cent of all firms employ fewer than 100 people and the majority of those employ fewer than ten workers.

Most businesses in the UK are small, single units catering for the needs of a local market.

A small, single business is likely to be a sole trader, partnership or private limited company, mainly concerned with generating profits for the owner.

Case study

Leather World is a small retail and manufacturing business started by two design students, Howard Bates and Lynne Robinson.

a small shop in a side street of a busy market town in the Midlands. They sell a wide range of genuine leather products, many of them designed and made on the premises and ranging in price from a couple of pounds for a bookmark to several hundred pounds for a hand-tooled satchel. Their designs and products are aimed at the younger market, although the more expensive items have a wider appeal. Lynne does most of the design work and manages the shop, while Howard makes the products and buys in the raw materials and some ready-made goods. All profits are shared equally. They now sell to other retailers in neighbouring towns and employ two production workers and a part-time sales assistant.

Activity

The rest of this section will help you to judge and classify a business more accurately.

1 **Analyse the operation of Leather World.**
  - **a** What is the purpose of Howard and Lynne's business?
  - **b** What market are they in and who are their products aimed at?
  - **c** What type of business organisation is it?
  - **d** How can you estimate its size?

2 **Select three small businesses in your area and describe each organisation's purpose, product, intended market and approximate size as indicated by the numbers employed.**

Industrial sectors

Trends

Changes are identified through information over time about sales, (un)employment levels or the rate of inflation. Changes in the three industrial sectors can also be described by using figures for:

- output – the volume or value of the goods and services produced
- employment – the number of workers in the industry.

It is easier to describe the trend in terms of percentage change, rather than use actual totals.

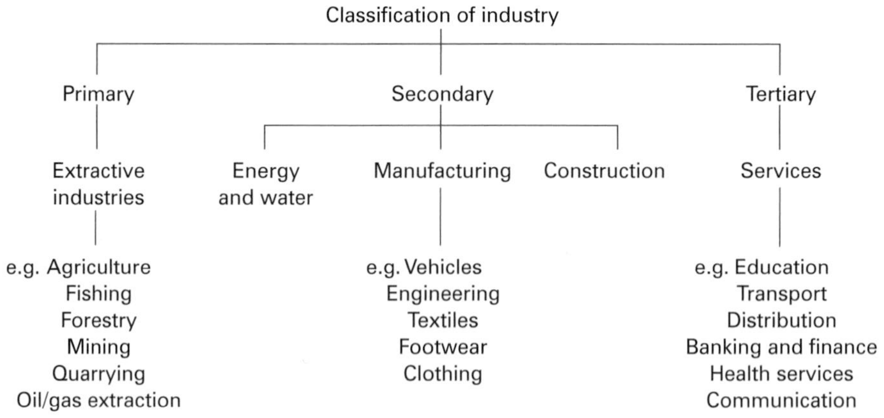

Businesses belong to one of three industrial sectors – primary, secondary or tertiary. Each sector has its own activities, trends and likely future developments.

The following factors influence change and development in each of the sectors and may cause expansion, decline or adaptation:

- Consumer demand for improved, higher quality products, greater choice and good value for money.

- Competition from those firms that adapt.
- Government policies and regulations regarding the quality, safety and promotion of products.
- Concern about the environmental effects of production.
- Rapid changes in technology.

The primary sector

Most goods start life as some form of raw material, taken from the ground, the sea or the fields. The main divisions of the **primary sector** are:

- mining and quarrying
- mineral oil and natural gas extraction
- agriculture, forestry and fishing.

Activity

Gross Domestic Product is the total value of a country's output over the course of a year

1 **Look at the table showing the primary sector between 1983 and 1993. What has happened to the sector**

a in actual terms

b as a percentage of Gross Domestic Product (see below)?

2 **How important is agriculture to the UK economy? Work out your answer as a percentage.**

Now check your answers with those given at the end of this study unit.

Gross Domestic Product by industry: primary sector £m

	1983	***1988***	***1993***
Agriculture, hunting forestry and fishing	5,429	7,153	10,373
Mining, quarrying, oil and gas extraction	20,234	10,866	12,147
Total primary sector	25,663	18,019	22,520
Gross Domestic Product	261,225	401,428	546,120

Source: Central Statistical Office

Mining and quarrying for stone products and coal

In recent years coal production has steadily declined as it has become more economical to import cheap surface-mined coal rather than extract it from the UK's deep mines. The production of electricity has also been switched to nuclear power and gas.

Mineral oil and natural gas extraction

The decline in mining has been partly offset by the rapid rise in the output of oil and natural gas from the North Sea in the 1970s and 1980s.

The future importance of this sector depends on the successful exploitation of further fields in the North Sea and the newly found fields off the west coast of Scotland.

Agriculture, forestry and fishing

The future for many small farming units, particularly low-productivity ones, such as hill farms, is not promising. The trend is for larger, more efficient commercial farms to be the main survivors as European Union (EU) subsidies are gradually scaled back.

Agriculture in the UK experienced growth in the 1960s and 1970s. But since 1984 agriculture has declined and by the 1990s it contributed less than 1 per cent of the UK's GDP.

The primary sector as a whole has generally declined since the 1960s. In 1964 it provided 5.8 per cent of the UK's total output, but by 1988 it produced only 3.8 per cent, of which 1.8 per cent was provided by oil and gas. In terms of employment, the primary sector created 5.1 per cent of all jobs in 1964, with more than 1.2 million employed. By 1988 this had fallen to 474,000, just over 2 per cent of all employment. The long-term trend is for this sector gradually to become less important as a creator of output and employment in the UK.

Activity

For this activity you will need to find data on the UK economy for the last 20 years. This is available in the publications of the Central Statistical Office (CSO), particularly in the *Blue Book*. This is the main source for details of the annual breakdown of national income and expenditure. Other good sources include *Economic Trends*, *Monthly Digest of Statistics* and the *Employment Gazette*.

Produce a report on a word processor showing developments in three different activities in the primary sector. The report should include data taken from some of the publications listed above. You will need to describe:

- typical activities in the sector
- the current growth or decline of selected industries
- the approximate value of the sector in the national economy.

At the end of the report list the resources you have used.

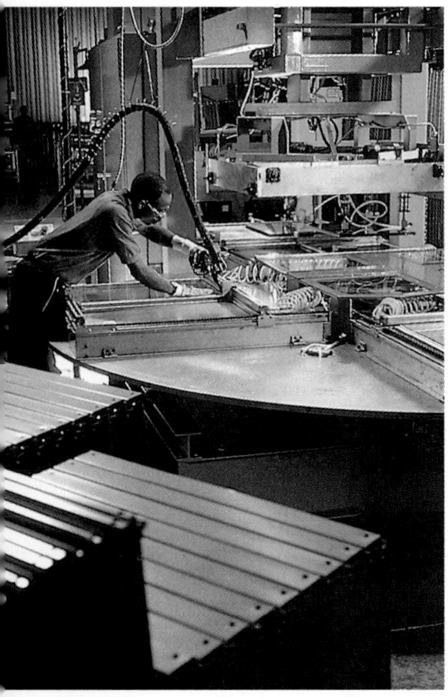

You may have found the above task quite difficult without some guidance and assistance. The amount of data available is huge and the way it is presented can be confusing. Even so, you should have been able to see that the primary sector is gradually becoming less important as a wealth generator or employment creator in the UK. This can be demonstrated by looking at the output figures, the sector's share of GDP or the numbers employed in the industry.

The secondary sector

The processing or manufacture to convert raw materials into products is known as secondary activity.

2.3 AN **C** **Activity**

1 **Look at the table showing the secondary sector between 1983 and 1993. What has happened to the sector**
   a in actual terms
   b as a percentage of Gross Domestic Product?

2 **Comment on the importance of the secondary sector.**

3 **Look at the figures for manufacturing in the table, then answer the same questions as for the secondary sector.**

Now check your answers with those given at the end of this study unit.

Gross Domestic Product by industry: secondary sector £m

	1983	*1988*	*1993*
Manufacturing	64,738	100,232	118,294
Electricity, gas and water supply	8,682	10,263	13,994
Construction	15,929	28,093	29,221
Total secondary sector	89,349	138,588	161,509
Gross Domestic Product	261,225	401,428	546,120

Source: Central Statistical Office

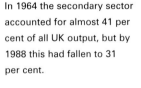

In 1964 the secondary sector accounted for almost 41 per cent of all UK output, but by 1988 this had fallen to 31 per cent.

Until 1973 output from both manufacturing and construction rose steadily at annual rates of 2.9 per cent and 1.8 per cent respectively. This growth was sharply reversed in the recession of the 1970s. By 1981 manufacturing and construction were operating at the same levels as in the mid-1960s. Since then manufacturing output has grown slowly, but its relative share of GDP has fallen, especially when compared to the growth seen in the services sector.

Overall, the secondary sector has become less important in terms of output and employment.

The tertiary sector

The products of the primary and secondary sectors need to be distributed to consumers. The services of transport, wholesaling and retailing perform that function. In turn, industry needs support from banking, insurance, education, communications and administration. All of these make up the **tertiary sector**.

2.3 AN **C** **Activity**

Look at the table showing the tertiary sector between 1983 and 1993.

a What is the growth of the sector as a percentage of GDP?

b Which industries within this sector have grown the most?

Now check your answers with those given at the end of this study unit.

The tertiary sector includes:

- wholesale and retail trade
- hotels and restaurants
- transport
- storage
- banking
- public administration
- real estate
- national defence
- education
- health services
- insurance
- social work
- refuse collection.

Gross Domestic Product by industry: tertiary sector £m

	1983	***1988***	***1993***
Wholesale and retail trade	33,491	55,862	78,348
Transport, storage and communication	19,727	34,072	46,263
Financial intermediation, real estate, renting and business activities	49,645	87,917	133,956
Public administration, national defence and compulsory social security	18,599	26,000	38,199
Education, health and social work	22,997	36,473	57,457
Other services, including sewage and refuse disposal	13,752	22,086	31,292
Total tertiary sector	158,211	262,410	385,515
Gross Domestic Product	261,225	401,428	546,120

Source: Central Statistical Office

Communications and financial services – finance, insurance, banking, business services and leasing – were the major contributors to expansion in the tertiary sector between 1964 and 1988. Financial services now account for one-fifth and services in general for two-thirds of all UK output. This is also reflected in employment which has grown from just over 11 million in 1964 to 15.5 million in 1988.

In general, three trends can be seen in UK business activity:

- a small primary sector accounting for less than 2 per cent of all activity
- a secondary sector declining in importance
- a growing service sector.

Distribution of GDP in the major industrial market economies

	% of GDP	
	1960	***1985***
Primary sector	6	3
Secondary sector	40	36
of which manufacturing	30	23
Tertiary sector	54	61

Source: World Bank

The table shows the decline of primary and secondary sectors and the expansion of the service sector in all of the industrial market economies.

Companies such as Nissan, Pioneer, Toyota, BMW and Samsung have shown confidence in the British economy by establishing new production plants in the UK.

Within the secondary sector manufacturing has declined much more than in other countries. This trend has worried economists, businesses and the government as it leads to job losses and increased imports. It is hoped that the recent improvements in productivity and the growth of inward investment from abroad will slow or reverse the trend.

Types of business ownership

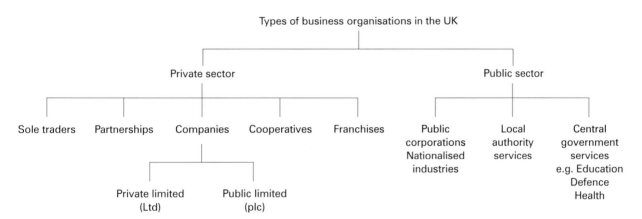

Types of business organisations in the UK

- Private sector
  - Sole traders
  - Partnerships
  - Companies
    - Private limited (Ltd)
    - Public limited (plc)
  - Cooperatives
  - Franchises
- Public sector
  - Public corporations Nationalised industries
  - Local authority services
  - Central government services e.g. Education Defence Health

There are many types of business unit ranging from the local self-employed sole trader to worldwide multi-national organisations. Each type of business has a role to play in the modern economy. The next section explores the purpose of each and the differences between them.

Private sector

Unincorporated businesses include all those where the owners are liable personally for debts. It is mainly made up of sole traders and partnerships.

The private sector is the part of the economy operated by firms that are owned by shareholders or private individuals.

Sole traders

A sole trader is the simplest form of business unit as there are few legal formalities necessary to start and little capital required. Sole traders are often found in activities where personal service is important and where large-scale production would be uneconomic. Examples include local retailers – grocers, butchers, newsagents, florists; local services – hairdressers, window cleaners, restaurants, garages; and local manufacturing – self-employed crafts people, small engineering companies.

Custom-made clothes

If trading under a name other than that of the sole trader, the business must register with the Registrar of Business Names. Depending on the type and size of

Sole traders are the most common form of business organisation but only account for a small percentage of the total output and sales in the UK. They are, however, important sources of employment, particularly in remote and rural areas. They also provide many of the personal and specialist services that large firms ignore.

activity, the owner may require a licence and to register with the Inland Revenue and HM Customs and Excise for VAT.

In general, the sole trader provides the capital for the business, bears all the risk and makes all the decisions. One of the main incentives, however, is that all the rewards in the form of profits belong to the sole trader.

This type of business has advantages and disadvantages for both the owner and the customer. Advantages for the owner:

- Business details may be kept private.
- The business is easy to establish.
- The owner has independence.
- The owner receives all of the profit.
- The owner generally has flexibility when making decisions.

Disadvantages include:

- **unlimited liability** – all losses are borne by the owner
- may lack business skills
- potentially long hours of work, especially in the early years
- potential lack of continuity of business
- limited capital for expansion
- historically, a high failure rate (approximately 40 per cent of all new businesses fail in the first two years).

Case study

Tony and Andrea Mason took over a small newsagents/general store in the late 1980s, situated on the outskirts of a large housing estate. It attracted a regular flow of customers for daily needs such as fresh food, newspapers and groceries. Tony and Andrea improved and extended the service by adding videos and a fresh-meat counter. A typical day involved Tony collecting the papers at 5 a.m., organising the newspaper deliverers and serving in the shop for the first few hours until relieved by Andrea and day staff. Tony then had to check the stock, order deliveries and collect goods from the wholesaler. Andrea combined duties in the shop with administering the accounts and dealing with the paperwork. The store stayed open until 10 p.m., seven days a week. This is typical of many sole traders in the retail sector.

Activity

Look in the advertisement section of your local newspaper and draw up a list of sole traders and their occupations. What special claims do they make about their businesses that would give them an advantage over larger organisations?

Activity

Nearly 19 per cent of all units in the retail sector are sole traders. Produce a survey of your local shopping area. This can be done as a group activity dividing the area into smaller sections. Individually, report on:

- names and activities of at least ten retail businesses
- the percentage that are sole traders
- the number of staff working in the sole trader outlets (remember that sole traders may still employ other people as assistants, for example in a florist or a newsagents)
- the number of years each sole trader has been operating.

Partnerships

A partnership is a legal form of business organisation where two or more people trade together under the Partnership Act of 1890. Many of the difficulties associated with being a sole trader may be overcome by forming a partnership. As the partners still have unlimited liability – each partner is liable for the debts of the other partners – it is common for partnerships to exist in family businesses or in professional areas such as law, insurance, accountancy and medicine.

Usually, the rights and responsibilities of each partner are written down in a partnership agreement, although this is not required by law. The agreement states:

- the capital supplied by each partner
- the sharing of profits and losses
- the voting rights of partners
- the rules for admittance and expulsion of partners
- the arrangements for dissolving the partnership.

Case study

CB Security is a small firm specialising in fitting, upgrading and servicing house-alarm systems. As a sole trader Chris Broom built up the business to one that employs seven people, two installation teams of three and a secretary/telephonist. In recent months Chris has found it very difficult to visit all of the prospective customers to provide quotes and handle the administration and accounts. This has resulted in some customers going elsewhere, quotations being sent out late and invoices and payments not kept up to date. Chris has also identified a larger, more central site for his workshop and office, but it would require a business loan. Most of Chris's profits have been ploughed back into buying more stock, equipment and vehicles. He is now considering forming a partnership, especially as he recently identified a growing market in the area for sophisticated alarm systems for industrial premises. He cannot explore this market without sacrificing time devoted at present to administration or visiting domestic customers.

Activity

Read the case study and draw up a list of advantages and disadvantages of Chris Broom expanding by forming a partnership. Identify the skills and resources that the new partner should possess.

Your analysis should have highlighted that partnerships allow businesses to bring in new people who can offer extra expertise, more capital or just share responsibility and workload. How many of the following did you identify as applying to Chris Broom's situation?
Advantages:

- injection of extra capital
- division of labour – specialists can be brought in such as an accountant, sales manager and purchasing manager
- shared responsibility – cover for illness, holidays and absence

- easy to establish
- business affairs still kept private

Disadvantages:

- unlimited liability
- disagreements over decision making and control
- lack of continuity as partners change and new agreements required
- limited to a maximum of 20 partners, except for solicitors, accountants and other specially exempted groups

Incorporated businesses

By **incorporation** a business establishes a separate legal entity. The main disadvantages of unincorporated businesses are a lack of capital (money put into the business) and unlimited liability. The Liability Act of 1855 and subsequent Companies Acts solved these problems by allowing the creation of a 'limited company' (sometimes referred to as a joint stock company).

Incorporated businesses differ from unincorporated ones in the following ways:

- Limited liability – shareholders are only liable for the value of the shares that they own.
- Incorporation – the company becomes a separate legal entity independent of its shareholders. The company can therefore own property, sue and be sued in its own right.
- Share capital – the company can raise capital by selling shares which provides it with extra finance for the business.
- Legislation – the company is subject to stricter legal control under the Companies Act regarding published accounts and registration.

The name of the company must be registered with the Registrar of Companies and it must have the word 'Limited' – often abbreviated to 'Ltd' – at the end. There are over half a million private limited companies in the UK ranging in size from small local businesses to multi-million pound concerns such as Littlewoods.

Limited company (Ltd) – This type of business must have at least two shareholders. They are not allowed to sell shares to the general public, but must offer them on a private basis. This is the type of business often chosen by family concerns as shares cannot be sold without the agreement of the other shareholders.

A limited company is formed to encourage people to invest in larger businesses with a fairly small amount of risk. The owners are only financially responsible for the amount invested in the company rather than risking their personal wealth. It is also a means of expanding the business by raising extra capital. Without the guarantee of limited liability, it would prove very difficult to persuade people, particularly outsiders, to invest in a business or a planned expansion.

Public limited company (plc) – Most public limited companies (plcs) start life as private companies which go 'public' in order to raise further capital for development and expansion. Again, there is a wide range of sizes from small local firms to multi-nationals such as ICI, BT and Glaxo. Although small in number, they account for most of the turnover, employment and capital investment in the UK. The principal purpose of creating a plc is to raise large amounts of capital to fund future expansion. This involves offering shares to the general public through a listing on the stock exchange.

Activity

1 **Identify the main differences between a limited company and a public limited company and discuss why businesses move from one form to another.**

2 **If you were the main shareholder in a large, family business what objections might you raise against a proposal to become a plc? What would be the benefits?**

Your discussion might have identified objections such as loss of control, the need to bring in specialists from outside the family, the expense involved and the risk of takeover. On the other hand, you might have suggested a number of benefits, including easier and cheaper availability of capital, the savings associated with increased production and the opportunity to expand operations. You may have listed the following advantages:

- limited liability
- easier to raise large amounts of capital (share capital or loan capital)
- shares transferable on the stock exchange
- **economies of scale**
- continuity guaranteed.

In fact, very few limited companies ever think about making the change to a plc.

Cooperatives

Principles of the cooperative movement:
- Anyone may become a member
- Each member is limited to one vote
- Members decide on profit distribution
- Members control the operation of the business

A cooperative is an organisation run by a group of people who each provide the finance, are involved in decision making and take a share of the profits. Cooperatives may be either retail, worker, employee or producer. They are organised largely for the benefit of their members.

The cooperative movement is important because it accounts for about 10 per cent of all turnover in the UK. Retail cooperatives had total sales in excess of £7 billion in 1993 and employed 81,000 people. In a similar way, the Cooperative Wholesale Society which supplies the retail stores had a turnover of £3.3 billion and employed over 40,000 workers.

Cooperative Retail Services (CRS) is the largest co-op in the UK with a turnover of £1 billion

Franchises

In 1976 Anita Roddick opened the first Body Shop in Brighton selling a range of natural cosmetics and toiletries. The bright window displays, prominent location sites and natural products were an instant success. In order to expand quickly, The Body Shop decided to **franchise** its products. This meant that it allowed other businesses – franchisees – to buy the rights to sell The Body Shop's branded goods. In exchange for an initial fee and a percentage of sales (royalties) the **franchisee** was given an area within which the franchise had sole permission to sell. The Body Shop – **the franchiser** – supplies the products, organises national advertising and provides management support. A franchise, therefore, is a business based on the name, advertising and trading method of an existing successful business.

Franchising is a major growth area in the UK economy. In 1992 there were over 100 different franchises registered with the British Franchise Association with nearly 19,000 retail outlets and a turnover of more than £5 billion.

BRITISH FRANCHISE ASSOCIATION

Examples of franchises are The Body Shop, McDonald's, Fast Frame, Kwik Fit, Tie Rack, Kall Kwik, Prontoprint, Dyno Rod, Kentucky Fried Chicken, Pizza Hut, Spar and Benetton.

Advantages for the franchisee include:

- the use of the trade name of the franchise
- the opportunity to sell well-known products or services
- an exclusive market area
- support in marketing, training and finance
- an established design of the retail layout.

Activity

1 **Visit a local franchise or find some information on franchising and briefly identify the advantages and disadvantages for:**

a the franchisee

b the franchiser.

2 **As a group, interview owners of several franchises and then compare the responses. Find out the backgrounds of the franchisees and their reasons for choosing a franchise as a means of starting a business.**

You may have found that some of the owners had limited business experience and therefore a franchise offered them the following advantages:

- tried and tested trading method
- less risk as the franchiser is already successful
- national advertising
- professional support
- consumer loyalty attached to the product.

Franchises are less risky than setting up on your own and have a much lower failure rate than other forms of business startup. There are, however, a number of disadvantages :

- limited area of operation
- annual fee based on total sales
- all supplies purchased through franchiser
- strict control on layout and decor.

Franchises are not limited to retailing, but may include manufacturing as well. The soft drinks giants Coca-Cola and Pepsi-Cola franchise the making of their products as do sportswear firms such as Adidas and Nike.

State-owned businesses: the public sector

The public sector is made up of public corporations (nationalised industries), government departments (for example, the Department of Health) and local government services (for example, council-run leisure centres). The emphasis here is not on making a profit but on providing a service for the community. Increasingly, this objective has become more commercialised with government agencies having to operate within strict budget guidelines and to rely on cost savings for extra funding rather than on increased government subsidy.

Public corporations

A public corporation or nationalised industry is an enterprise which is owned by the state but offers a product or service to the general consumer. Examples include British Rail, the Bank of England, the BBC and the Post Office. The main features of a public corporation are:

- It has a separate legal identity.
- It is responsible to a government minister for the industry and overall strategy.
- A chairperson and board oversee the day-to-day running.
- Its assets are owned by the government.
- It is watched over by a consumer council to protect the interests of customers.
- It is subject to investigation by a Select Committee of MPs.
- Financial targets, such as a return on capital, are set.
- It must take account of wider social issues.
- It may be audited for efficiency by the Audit Commission.

Local authority undertakings

These are the many services provided by local authorities for the benefit of the local community. They are partly funded by central government grants, local taxes, business rates, borrowing and sometimes charges. Examples include education, the fire, police and ambulance services, parks, libraries, housing and leisure facilities. Some of these services are provided free of charge to the user, such as libraries and refuse collection, but others may charge a small or a commercial fee, such as swimming pools and leisure centres.

Business links

Any business, no matter how large, is only one small part of the total economy. Businesses are affected by changes in the economy over which they have little or no control. Each business must know what is likely to affect it and how to react to changes in society and in the economy.

The general business environment

The business environment is made up of all the factors which lie outside an individual firm's control, but which have an effect on its business performance.

Activity

As a group, hold a brainstorming session to identify all the factors that can affect a business. Write down your answers – as single words or short phrases – on a large sheet. When you have run out of ideas, take each of your answers and talk about how it could affect the business. Remember, some factors may have a direct effect on customers which then indirectly affects sales, for example, changes in interest rates.

Your discussion will have shown that all firms operate in a dynamic business environment. How many of the factors you listed could be included in one of the following categories?

- Technology – developing technologies lead to new products. For example, in the music industry compact disks and cassettes have largely replaced records.
- Government legislation – new laws and regulations about safety, pollution and advertising must be followed or the business will face criticism, fines or even closure.
- Demography – the size and age composition of the population is an important influence on the market. With an ageing population the demand for private health care, retirement homes and nursing homes has greatly increased.
- Economic and financial climate – changes in interest rates, taxation and exchange rates can create a boom or a recession. The high interest rates of the late 1980s created a long, deep recession during which many firms closed because of falling sales and rising financial costs.
- Consumer pressure groups – the general public is more aware of environmental concerns and is now likely to put pressure on businesses to follow acceptable practices. The fear of further damage to the ozone layer led to some consumers boycotting aerosol products that contained CFCs. Businesses producing these goods were forced to react quickly or face falling sales.

- Competition – the behaviour of competitors can greatly influence a firm's activities. The price cutting of own-brand cola drinks by leading supermarkets forced Coca-Cola and Pepsi-Cola to adopt a more aggressive strategy on pricing.

Case study: Nissan
Nissan chose Sunderland as its main European assembly base because the area had a pool of unemployed labour, good access to the UK market via the motorway network and a route to mainland Europe through the east coast ports. Nissan particularly wanted to expand into Europe, but faced a limit on imported cars from Japan. By building in the UK, Nissan can claim that its cars are British manufactured and so has unlimited access to the rich market of the European Union. Sunderland satisfied Nissan's objectives with respect to location, market and future growth.

The local business environment

As well as being aware of the general economic environment and how it can affect performance a business must also decide on:

- location – the particular area it is to produce and sell in
- target market – the goods or services that it wants to produce for its identified customers
- company objectives – the short-, medium- and long-term goals that it wants to achieve.

Case study

Running Free is a newly opened, dedicated running sports shop catering for the total requirements of athletes and fun-runners. Philippa North, the owner, is a keen cross-country runner who was dissatisfied with the service of general sports shops. She identified a gap in the market for a specialist running shop located midway between Leeds and Bradford which would serve the whole of West and North Yorkshire. Philippa had to set up links with a wide range of organisations. To begin with she had to establish trading terms with a large number of sports suppliers. These included not only well-known brand names such as Nike, Adidas and Puma but small firms that supplied the more unusual items like maps, running guides and books. She had to negotiate the terms of supply, which included discounts, delivery times and periods of credit. It was also important to establish links with potential customers. These included athletics clubs, schools and the local sports clubs. Nearby housing estates were targeted to receive a discount leaflet on a rotational basis. Running Free could not rely just on passing trade to build up its reputation and a loyal customer base.

The fast-food chain McDonald's buys processed raw materials for its food and drink products. These are transported and sold through an international chain of retail outlets. The products are widely marketed through national advertising, using television, radio, magazines and posters. Cash services are provided by the banks. Outlets are insured against fire, damage and theft.

No business operates in isolation. All need the products or services of other businesses. In general, businesses can be grouped into one of four activities:

- Manufacturing – the transformation of raw material into products required either by individuals or other companies.
- Transport and distribution – the provision of air, sea or land transport for the firm's input and output is the job of the transport industry. The distribution centre provides alternative methods of getting the product to the final consumer, for example, by mail order or through a wholesaler.
- Retailing and wholesaling – the final process of selling the goods or services. This could be through small outlets (independent retailers) multiples, department stores, shopping centres, hypermarkets or cooperatives.

- Services – this includes banking, finance, insurance, communication, import and export services, advertising and retailing.

A business often requires products or services of firms in other sectors.

Small businesses are linked to their raw material suppliers, their service providers and their transport and distribution network. Most important of all, they need to be linked to their customers.

Activity

Produce a detailed diagram of business links for a local business. You can do this by observation, but it is also a good opportunity for you to interview a local businessperson. Before the meeting, prepare a list of questions to make sure that you cover all areas. Your diagram should show where all of the business's inputs come from, i.e. its product and service providers and who it supplies its own goods to.

2.2, 2.3, 2.4 C © **Assignment**

1 **Identify a local or national business and produce a report describing it in terms of:**

- the type of business, its product or service and its industrial sector
- the business environment it operates in
- its main purpose (for national businesses, try to obtain an annual report which contains much of this information in the chief executive's and directors' reports)
- the firms that provide services and goods for the business
- its link with other businesses – you could do this as a diagram.

Where appropriate, illustrate your report with tables and diagrams, for example, to show trends or market share.

You should also include in your report information on developments in the sectors, their typical activities and their importance to the national economy.

2 **Identify seven examples of businesses with different types of ownership and identify the differences between them. Your list should include at least one public-sector business, and at least one small, one medium and one large private sector business. For a small local firm you will need to undertake some form of interview and data research. For a large national organisation choose one that has a branch nearby so that printed information can be combined with a visit.**

2 The business environment

All businesses are influenced and changed by their environment, the law, competition, location and resources available. This section looks at the reasons for choosing particular locations. You will see that both human and physical resources are important. Success of a business depends on accurately identifying market demand and on producing and selling the required product. You will be asked to look at markets for products and to propose product development to meet market demand.

Location

Location plays an important part in a firm's success. A good location can help to keep down the unit cost of production and make the end product more competitive.

Case study

Tom Skeith, managing director of TS Transport has called a management meeting to discuss the possible sites for a European depot. Satish Patel, the service manager, says they require a site of at least 20 acres within 2 miles of a motorway somewhere in central Europe. He also stresses that suitably qualified and experienced mechanics will be needed to provide a 24-hour service for the large European fleet. The sales manager, Janice Denton, wants the site to be close to the company's major customers in northern France and southern Germany, but Tom feels they should also be looking to find business in eastern Europe. Fiona Hughes, the financial controller, has identified six areas which qualify for government or EU assistance for newly located businesses. She says this would greatly reduce the initial setup cost and reduce running costs for five years. The meeting decides to concentrate its research on eastern France and northern Italy. Each manager is given an area to examine for potential sites.

Activity

Make a list of the important location factors affecting TS Transport. Would the factors be different if the business was:

a a food-processing plant
b an iron and steel foundry
c a financial consultancy?

Some of these factors may conflict such as the need to be near to a bulky raw material or to the market. Each firm must carry out a cost-benefit

Cost-benefit analysis takes into account all economic and social costs and benefits of a venture.

analysis weighing up the advantages and disadvantages of alternative sites. The purely economic factors may also be influenced by non-economic ones such as the availability of grants from the UK government or the European Union.

Deciding on location

Factors influencing the location of a business range from the availability of input resources – labour, raw materials, premises – to the existence of good transport facilities or government assistance. Established firms may also want to relocate in order to expand, to reduce costs, to upgrade facilities or simply to be nearer the market. Several government departments and private companies have moved out of London to reduce costs. Large retailers such as Sainsbury's, Asda and Morrisons have moved to the edge of towns in order to provide a better service in the form of one-stop shopping.

When discussing location or relocation, a business must consider the following factors.

Nearness to raw materials

Birds Eye, for example, is located in the farming belt of East Anglia.

Many of the traditional raw materials such as coal, iron ore and timber are heavy and bulky. A firm using any of these may decide to locate near to the source of the material so that the cost of transport is kept to a minimum. It is important for firms handling perishable goods, as in the canning and freezing industry, to be close to their products.

Businesses that rely on the import of high bulk, high weight raw materials may prefer a location close to a port. Generally, the raw material factor has declined in importance with the continued improvement in transport and the increased use of lighter materials such as plastics and alloys.

Availability of labour

The Nissan car assembly plant in Sunderland and the Pioneer electronics factory near Wakefield are able to use a local pool of semi-skilled and skilled labour.

Depending on the type of business, a firm may require a plentiful supply of cheap unskilled labour or the availability of highly skilled, experienced workers. This is one of the main reasons for the location of computer specialist and technical firms along the M4 corridor where there is an abundant supply of experienced staff.

Availability of land

This may be one of the most costly elements in a location decision. The amount of land needed depends on the type of business and its size of operation. Some processes require large areas of flat land, for example, oil refineries, chemical plants, distribution centres. Others require remote locations for safety reasons, such as munitions factories and nuclear-power plants. Businesses involved in the service sector prefer locations in or with easy access to areas of high population.

Availability of transport services

Distribution becomes important when the inputs or finished goods are heavy, bulky or perishable. A business must compare the cost of raw material transport with that of servicing the market. Access to rail or sea terminals or the motorway network are important considerations. For businesses with a wide distribution area such as supermarket chains, car assembly plants and soft drinks manufacturers, it is essential that their sites are located close to motorways and where possible, at the junction of several motorways. The opening of the Channel Tunnel may act as a magnet for firms who wish to have easy access to mainland Europe.

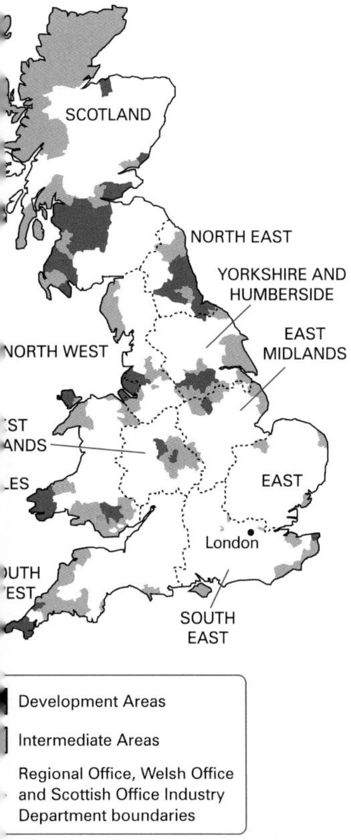

Nearness to markets

London and the South East experienced rapid growth as more and more firms located close to this large, prosperous area. Businesses that supply parts or services to other companies benefit from locating close to their principal clients. For example, many agricultural machinery firms are based in the farming areas of East Anglia. The corner shop is a good example of a business locating close to its market as its appeal as a convenience store is its main attraction. Other personal services that need to be near their markets include GPs, dentists, hairdressers, car maintenance firms.

Government assistance

External assistance is available in some designated areas from local government, central government or the European Union to encourage firms to move to locations of high unemployment. These designated areas are known as development areas, intermediate areas and enterprise zones.

The type of incentive depends on the area's designation, but may include some or all of the following:

- grants for plant and machinery
- low rental sites
- tax allowances
- relocation expenses for key workers
- management advice and consultancy
- assistance with training
- easier and faster planning permission.

In addition to the regional policy of the UK government, the European Union also helps through its:

- European Regional Development Fund – for infrastructure projects such as roads and telecommunications
- European Social Fund – for training
- European Agricultural Guidance and Guarantee Fund – job creation in rural areas.

Other influences

- The climate. Agriculture and horticulture require particular climatic conditions.
- Nearness to service companies. It may be important to locate close to firms that supply technical and support services.
- Local specialist educational facilities. Training costs can be significantly reduced if local colleges and universities offer appropriate courses, for example, textiles in Manchester and Leeds and engineering in the Midlands.

Government constraints

The government also restricts the areas where businesses may locate in order to protect the environment, maintain the greenbelt or limit urban sprawl. It does this through the Town and Country Planning Act. This act requires businesses to obtain planning permission and an industrial development certificate. These are more readily available in areas of high unemployment, but are harder to obtain in crowded areas such as the South-East.

Costs and benefits

For every potential site the business needs to prepare a *cost-benefit analysis* weighing up the advantages and disadvantages of each. The site chosen will be the one that provides the best overall result and not necessarily the best in every category. All of the factors mentioned above have to be considered, assessed and ranked in order of importance towards the final choice. This was the situation facing Coca-Cola and Cadbury Schweppes when deciding where to locate their joint venture in the world's largest and most technically advanced carbonated soft drinks factory.

The team that can

It was in January 1987 that Cadbury Schweppes Plc and the Coca-Cola Company decided to merge their UK soft drink manufacturing, distribution and marketing interests in a joint venture, Coca-Cola Schweppes Beverages Ltd (CCSB), 51 per cent owned by Cadbury Schweppes and 49 per cent owned by Coca-Cola...

CCSB had an excellent network of canning and bottling plants and depots covering the whole country. They were however determined to achieve a quantum leap forward to state of the art production facilities for the nineties and beyond, which any competitor would be hard put to match, let alone improve upon, even if they were prepared to match CCSB's largest ever £75 million investment in this industry.

Three factors were to be critical in the choice of location, the right site, first class communications and local availability of a highly skilled labour force, for this plant was to be far removed from the traditional low tech soft drinks factory.

On these criteria it rapidly became clear that the Wakefield 41 Industrial Park outscored any competition. The sixty acre site, with services already installed, could easily accommodate the giant factory, with plenty of space both for future expansion within the present factory and for extensions. Part of the site was made available for can manufacturers Nacanco, whose presence was an essential part of the strategy.

Communications were superb. The excellent rail service and convenient airports at Leeds/Bradford and Manchester were important, but the road network was the key. The distance to Junction 41 of the M1 is one mile, with a further mile to the M62 intersection and thus a quick motorway connection to the A1...

The third factor, skills availability, was equally important. The factory is not a user of labour on a large scale, it is far too automated for that...The skilled technician has replaced the unskilled line operator and CCSB have had no problem at all in finding the right skills and motivation they need from an area with strong engineering and heavy industrial traditions.

Business Link, June 1992

Activity

Read the article on Coca-Cola Schweppes Beverages Ltd (CCSB) and then answer the following questions. You will need a motorway map of the UK. Find junction 41 on the M1 motorway.

a What were the reasons for the construction of a new £75 million soft drinks factory?

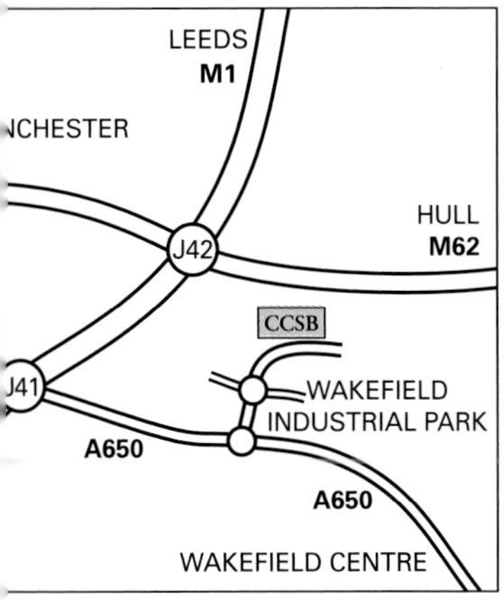

b What location factors were considered the most important by CCSB? How was the Wakefield site able to satisfy these requirements?

c Look at the motorway map. From junction 41 on the M1 find suitable routes to supply soft drinks to:

- Liverpool
- Birmingham
- Bristol
- Glasgow
- Newcastle.

The business environment

Case study

JCT Ltd is a large bottling plant on the outskirts of a northern city. It employs 130 people on a rotating three-shift system for continuous production. As a drinks producer it is required to adhere to all the laws concerning food products which involves regular quality testing and strict hygiene conditions. JCT is the largest single user of water in the area and it must ensure that it does not discharge cleaning chemicals and waste products into the general water supply without first filtering out impurities. All employees are expected to be multi-skilled and to work morning, afternoon and evening shifts in rotation. In return the labour force expects to be well rewarded both in terms of salary and working conditions. The continuous arrival and departure of delivery vehicles has to be carefully monitored so as to cause the minimum inconvenience and noise to residents living near by. The drinks industry is fiercely competitive with several international firms such as Coca-Cola, Cadbury Schweppes, Pepsi and Seven-Up trying to capture a greater share of the market. JCT must, therefore, strive to improve productivity and reduce costs in order to remain competitive and retain its market.

Every business operates in a competitive environment and must take account of the actions of its main rivals and the demands of its customers.

Businesses also have certain obligations to society. Some of these obligations are enforced by law such as health and safety regulations and employment conditions. Others are imposed by public opinion and pressure groups and may concern the environment, the quality of the product and relations with the local community. Failure to take these into account might result in prosecutions, fines or closure for breaches of the law or public outrage and falling sales for ignoring the views of society. A company must balance the need to remain competitive with the demands and standards expected by society.

The competitive environment

In the competitive environment, not only are a company's own actions important, but so are those of its rivals. All firms are attempting to gain a greater share of the present market as well as to enlarge the market by attracting first-time buyers. Increased competition often forces companies to look for cost savings that they can pass on to their customers, but in doing this businesses must not neglect their obligations towards the government and society as a whole.

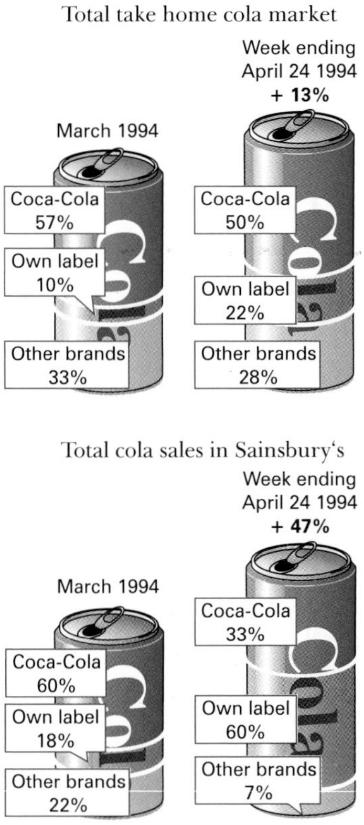

Taken from an article by Stephen Buck (Director of Taylor Nelson AGB plc) *The Times 11.5.94*

Activity

In April 1994 Sainsbury's supermarket chain launched its own-brand cola drink, Classic Cola. Look at the diagram showing the effect on the total take-home cola market and cola sales in Sainsbury's.

a What happened to the size of both markets following the major marketing of Classic Cola by Sainsbury's?

b What happened to Coca-Cola's share of the market?

c What happened to the other cola brands?

d Classic Cola was sold at a price significantly cheaper than Coca-Cola. What does this tell you about the preferences of the cola consumer?

Check your answers with those given at the end of this study unit.

The legal environment

All firms must fulfil certain legal requirements. These may include:

- providing a healthy and safe working environment
- treating all employees fairly without discrimination of sex, religion or race
- providing adequate liability insurance
- complying with regulations on pollution – noise, sight, air, land, water
- describing goods correctly and accurately, particularly their quantity and quality.

Activity

1 **Find out which legislation covers each of the legal requirements listed above.**

2 **All public and business premises must comply with fire regulations. Look around your school or college for evidence of compliance with these regulations. Make a list of the special equipment or signs that are required. What does this mean to a business in terms of cost?**

You should have noticed fire exit signs, fire extinguishers, fire blankets, emergency lighting and emergency exits. What may not have been obvious is that businesses must have a written fire evacuation procedure, an appointed fire officer, regular fire evacuation practices and equipment inspections. All of these add to the costs of running a business and form part of the price of the final product.

Examples of environmentally unfriendly behaviour include:
- the use of environmentally damaging materials or processes, for example CFCs in aerosols and pesticides on farmland
- the use of scarce natural materials such as hardwoods from South America
- the use of non-recyclable materials
- the destruction of wildlife sites for building or raw material extraction
- the pollution of the air, water or land

The natural environment

A large part of society, particularly young people, have become increasingly concerned about the effects on the natural world of large-scale production and consumption. A business must ensure that its products and processes do not harm the environment.

The local environment

Businesses do not operate in isolation, but are part of and responsible to the local community. Production processes may be noisy, factories can be an eyesore, waste can be harmful and extra traffic a hazard. Organisations must plan carefully to minimise the negative impact on their surrounding area and to maximise the benefits in order to build a good working relationship with the local community.

Questions of ethical behaviour may occur in the following situations:
- the provision of wheelchair access to workplaces and retail outlets
- the exploitation of cheap labour in the Third World
- the use of experimentation on animals
- dealings with armaments, alcohol or tobacco manufacturers.

The ethical and social environment

The general public expects businesses to follow certain guidelines in their everyday operations. These values and principles may be referred to as business **ethics**. They may be adopted willingly by the firm as part of its business culture or forced upon it by consumer or public pressure.

In 1994 British Gas awarded its chief executive a pay increase of 75 per cent from £270,000 to £480,000 per year. Two months previously British Gas sales staff had been told that their £13,000 annual salary was uncompetitive. A programme to cut the work force by 25,000 was also announced.

Activity

As a group, discuss whether British Gas acted ethically or fairly towards its:

- chief executive
- sales staff
- employees
- shareholders
- customers.

When looking at questions of moral behaviour, there is often no one right answer. Each business must decide on the likely reaction of its customers and the public at large and weigh these against the costs and benefits of carrying out a particular action.

Markets and products

All firms serve a market made up of customers who have needs and wants. One part of the market is made up of consumers and the other part is made up of producers who are willing to employ resources in order to make the goods and services wanted by the consumers. The interaction of the demand for products and their supply determines the:

For example, the UK market for DIY products was worth £6.4 billion in 1993. The major suppliers were B&Q (£1,150m), Texas (£690m), Do It All (£390m), Homebase (£280m) and Wickes (£230m). Between them they accounted for 43 per cent of the total market for DIY materials.

- type of market
- size of market
- market price
- value of the market.

The success of each business in accurately providing for the needs and wants of the market decides how large a share of the market the firm will obtain. In the example B&Q is the market leader with 18 per cent of the market. The total market can be broken down as follows:

- International markets – trade is conducted worldwide in a particular product. This market is dominated by large multi-national corporations that sell goods in many countries. Examples include Ford, ICI, IBM, Shell and Coca-Cola.
- The UK national market – mass produced goods are advertised, distributed and sold throughout the country, for example Cadbury's chocolates, Jaguar cars, Dunlop sportswear.
- Regional markets – a product or service is only available in a restricted area, for example, some breweries, bakers and car dealerships.
- Local markets – supply and demand is restricted to a small area, for example, the corner shop, local repair garage or hairdresser.

It is essential that a business understands its market, especially in a dynamic economy where the needs and wants of consumers are constantly changing.

Activity

For the following categories of products identify two companies that supply the items locally, regionally, nationally and internationally (some items may not be supplied in all of the market categories).

For example, beer may be supplied locally by a small brewer such as Robinsons of Stockport, regionally such as Tetley's in the north of England, nationally by Whitbreads and internationally by Fosters of Australia.

a coach travel
b furniture
c ice-cream
d used cars
e hairdressing
f air travel
g newspapers
h clothing
i two product groups of your own choice

When you have finished compare your answers with another member of your group. Are you satisfied that they are all correctly described? Have you discovered extra examples?

The value of the market

The total value of the market is found by multiplying the number of items sold by the average price obtained. For example, in 1994 the UK new car market was worth approximately £20 billion, the European soap powder market was worth £6 billion and the UK market for wrapped ice-creams was worth £240 million. It is not just the current value of the market which is important, but its future value. Expanding markets are more attractive than stagnating or declining ones. For example, the markets for computer games and compact disks are steadily growing, whereas those for board games and records are declining.

Activity

As a group, discuss which of the following product markets you think are declining, which ones are stable and which are expanding. Suggest reasons for each.

a compact disks
b hats
c running shoes
d exotic fruit
e meat
f private pensions
g residential care for the elderly
h adventure holidays
i personal computers
j rail travel
k garden centres
l sewing machines

You might have found it quite difficult to decide what was happening to some of the items. With rising living standards a growing number of people can afford more luxuries and are able to travel more widely. As the cost of clothing falls it is easier to replace than repair. The population of the UK is becoming older as well as richer. These changes affect the demand for goods and services.

The share of the market

The market share is the percentage of all sales within a market that are held by one brand or one company. Most markets are normally too large for one company or one product to dominate entirely (unless they are state-owned or state-sanctioned monopolies). Each business aims to secure a certain percentage of the total sales. This can be measured by volume – amounts sold – or by value – the revenue generated. A firm achieves a market share by persuading consumers to buy its product rather than those of its rivals. This is done through a mix of:

- advertising
- special features

- customer service/after-sales service
- pricing
- special promotions, including limited offers, competitions and free samples.

The more successful it is at this the more repeat sales it will have from a loyal customer base. In 1994 the main quality newspapers attempted to gain extra market share through aggressive price cuts and television advertising.

Case study

UK washing detergent market share **%**

	30 Apr. 1994 (At Power's launch)	***11 Jun. 1994 (At Power's peak)***	***24 Dec1994 (Unilever decides to replace Power as its lead detergent brand)***
Procter & Gamble (eg. Ariel)	50.6	50.0	52.8
Unilever	32.6	33.2	31.0
Persil brand total	26.5	28.9	26.0
Persil Power	0.8	4.5	2.3

Source: Neilsen, *Financial Times* 1995

Unilever's launch in 1994 of Persil Power in the UK and Omo Power on the continent was at first a success. The company captured 4.5 per cent of the market and improved Unilever's share of the £6 billion detergent market to 33.2 per cent. Unfortunately, the powerful 'accelerator' ingredient in the product damaged certain fabrics. This was exploited by Unilever's competitor Procter and Gamble. Persil Power was replaced by 'New Generation' Persil. Procter and Gamble and Unilever account for over 83 per cent of the detergent market and both work hard to protect their share.

2.3 C, 2.3 AN **C** **Activity**

Present the information about market share in the detergent market in the form of a pie chart. What are the different sizes of pie for Persil between 30 April and 24 December 1994?

Different markets

Businesses provide goods for three main markets – the consumer market, the industrial market and the government market.

The *consumer market* is made up of all the items sold for final consumption. They can be classified as:

- **consumables** – single-use products such as food, toothpaste, make-up, film and medicines
- consumer **durables** – multi-use products that have a reasonable life-span such as televisions, lawnmowers, furniture, cars and cameras.
- consumer services – personal services for the individual consumer such as insurance, hairdressing, professional decorating, dental care and leisure activities.

The *industrial market* includes the goods and services needed by businesses in order to create the final consumer products. They can be classified as:

- **capital goods** – items needed as part of production such as machinery, computers and vehicles
- producer consumables – items bought frequently for immediate use such as lubricants, stationery, raw materials and packing materials
- producer services – activities that help the business such as insurance, transport, banking, advertising, retailing and finance.

The *government market* consists of all the government units that purchase or rent goods and services in order to perform the function of government. These 'units' vary in size and include:

- supranational organisations – for example, the United Nations and the European Union purchase telecommunication equipment, excess food stocks, office accommodation and translation services.
- national bodies – for example, central government departments such as the National Health Service (NHS), the Ministry of Defence and the Department for Education. The NHS uses the services of doctors, nurses and auxiliary staff as well as medical equipment, medicines, foodstuffs and energy.
- regional and local councils which provide services and amenities tailored to the needs of a particular area, for example fire protection, police, road maintenance and leisure services.

2.1, 2.3 C **C**

Activity

As a group, prepare a series of visual aids to show the types of goods and services provided for the three markets: consumer, industrial and government. On A2-size paper produce a collage of pictures illustrating the goods in each market and, if possible, in each sub-category, for example, consumables, consumer durables and services for the consumer market. Use cuttings from magazines, newspapers, leaflets and catalogues. When you have completed both projects prepare a three-minute talk on each market (you could do this with a partner) explaining:

a the types of products in the market

b the range available of one product, for example, washing powders

c the market leaders (the best-known brands).

Satisfying market demand

Demand is the desire to own a product or consume (use) a service backed up by the ability to pay for it. Many consumers would like to have a Rolls-Royce but few can 'demand' one. A business must focus its attention on those in the market that are potential buyers of the product. Successful targeting of this group is the key to sales growth and profitability. The product must also accurately reflect the views of the customer as to its features, style and price. The business must be 'market' orientated, putting the desires of the customers at the centre of all its operations. Many businesses follow a logical approach to the design, production and selling of their products:

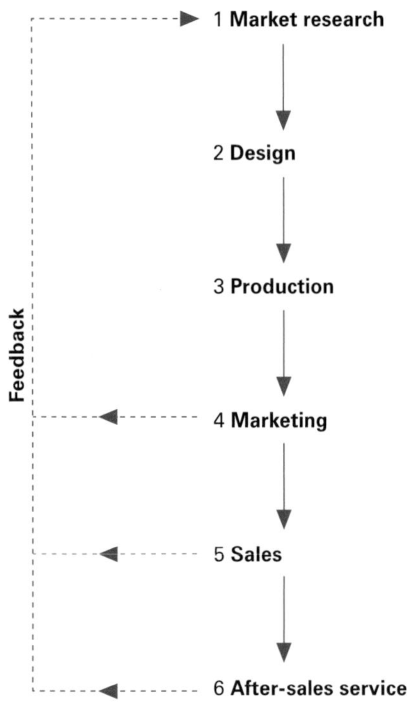

Key
1 to find out customer likes/dislikes
2 incorporating wants/needs of customer; prototype tested on market
3 feedback from early sales
4 advertising, exhibitions, in-store demonstrations, free samples
5 promotions
6 advice, complaints, repairs, feedback

Marketing activities may include:

a advertising – a choice of television, radio, newspaper, poster, direct mail shots, etc.
b special events – in-store demonstrations, press conference, free gifts, trial packs, celebrity support, etc.
c sales literature – display stands, point-of-sale leaflets, articles in trade magazines, banners, etc.

1 Market research involves the gathering of data on the lifestyle, age, income, taste and habits of potential customers and what they think are the key features of the product/service they want or need.

2 Design involves putting together the three key design elements in the best possible way:

a aesthetic appeal of the product
b function (the ability to perform a task)
c economic manufacture.

3 Production is largely decided by the size of the market and the type of product. For example, uniform items with mass demand, such as soft drinks and car assembly, tend to be produced using continuous production-line techniques.

4 Marketing is the function of a business that links the firm with its consumers in order to get the right product to the right place at the right time and the right price. Marketing is often referred to as the 'marketing mix' or the 'Four Ps' (product, price, promotion and place). Assuming that market research and production have created an acceptable product, its price is competitive and it is available for customers to buy, the business must find an effective way of 'promoting' the item. This may involve a variety of activities to inform the buying public about the product.

5,6 Sales promotion boosts demand through incentives and after-sales service encourages customer loyalty and repeat purchases.

The need for new products

The product life-cycle (PLC)

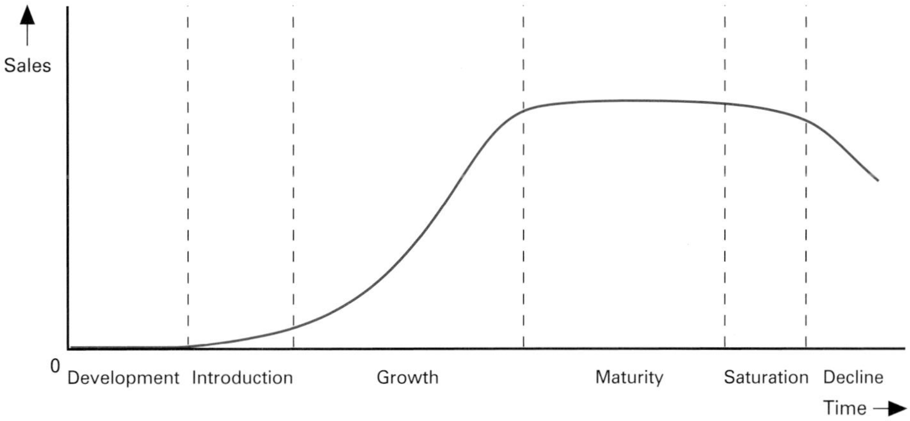

Extension strategies are techniques to improve sales such as:
- extending the product range – different sizes, associated products
- added qualities – larger, brighter, more powerful
- finding new markets – for example, the VW car in South America
- new packaging
- new advertising and slogans – the slogan 'Now there's more to Mars' replaced 'A Mars a day helps you work, rest and play'

In 1994 Mars introduced two new chocolate bars to its Galaxy range – 'Galaxy caramel' and 'Galaxy hazelnut'.

Extension strategies have also been applied to products such as detergents.

All products have a lifespan. The market for some products is very short (fads, crazes and fashion), but others can last for many years with only minor alterations. The **product life-cycle** (PLC) shows the different stages that a product passes through and the relative amount of sales at each stage.

The mature stage of the PLC is where sales have peaked and levelled out but can be kept going by using strategies to extend the life of the product.

Eventually, sales of a product decline and at some stage it must be 'killed off', i.e. production stopped.

Successful businesses have a range of products with sales of some items growing and steady sales of other products in order to balance any decline in sales turnover from products coming to the end of their life-cycle.

New technologies

Research and development create a range of new possibilities from which products emerge. Examples include:

- new materials – cloth with improved properties (warmth, non-crease, stretch) such as Goretex and Lycra, and optical fibres allowing telecommunications to travel at the speed of light
- new processes – plastic moulding altered the shape of goods like cars, music centres and televisions
- new components – the silicon chip has allowed goods to be computerised and miniaturised.

Changes in consumer demand

The pressure of time on people at work has led to the demand for fast-food, lap-top computers, mobile phones, cash points and telephone banking.

This is one of the most important influences for change. Firms now concentrate on making goods that are carefully tailored to consumer demands which are influenced by social attitudes and behaviour.

Rising standards of living have increased the demand for leisure centres, overseas holidays and DIY materials.

Increased awareness about healthy living has led to a demand for low-calorie foods and foods with low-fat content and no additives, more sports equipment and clothing.

Concern for the environment has influenced the development of goods that do not damage the environment or harm animals.

Assignment

2.2, 2.3, 2.4 Ⓒ
2.1, 2.2, 2.3

1 For this part of the assignment you will need maps of Europe showing population densities, climate and major transport links by road, rail and air.

a EuroDisney was built on a site east of Paris. Using the maps, explain why you think this site was chosen. The south of France, northern Spain and the UK were also considered as possibilities – give reasons why you think they were rejected.

b From a local travel agent obtain brochures about the Paris location and identify its advantages. Present your findings in a report, together with maps and brochures, to show the advantages and disadvantages of the Paris location.

2 Choose a business and one or two of its main products. For these, describe the market, the demand for the product(s) and what the business does to improve its market position. You should find out about competitive products and the effects of the business environment. Illustrate your report with diagrams where appropriate.

3 Suggest at least two new products for development which would meet the market needs of a specific group of people such as students, children, the disabled in, for example, fashion, transport or leisure. These can be completely new products or products developed from an existing product.

a Choose two of the products and develop a full description of them with sketches where appropriate.

b Survey the market using a brief questionnaire to gather information on the proposed product including:

- reaction to the product – likes and dislikes
- features that are missing
- frequency of purchase
- maximum price prepared to pay
- rival products.

Present your findings in a word-processed report using charts, diagrams and sketches where appropriate.

If only one product can be developed, comment at the end of the report on which item you feel has most chance of success.

4 Write a summary of the legal, environmental and public influences on business organisations.

3 Employment

The employment market in the UK and the rest of Europe is undergoing major change. You will be aware of the shift away from full-time employment to more flexible working. In this part of the unit, different working conditions are compared. You will gain a broader view of employment across Europe by investigating working conditions. The reasons for regional differences in employment are looked at, as well as the major impact of technological change on working practices and on numbers employed. In the UK workers are expected to be more adaptable, better educated, better trained and more skilled so that British companies can win orders in the face of growing foreign competition.

Employment in the UK

The labour market is like any other market for goods or services in that it is made up of buyers of labour services (employers) and suppliers of labour (employees). The supply and demand for each type of labour decides the price of labour (the wage or salary).

In recent times people chose an occupation, trained for it if required and expected to follow the same career for the rest of their working lives, often with the same firm. Today's labour market is very different. Skills need to be updated constantly and working practices have become more flexible.

Typists have become word-processor operators. Many jobs in banks instead of being undertaken by people are now done by computer. Bus drivers nowadays both drive and collect fares so removing the need for conductors.

The modern labour force have to expect rapid change in their occupations, the businesses they work for and the industry they work in.

A new entrant to the labour force, whether skilled or unskilled, can expect to choose from the following types of employment.

Employment by an organisation

This is the most common form of employment and includes the following categories:

- Full-time employment – a person is employed for a full working week. In 1993 12.8 million males and 6.2 million females were in full-time employment.
- Part-time employment – a person is employed for less than the full week, normally on an hourly basis. The period of work may be a small number of hours each day or a few days of the week.
- Permanent employment – for a job to be permanent, the employer must provide a commitment to continued employment. This gives the worker a greater sense of job security and the employer a 'core' work-force. This

Part-time employment is more common among women with over 5 million employed part-time in 1993 compared to 886,000 men.

Permanent jobs often integrate training and career development.

can apply to part-time work as well as to full-time jobs.

- Temporary employment – the period of employment is only guaranteed for a short period of time, often to cover busy seasonal demand, for example, hotel staff in holiday resorts.

Activity

Look in local newspapers or visit the local job centre to find three job advertisements illustrating each of the four categories of employment. Some of them will be a mix of types such as part-time permanent or temporary full-time. Group these into a fifth category for mixed varieties. What do you notice about the frequency of each type? What conclusions can you draw about your local employment market?

You may have found that there are more opportunities for temporary employment, perhaps holiday-related. Or the emphasis may be on skills and experience in a particular area such as horticulture or financial accounting.

Self-employed

Self-employed workers are those who earn a living by running their own businesses. Examples include plumbers, gardeners and freelance translators. Many professionals also operate on a self-employed basis such as accountants, dentists, solicitors and doctors in private practice. They may employ other people, but the risk and rewards are their own.

Recent changes in employment patterns

Research has shown that the employment market has changed greatly in recent times. Some of these changes are:

In 1977 there were just over 4 million employed part-time but by 1991 this had risen by more than one million. Women account for two-thirds of the increase.

The banking, distribution and finance part of the service sector tends to employ women, many of them in part-time flexible working.

- a decline in full-time male employment
- an increase in full-time female employment
- an increase in part-time employment. The overall decline in full-time employment has been partly offset by an increase in part-time work.
- a decline in employment in the production industries. The 1980s saw a decline of over 2.7 million jobs in the production industries.
- an increase in employment in the service sector. In the same period services provided 2.6 million more jobs.
- an increase in temporary employment. This includes not only unskilled and semi-skilled staff but increasingly professional staff who are hired through agencies or on fixed-term contracts.

Information on employment can be found in the following government publications:

- *Regional Trends*
- *Labour Force Survey*
- *Employment Gazette*
- *Social Trends*

All are published by HMSO and are available at most reference libraries.

- an increase in **flexitime**, home working and job sharing.
- an increase in self-employment. Between 1977 and 1991 the number of workers in self-employment increased by 1.3 million of which nearly one million were male.

Activity 2.4 C, 2.2 AN ⓒ

Look at the table on full- and part-time employment for the period from 1990 to 1993 and the table showing numbers in employment and self-employment in 1989 and 1992. Calculate the percentage change in:

Full- and part-time employment in the UK: by sex

Thousands

	Males		*Females*	
	Full time	***Part time***	***Full time***	***Part time***
1990	14,109	789	6,479	4,928
1991	13,686	799	6,350	4,933
1992	13,141	885	6,244	5,081
1993	12,769	886	6,165	5,045

Includes employees, self-employed, those on government training schemes and unpaid family workers.

Source: *Social Trends 1994. Crown copyright*

Numbers of people in employment, 1989 and 1992

Thousands

	1989	***1992***
Employed	22,670	21,835
Male	11,999	11,211
Female	10,671	10,624
Self-employed	3,253	2,989
Male	2,487	2,256
Female	766	733
Unemployed	1,785	2,723
Male	1,276	2,088
Female	510	634
Workforce	28,480	28,174
Male	16,346	16,038
Female	12,134	12,136

Source: *Annual Abstract of Statistics*, 1993

a male full-time employment
b female full-time employment
c male part-time employment
d female part-time employment.

Comment on the trends in the 1990s and then compare your answer with the one at the end of this study unit. You may also want to look at the tables on pages 43 and 44 and compare the differences found between the different industries and trends.

The employment package

Accepting a job is about accepting not only a wage or salary but a whole employment package. This includes the working environment, salary, training and fringe benefits when assessing the true value of a job. What is important to you in employment? For some it will be the financial terms of the job, but for others it may be a mixture of job satisfaction, career prospects and the availability of training.

Physical working conditions

The working environment varies a great deal between sectors, industries and organisations.

For example, jobs in agriculture, fishing and industries such as oil exploration and mining often involve outdoor work and are therefore affected by the weather. In agriculture the hours of work are dependent on the season, weather and the demands of animals and crops. Primary-sector work is often dirty, sometimes dangerous, as in mining, and can involve the handling of hazardous chemicals.

Working conditions in the secondary sector can vary widely depending on the industry and the organisation. Industries such as iron and steel are just as dirty and hazardous as the primary sector, while the manufacture of computer microchips is clean. The construction industry can be involved in outdoor work in remote locations or the refurbishment of interiors.

The service sector includes commercial services such as banking, transport, finance and insurance as well as personal services such as hairdressing, dentistry, window cleaning and landscape gardening. As the range suggests, many of the jobs will be indoors in an office environment, whereas others will be outside and may involve working unsocial hours, for example, police, market traders.

Each of the above sectors can involve workers in a manual occupation, an administrative job or a managerial post. The actual working conditions therefore depend on the sector, the position held and the attitude of the organisation to the environment of its employees.

Case study
Chantal Cooke is a highly successful senior accountant whose salary is fixed for the year but she also receives a bonus depending on the success of her department and the company as a whole. Selwyn Crawford is a self-employed builder who only receives an income if work is available and it can be carried out profitably.

Financial rewards

One of the most important aspects of a job is its financial rewards as this provides workers with the ability to buy the goods and services they require. Unfortunately, it is not always easy to compare accurately the financial rewards of different jobs if there are also other benefits attached to the post such as subsidised meals, social facilities and medical care.

The principal financial rewards for employment are:

- wages – paid on an hourly, daily or weekly basis and usually consisting of an agreed flat rate for a specific working period.
- salary – a fixed monthly payment made by an employer for professional

or office work as opposed to manual work. Salaried workers may be expected to work longer hours without being paid for overtime as one of their responsibilities for ensuring a job is completed.

- extra payments – many workers have the opportunity to earn additional payments such as:
- – overtime – a reward for working beyond the normal agreed period, usually paid at a higher hourly rate.
- – bonus payments – rewards for achieving agreed productivity or output levels.
- – commission – a payment to sales staff directly related to the volume and value of sales. This may be paid in addition to a basic wage or at a much higher level instead of a wage. The weekly wage will then be directly related to the success of the employee as a salesperson.
- – profit sharing – a scheme where workers obtain a share of the annual profits of the company either in cash or as shares.
- – expenses – repayment by the company of money spent by employees in the course of business, for example, using own car to visit a customer.

Activity

Using a spreadsheet produce a matrix from information about jobs in your area. Under the headings of 'Wages/salary', 'Additional payments' and 'Other advantages' (subsidised meals, travel allowance, medical care, etc.) compare the merits of at least five jobs in a similar occupation. How different are the rewards?

Travel to work

A future employee must consider seriously the impact of travel to and from the workplace for the following reasons:

- Time – how much of the day will be spent in non-income generating travel? Commuters to London who live outside the city spend many hours on the train or in a car.
- Comfort – how easy is it to reach the workplace? Public transport may not provide a direct route to the employer's site, requiring several changes of bus or train. Similarly, the route, even if direct, may be very popular and therefore not very comfortable in the rush-hour.
- Cost – this is an important consideration because travel to and from work is not normally an allowable expense and must be paid for entirely by the employee.

Hours of work

The traditional standard working day or week has largely disappeared in the UK. It is estimated that nearly three-quarters of all workers are now involved, in some way, with flexible working arrangements. The options are:

This system allows working parents, for example, to schedule their day around the needs of children as well as those of the employer.

This is common in manufacturing where continuous production techniques require the factory to be operational 24 hours per day.

- flexitime – an agreed number of hours per week or month worked at times that are more suitable to the employee.
- unsociable hours – employees involved in the hotel, restaurant and leisure industries may be required to work evenings. Similarly, many delivery workers start very early in the morning, for example, milk and postal deliveries.
- shift work – regular work that takes place during non-standard working hours, for example, midnight to 8 a.m. This is essential in services such as the police, fire brigade and hospitals.

Safety

One of the concerns raised about the privatisation of the coalmines regards the level of safety that may be maintained by a cost-conscious, profit-minded private sector company.

Some occupations are dangerous, for example deep-sea diving, off-shore fishing, fire fighting and mining. The employee must accept that there is a degree of risk, but should also make sure that the employer provides adequate protection, often as required by law. Many firms go beyond the basic safety requirements as accidents and hazards add costs to the business.

Job security

In times of recession companies reduce their work-force in the face of falling demand. Your job security will depend on:

- your job status as a 'core' or **'peripheral' worker**
- the general economic climate
- the ability of the company to remain competitive
- the impact of new technology.

It is not just the immediate rewards that are important but also the long-term prospects. One of these is job security. Occupations in medicine and education tend to be fairly secure with good prospects for long-term employment. Manual workers, semi-skilled workers and those employed in fast-changing industries or those industries quickly affected by economic conditions are not guaranteed permanent employment.

Career opportunities

A career is a profession or occupation chosen by a worker as a lifelong goal or path such as medicine, carpentry or design. Every career path has different levels, each of which requires specialist training and skills. At one end of the scale are unskilled manual workers who can be employed on a wide range of tasks, but only at a low skill level. The opportunity for high financial reward is limited. At the other end are highly trained, skilled workers who are well paid for their abilities such as surgeons and lawyers. It is important for the employee to choose both an occupation and a company which offers career advancement. This is one of the advantages of joining large organisations where there are many positions and a programme of staff development and promotion.

Training

The amount of training and qualifications can directly affect the long-term prospects of employment. In the 1990s unemployment rates for unqualified workers were twice as high as those who had A levels or GNVQ equivalents and five times as high as those with degrees and professional qualifications.

In the modern economy all workers must have some skills, at the very least the ability to read and understand basic instructions. Increasingly though, much higher qualifications are required by employers. The labour force in the UK generally has attended school to GCSE (GNVQ 2/ NVQ 2) level and followed a national curriculum. Employers may expect higher academic or vocational qualifications such as A levels and GNVQ courses and university degrees or professional awards. Whatever the starting point, the employee is expected to upgrade and update their skills. It is important for prospective employees to enquire about the availability of training.

The impact of new technology

Workers constantly have to adapt to new products, processes and practices as a result of new technology. It is an advantage to be employed in a company that uses the latest equipment and regularly upgrades its employees' skill levels accordingly.

Activity

1 **Design a questionnaire about working conditions using the categories above to interview up to seven friends or relatives in work about their jobs. Make a note about what they consider are the important features of the job. Produce a 'job profile' for each one listing the main features. Find out about their attitude to their journey to and from work. How do they rate their experiences in terms of time taken, comfort and cost? What conclusions can you draw from your survey? What does it tell you about people's motivation to work?**

2 **Look at the photographs of different occupations. Match the following list of wages and salaries to the occupations and say why you think it is a suitable reward. £12,000, £15,000, £18,000, £25,000, £32,000, £36,000. Remember that different jobs receive different pay because of skill levels, experience, responsibility, labour shortages, regional differences and productivity levels. These are known as pay differentials.**

Check your answers with those given on page 48.

All the people represented in the list are trained and skilled in different ways. How did you explain the differences in salaries? Perhaps you considered the amount of responsibility and the decisions each has to take. There is no correct answer as it depends on your view of the value of the occupation's contribution to society.

Regional differences in employment

Geographical, economic, human or governmental factors affect and decide the level of employment in different regions. All economies undergo periodic changes particularly in the demand for certain goods and services. This can result in some industries declining and others expanding, which in turn affects the areas they are located in. The next section looks at the impact of natural resources, investment, labour skills and labour supply on the level and type of employment in different regions.

Reasons for differences in employment levels

A region is a part of a country with certain characteristics (physical, economic, political) which give it an identity. In the UK these, for historical reasons, are based on the counties. Regions differ for a number of reasons.

Natural resources

The type of industry and the level of employment in a region can be affected by the presence of natural resources that are profitable to exploit such as coal, gas, oil, woodland and forests, fertile agricultural land, fish and water (rivers and lakes).

2.2, 2.3, 2.4 C ©
2.3, AN

Activity

1 **Find out the main natural resources of your region. This information can be obtained from local authorities, the local Chamber of Commerce, the Training and Enterprise Council or a geography textbook. What are the important industries in the area near your school or college?**

2 **You are a careers consultant and need to find out the types of employment available, by sector, in your region. This should include opportunities for employment and self-employment in both the private and public sectors. Add numerical data where appropriate and present your findings as a report. Keep the report in your portfolio.**

Level of investment

Regions differ as to their prosperity and wealth. London and south-east England, for example, are very prosperous and heavily populated. This region produces 40 per cent of the UK's total output – as measured by the Gross Domestic Product – and can therefore create greater employment opportunities. Investment over many years means better infrastructure such as transport systems, power supplies and educational facilities. This acts as a magnet for new firms. Areas that are more remote, less populated and less developed are not as attractive to new firms.

Supply of labour and skills

Businesses are attracted to regions not just by a good infrastructure but also by the availability of labour. A plentiful supply of labour is an important factor in the location decision. The numbers available for work differs from region to region and from country to country as the tables below show. As well as the total labour supply available new firms are concerned about the skill levels of the workers.

Unemployment rates by country %

	1985	1988	1992
UK	11.2	8.5	9.9
Belgium	11.3	9 .7	7.9
France	10.2	10.0	10.3
Germany (since Oct. 1990)	7.2	6.2	4.6
Italy	9.6	11.0	10.5
Netherlands	10.6	9.2	6.8
Portugal	8.5	5.7	4.1
Spain	21.4	19.1	18.1
Australia	8.2	7.2	10.7
Canada	10.4	7.7	11.2
Finland	5.0	4.5	13.0
Japan	2.6	2.5	2.2
Sweden	2.8	1.6	4.8
USA	7.1	5.4	7.3

Source: *Social Trends 1994. Crown copyright*

Unemployment rates in the UK: by region %

	1990	1991	1992	1993
North	8.6	10.6	11.2	11.2
Yorkshire & Humberside	6.8	9.1	9.9	9.8
East Midlands	5.1	7.8	8.7	9.0
East Anglia	3.8	6.2	7.1	8.3
South East	3.9	7.4	9.4	10.3
South West	4.5	7.7	9.1	9.2
West Midlands	5.9	9.0	10.7	11.6
North West	7.5	9.9	10.1	10.9
Wales	6.6	9.2	8.9	9.5
Scotland	8.0	9.2	9.5	10.1
Northern Ireland	13.7	14.1	12.1	12.5

Source: *Social Trends 1994. Crown copyright*

People are often reluctant to leave areas where they have grown up, even when jobs are scarce, so pockets of high unemployment develop. Some regions (East Anglia and the South East) have consistently had unemployment rates below the national average whereas others (Scotland and the North) have stayed above the national average. The West Midlands has moved from being a region of low unemployment to one of above average yet Wales has done the reverse.

Changing employment patterns in UK regions

Over time some industries decline and new industries emerge. This is caused by changing consumer demand and increased competition from abroad.

In the past 50 years the UK has experienced three main changes that have affected the pattern of employment in the regions.

1 Its population has become wealthier and, as a result, has demanded an increased number of services. These services have tended to be located in south-east England, which has led to a growing demand for labour in the region.

2 The direction of trade has changed adding further employment to the areas bordering mainland Europe but, more importantly, leading to a decline in the ports on the west coast.

3 The UK has lost much of its manufacturing sector to foreign competition. This has led to the decline of traditional heavy industries such as iron and steel, shipbuilding and engineering. Areas such as Belfast, central Scotland, South Wales and Tyneside in the North East have suffered badly and tend to have above-average unemployment.

Activity

The table shows the structure of employment in the UK between 1978 and 1991. Calculate the actual and the percentage change in each industry and in total employment. Comment on the changes and where possible suggest some of the reasons behind them.

Employees by industry ***Thousands***

Year	*All industries and services*	*Manufacturing*	*Energy and water supply*	*Construction*	*Service*	*Agriculture, forestry and fishing*
1980	22,511	6,807	1,265	1,229	12,840	370
1984	21,242	5,542	633	989	13,737	341
1988	22,258	5,195	485	1,047	15,218	313
1992	21,848	4,498	402	911	15,758	279

Source: *Annual Abstract of Statistics*, 1993

Patterns of employment in Europe

In the same way that regions can experience different rates of employment and unemployment so can countries. The reasons may range from structural change in industries to a more positive attitude by governments towards job creation and industry incentives.

Activity

Find information about the percentages of people in employment in two different EU regions (one UK and one other EU region) and explain why there are large differences.

Regional policies

Since 1988 small companies in assisted areas, which employ fewer than 25 people, have been able to apply for Regional Enterprise Grants, including:

- an investment grant – 15 per cent towards fixed assets to a maximum of £15,000
- an innovation grant – 50 per cent of development costs to a maximum of £25,000.

To prevent the poorer regions from becoming steadily poorer, the government and the EU introduced programmes of assistance – regional policies – to help the worst-hit areas.

Government assistance: UK regional policy

The **regional policy** of the UK government has tried to correct the regional problem by a mixture of financial, practical and information assistance to attract new firms into areas of high unemployment. Areas with above-average unemployment are designated as either development areas or intermediate areas. Look back at the map of assisted areas on page 23. As such, they are eligible for Regional Selective Assistance (RSA) which may include discretionary grants towards:

- capital related projects – for land purchase, site preparation or the purchase of plant and machinery
- job related projects – to cover the costs of hiring and training staff.

These incentives are meant to attract new firms into areas of high unemployment so providing extra employment.

European Union regional policy

Other funds include European Social Fund – for training costs and the European Agricultural Guidance and Guarantee Fund – to promote job creation in rural areas.

The European Union also assists areas of high and persistent unemployment through the European Regional Development Fund – this finances infrastructure projects such as transport links and telecommunications. Between 1975 and 1990 the UK received £3.6 billion.

2.2, 2.3, 2.4 C
2.3, AN
2.1, 2.2, 2.3 IT

Assignment

1 Using information already gathered together and with further research describe:

a the main industries of your region (brief description of location, products and firms)

b the types of regional employment (male/female, full-time/part-time employment by age)

c employment by industrial sector.

Add graphs and explanations and, where possible, identify trends including growth or decline in the sectors. Word process your report if possible and use graphics packages to produce your graphs and visual aids.

2 Choose another region and complete a similar survey. If possible, select a region from another country as this should help you to increase your knowledge of European business developments.

Compare the two regions and identify any differences and similarities.

Now prepare and deliver a presentation of your findings supported by visual aids (these should include graphs, bar graphs, pie charts or pictograms to highlight important points). Remember to highlight the similarities and the differences rather than providing a factual description.

3 From the seven people interviewed for the activity on page 41, identify two companies which would allow you to look at their working conditions, using the headings in this section. Compare

the two business organisations and present your summary comparison in report form. Add your descriptions of the types of employment from the activity.

Summary

This unit has looked at the purposes and types of business organisation and the industrial sectors in which they operate. We discussed advantages and disadvantages of types of ownership and the links between businesses. You should now have an understanding of the many factors making up the business environment; social, legal, ethical and the relationship with the customer.

The final part of the unit introduced employment patterns and opportunities, and the working conditions making up the employment package.

Review activity

You have now completed your work on this study unit and should spend some time reviewing what you have achieved.

1 Grading themes

For Intermediate GNVQs, you can achieve a higher grade depending on how much initiative and independent action you take in the areas of:

- planning
- information gathering
- evaluation
- quality of outcomes.

Action planning
Look over the assignments you worked on for this unit.

- Did you complete detailed action plans for each assignment?
- How much support did you need from your teacher/tutor to complete the plans?
- Did you regularly review and update your plans?
- How successful were you in achieving your plans and targets?
- What would you have done differently?

Information gathering
Look over all the assignments you worked on for this unit.

- Did you successfully identify the sorts of information you needed to complete activities and assignments?
- Did you succesfully gather the information you needed? How did you do this?

- How would you assess the quality of information you gathered? Was it:
  - useful and relevant
  - appropriate for your needs
  - accurate and complete?
- Were there any areas where you were not able to gather the information you needed?
- Why was this?
- What would you have done differently?

Evaluation

Evaluation is an important part of your GNVQ. It is one of the grading themes that will enable you to obtain a Merit or Distinction. As part of your evaluation, you should consider the following questions.

- Have I completed all the performance criteria for each element?
- What have I learned from this unit?
- How do my achievements compare with my Action Plan?
- What sources of information did I use and how did I access them?
- Is there anything I would do differently if I had to do it again?

Outcomes

- Did you present complete assignments that covered all of the areas mentioned in them?
- Did your assignment work show that you identified and selected only the appropriate parts from all the information you collected?
- Did you use business language and vocabulary accurately in your work to put information and points across clearly to your target audience?

2 Performance criteria and range

Look at the standards for this GNVQ unit. Work through the performance criteria for each element and check that you have done work to help you meet each one. Do this by noting down the relevant performance criteria number against the work.

Finally, check through the information given under the range.

3 Core skills

This unit has covered the following core skills:

- Communication Level 2: 2.2, 2.3, 2.4
- Application of number Level 2: 2.1, 2.2, 2.3
- Information technology Level 2: 2.1, 2.2, 2.3

Answers to activities

page 7 You should have seen that in actual terms the primary sector has declined only slightly over the ten years to 1993, but as a proportion of GDP it has suffered a serious drop. Even the agricultural sector which grew by £4,944 million in actual terms suffered a fall as a percentage of GDP.

1 a A decline of £3,143 million
  b 9.8 per cent in 1983 to 4.1 per cent in 1993.

2 Agriculture has fallen from 2.1 per cent of GDP in 1983 to 1.9 per cent in 1993.

page 9 In actual terms the secondary sector has almost doubled over the ten years to 1993, but as a proportion of GDP it has suffered a decline of almost 5 per cent.

1 a An increase of £72,160 million
  b 34.2 per cent in 1983 to 29.6 per cent in 1993, a fall of 4.6 per cent of GDP

2 The secondary sector, in particular manufacturing, is now less important to the UK.

3 Manufacturing has risen in actual terms by £53,556 million, but has fallen from 24.8 per cent in 1983 to 21.7 per cent of GDP in 1993.

page 10 As a percentage of GDP the tertiary sector has grown from 60.6 per cent in 1983 to 70.6 per cent in 1993. Finance (170 per cent), education (150 per cent) and transport (135 per cent) have grown the most.

page 26 Both the take-home market (by 13 per cent) and Sainsbury's market (by 47 per cent) grew as a result of marketing Classic Cola. Other brands suffered declines in both markets, particularly in sales at Sainsbury's. Coca-Cola fell from 60 per cent to 33 per cent and other brands dropped from 22 per cent to 7 per cent. Classic Cola increased its share from 10 per cent to 22 per cent in the take-home market and from 18 per cent to 60 per cent in Sainsbury's.

page 37

a Male full-time employment decreased by 9.5 per cent.
b Female full-time employment decreased by 4.8 per cent.
c Male part-time employment increased by 12.3 per cent.
d Female part-time employment increased by 2.4 per cent.

The percentage of males self-employed decreased from 15.2 per cent in 1989 to 14.1 per cent in 1992. The percentage of females self-employed decreased from 6.3 per cent in 1989 to 6.0 per cent in 1992. The decrease in full-time employment has been greater for men. Part-time employment has increased, particularly of males. Full-time jobs are being replaced by part-time working.

You might find slight discrepancies between the totals in the two tables. This is due to differences in sources and definitions such as 'self-employed'.

page 41 Industrial employee: £12,000, nurse: £15,000, chef: £18,000, architect: £25,000, barrister: £32,000, business executive: £36,000.

page 44 a UK 2.2 per cent; Belgium 2.9 per cent; Luxembourg 3.1 per cent; Greece 21.9 per cent; Ireland 13.8 per cent; Portugal 11.5 per cent.

b Norway 70.9 per cent ; Sweden 70.2 per cent.

c Germany 39.1 per cent.

Glossary

batch production the manufacture of a limited number of identical products

capital goods those items required by firms to assist production, such as machines, computers, tools and vehicles

consumables any product that can only be used (consumed) once

cooperative a business organisation which is owned and run by its members

core workers those employees considered permanent and essential to the firm; usually highly skilled and well rewarded

durable goods any product which can be used repeatedly for a long time such as televisions, cars, furniture

economies of scale the reduction in costs which can be gained when a firm expands its operations

employment working on a paid basis to perform a job or tasks specified in a contract of employment

ethics a set of values and principles which influence the behaviour of individuals and groups in society

flexitime completing an agreed number of hours of work at times to suit the employee and the firm

flow production the mass manufacture of a standard item using a continually moving process

franchise a concession by the owner of a product brand or service to another business to produce and/or sell its goods and services in a particular area

franchisee the purchaser of the local rights to a business

franchiser the holder of the franchise who sells the local rights of a business to franchisees

Gross Domestic Product (GDP) the total value of a country's output over the course of a year

incorporation the process of establishing a business as a separate legal identity

job production a means of producing a unique item for a specific customer

limited company a business organisation that has a separate legal identity from its owners and where liability is limited to the shareholders' investment in the business

market share the proportion of all sales within a market that are held by one company or one product

market where buyers and sellers can communicate to sell goods and services

marketing the function of business that links the firm with its customers and consumers to get the right product to the right place at the right time and the right price

merit goods considered by the state to be essential and likely to be underprovided by the private sector, for example, health care and education

mission statement a document summarising the objectives or purpose of a business so as to provide a common purpose

objectives a statement of what an organisation wishes to achieve through its operations

partnership a business organiation owned by between two and 20 people

peripheral workers those employees considered to be temporary and non-essential; usually hired and fired as demand for the product dictates

primary sector industry that extracts raw materials, i.e. mining and quarrying, mineral oil and natural gas extraction, agriculture, forestry and fishing

private sector the part of the economy owned and controlled by individuals and corporations

product life-cycle the different stages of the life of a product, such as development, launch, growth, maturity and decline

profit the surplus remaining from revenue after all costs have been deducted

public corporation an enterprise that is owned by the state – a nationalised industry

public sector the part of the economy owned and controlled by the state

public services services and goods provided from public funds and from which all individuals can benefit such as defence and street lighting

regional policy the government's attempt to correct imbalances of income and employment by stimulating the less prosperous areas through investment and the attaction of new industries

sales revenue income from sales

secondary sector industry that processes raw materials into finished goods

services assistance provided for individuals and businesses, such as banking, insurance, transport, communications, advertising

social costs the total costs to society of production, including effects such as pollution, congestion and environmental damage

sole trader a business organisation owned by one person

tertiary sector industry providing services

Training and Enterprise Councils (TECs) goverment-funded bodies which organise training in a local area

unlimited liability the owner of a business is personally responsible for its debts

People in business organisations

GNVQ

Contents

Introduction 52

1 How organisations work 52

2 Responsibilities and rights of people in business 66

3 Job roles in business organisations 79

4 Preparing for the world of work 86

Summary 95

Answers to activities 97

Glossary 98

Leo Cullum
"IT'S COME TO OUR ATTENTION THAT YOU HAVE A LIFE OUTSIDE THE OFFICE."

LONGMAN

Introduction

In this unit you will be looking at how individual business organisations operate and how they try to achieve fair and productive relationships with their employees.

Since the late 1980s and the collapse of the planned economies of Eastern Europe, the business environment has changed. The broad types of businesses we shall be discussing in this unit are the essential parts of this new environment and have become models for organisations all over Europe. Most countries are now busy trying to transform their economies by forcing businesses to become more competitive, more efficient and more quality-conscious.

Similarly, in the UK and many other countries in Europe, large state-run organisations have had to become more competitive – by being privatised, by having to face new competition or both.

This means that when you enter the world of work, the organisation you join – whether it is the Civil Service, BSkyB Television or the corner shop – will be following one of the broad patterns we shall examine in this unit.

1 How organisations work

Organisations are made up of different parts that operate together to achieve a desired objective. If you plan to work successfully within any business, large or small, it is vital that you understand the main business functions and the different ways in which they can be organised. You need to know what activities each department is responsible for and how each department relates to other parts of the organisation.

Structures and functions

The 'structure' of an organisation is the way it is arranged internally – what departments or sections it has and how these relate to each other. A good way to understand the structure of a business is to draw an **organisation chart**. This example shows a basic organisational structure for a typical business.

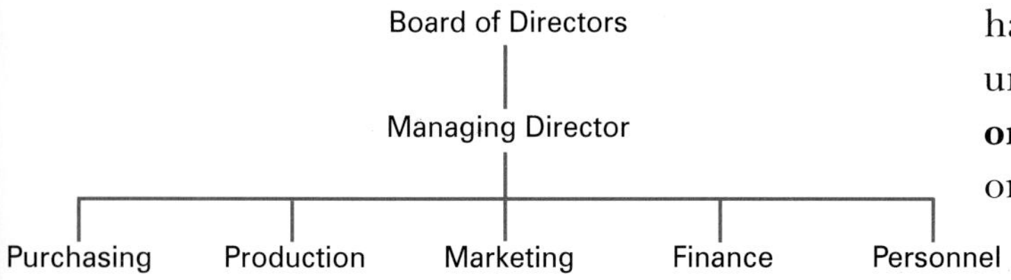

From the chart you can see that the organisation is divided into a number of departments. Each department takes responsibility for one **function** of the business.

For instance, people in the personnel department are concerned with activities like recruitment, training and health and safety, whereas marketing is responsible for such activities as market research, advertising, promotion and selling.

All organisations aim to achieve a particular purpose: for example, manufacturing goods, selling goods, providing a service or a combination of all three. The structure of the organisation will depend to a large extent on its purpose, but will also be determined by other factors. Some of these are:

- the size of the organisation
- the markets in which it operates
- the attitudes and beliefs of the people who own or control it
- the background and traditions of the organisation
- its goals and aspirations for the future.

As a general rule, we can say that the smaller the business, the simpler its structure will be. An organisation chart of a multinational organisation like ICI will be bigger and more complex than that of a national organisation like B&Q. This, in turn, will be more complex than the chart for a local engineering company, for example.

We'll start by looking at size and the way this relates to organisational structures. Businesses can be broadly divided into ones that are:

- *local*, that is, operating in a defined local area
- *national*, that is, operating within the boundaries of a single country or
- *multinational*, that is, operating across several countries.

Activity

Think of an example of a local organisation, say what it is called and describe briefly what it is in business to do.
Now do the same for a national and a multinational organisation.

Each of the organisations you have identified has a distinct internal structure which defines the relationships between the units and departments that make up the business.

Small organisations and sole traders

In a small organisation, the owner directly manages all the activities of the business and the people who work there. A **sole trader** operates alone, the **proprietor** personally carrying out all the functions of the business.

It is hard for the simple structure of a small business to coordinate the activities of more than about ten people. When the business expands and starts to become more complicated, other people will have to take over at least some of the functions carried out by the proprietor.

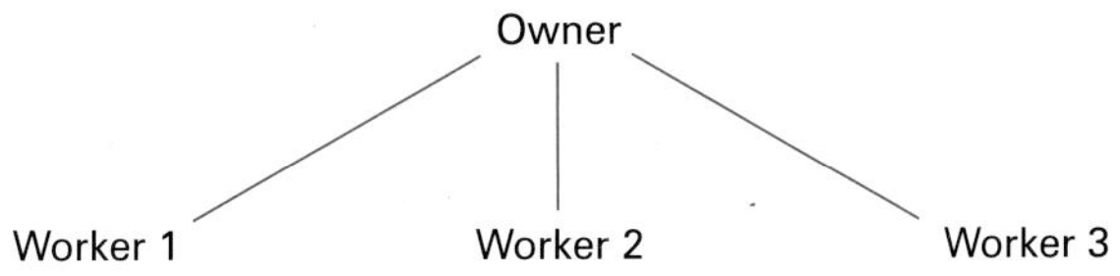

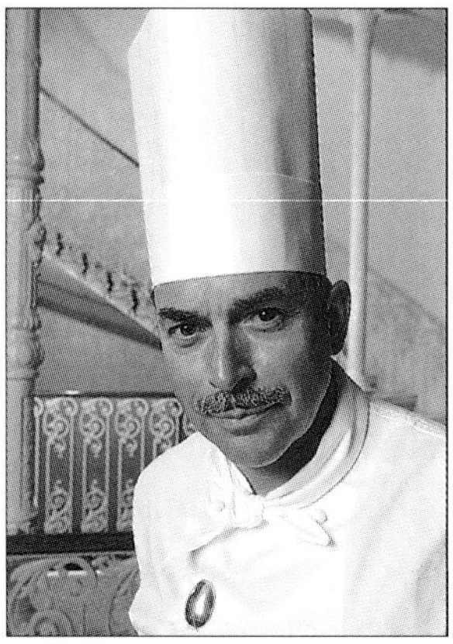

Activity

Case study

Aldo Bertorelli started making pasta for a few local restaurants in his kitchen at home in 1988. By 1990 he had moved into larger premises and was selling directly to the public as well as supplying a wider range of restaurants and hotels. He now had working for him:

- Sandra and Bruno, making pasta
- Roberto, making deliveries
- Anna and Gabriella, working in the shop.

Describe the functions of the three areas described in the case study above.
Draw an organisation chart showing the structure of the business, using the earlier examples to help you.
What problems would Aldo face if he expands?

Sandra and Bruno are in *production*, Roberto is in *distribution* and Anna and Gabriella are in *sales*.

Your organisation chart should look something like the chart on page 97.

If Aldo Bertorelli decides to expand his business, he will probably find that he is no longer able to directly manage all the business functions himself. It is likely that he will have to introduce a production supervisor or a shop manager. In addition, he will almost certainly have to employ people to take on some of the functions not directly related to making and selling the product – for example, a wages clerk or a secretary.

Larger organisations

In larger organisations, a simple structure is no longer an effective way of running the business. The increased size of the business means that people need to be specialists in different areas. For example, while in a small business the functions of marketing and finance may well be carried out by the owner, larger organisations will need people who have the expertise to manage each of these functions.

All but the smallest businesses have structures with several layers, or a **hierarchy**, of management. The following example shows an organisation chart for Precision Engineering Limited, a medium-sized engineering firm employing about 50 people.

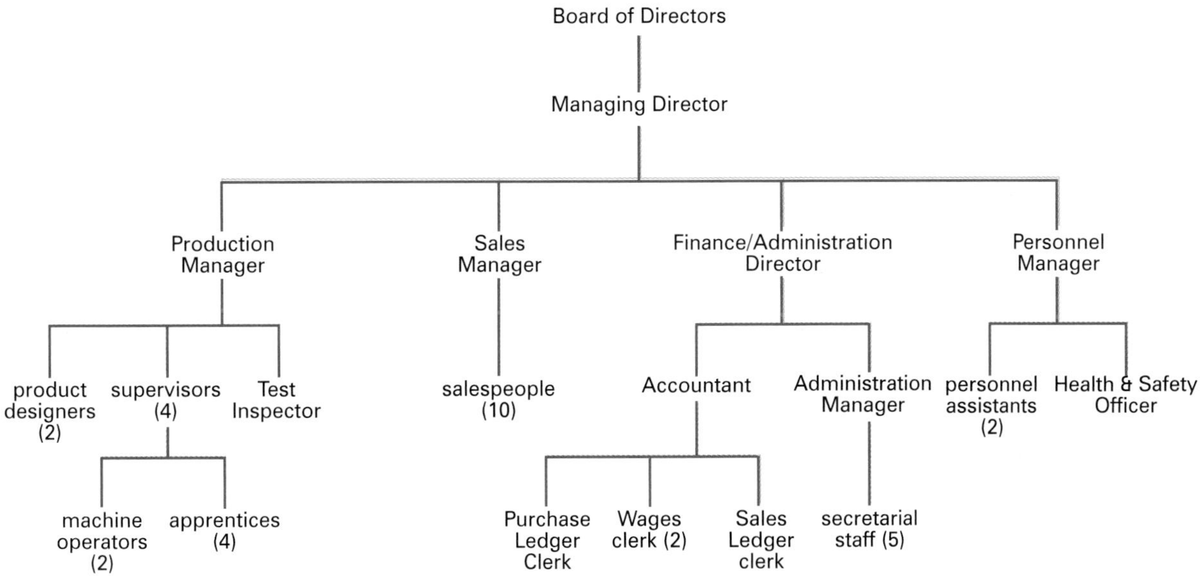

The chart shows that at Precision Engineering there are four levels in the management hierarchy:

1 the Board of Directors
2 the Managing Director
3 functional managers (production, sales, finance and personnel)
4 first-line managers (supervisors, Accountant, Administration Manager).

The pyramid structure

Almost all organisations – however large or small and however many levels there are in their management hierarchies – have structures that look like pyramids. In other words, they are broadest at the bottom.

Power and decisions flow down through the organisation, with managers and supervisors at each level passing on instructions to the people in their **spans of control.**

Structures and information

All organisations rely on high-quality information to operate efficiently and to supply products that meet the demands of the market. Some of this information comes from *outside* the organisation, but most of the information that tells managers how well the organisation is performing comes from *within* it.

Information generally flows from the bottom of the organisation up to the top. Senior managers need to know how the organisation is performing so that they can make decisions and take action for the future. Information about, for example, productivity, expenditure, customer complaints, staff absences or health and safety is collected by managers at each level from the departments or units below them. This is then processed and passed on up to higher levels for analysis and action.

Hierarchical and flat structures

The exact shape of the pyramid structure can vary widely between different organisations. In general, though, there are two main types of pyramid structure:

- hierarchical
- flat.

Hierarchical structures

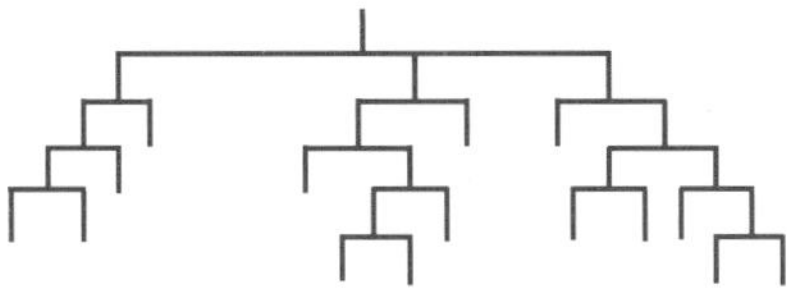

In these organisations each manager has a small span of control, and information in hierarchical structures is passed easily from layer to layer. But, because chains of command are long, implementing decisions can be a slow process.

Flat structures

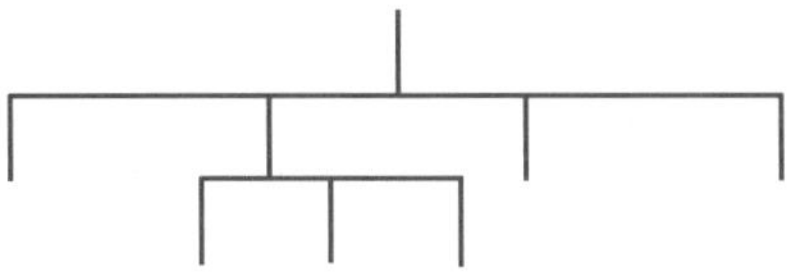

People in the organisation are given a lot of freedom, and are expected to use their own initiative rather than being told exactly what to do by their managers. Decision making is often devolved, rather than delegated to lower levels, and staff may be expected to undertake a wide variety of tasks.

In the 1980s and early 1990s many organisations have moved towards a flatter type of structure. There are several advantages to be gained by doing this:

- administrative costs are lower because there are fewer layers of management
- the organisation can react faster to changing circumstances because decisions can be made and implemented quickly
- employees are more motivated and will achieve better performance because they participate in the decisions that affect their actions.

The Civil Service and the Armed Forces are examples of hierarchical structures in which job roles are tightly defined within a formal framework.

An example of an organisation that is painfully struggling to make a flatter structure work well is the National Health Service. Decision making now occurs at lower levels, individual departments and units are responsible for managing their own budgets and performance targets are constantly monitored to make sure that overall goals are being achieved.

However, flatter structures do not automatically mean lower costs, bigger profits and a more enthusiastic workforce. It is extremely difficult to design and operate systems of control that make sure that everyone is pulling in the same direction – towards the organisation's goals and objectives.

Even organisations that have traditionally been thought of as being typically hierarchical – such as the Civil Service – are, in some areas, seeking to introduce flatter structures and a more devolved approach to decision making.

Activity

Look at the following list of statements and then note down on a separate piece of paper whether or not you think the organisation described in each one is hierarchical or flat.

1 The organisation expects staff at all levels to take responsibility for the performance of their departments.

2 **Management provides staff with detailed instructions about how to perform their tasks.**
3 **Decisions are taken at a high level of management.**
4 **Managers devolve power and authority.**
5 **The organisation is slow to respond to external pressures.**
6 **The organisation's administrative costs are a small percentage of its annual turnover.**

Now check your understanding against the answers on page 97.

Matrix structures

Another type of structure is becoming more widespread as organisations try to develop more flexible ways of dealing with pressures and problems. This is the **matrix structure**.

	Marketing Manager	Finance Manager	Personnel Manager	R & D Manager	Manufacturing Manager
Product A Manager	Marketing team	Finance team	Personnel team	R & D team	Manufacturing team
Product B Manager					
Product C Manager					
	Marketing staff	Finance staff	Personnel staff	R & D staff	Manufacturing staff

A parallel system of management runs alongside the traditional vertical chain of command. For example, a company manufacturing several main products would have a manager responsible for each product in addition to a manager for each function (production, distribution, finance, personnel, etc.).

The second, horizontal management line is not always related to products. It can, for example, be based on projects or geographical areas.

Employees in matrix structures therefore have *two* line managers:

- their *functional* managers, for generalised information, training and support relating to that function
- their project, brand or area manager, for all activities associated with that project, product or brand.

For each product, there will be a team that is made up of people from each functional area. Although staff may have general duties in their functional area, their primary loyalties and their main activities will be directed to the particular product. Although this system seems to fly in the face of one of the oldest principles of management – that an employee should only have *one* manager – it has worked extremely well in practice in a wide variety of organisational contexts.

Departments in organisations

In the section so far we have been exploring how organisations design or develop structures that enable them to meet their business objectives. We now move on to look in more detail at the specific departments that are found in most businesses.

Activity

Write down the names of the main departments (or functions) that you think would be found in an organisation manufacturing sports goods. Two are listed below to start you off:

- personnel
- finance.

The main departments found in the vast majority of businesses are:

- personnel (or human resources)
- finance (or accounts)
- production and design
- sales and marketing
- administration
- distribution (or logistics).

The following departmental names are less common, but you may well come across them when you talk to businesspeople:

- research and development
- purchasing
- computer (IT) services
- customer services
- transport.

Personnel

People are not only essential to the organisation, they are also very expensive: pay often accounts for more than half the organisation's costs.

A human resources or personnel department is vital because it deals with people, *the* most important resource. The function is concerned with employing the right people, with the right skills, at the right time and ensuring that those people are able to give of their best.

Activities undertaken within the personnel function are:

- *recruitment* obtaining the right people for jobs that fall vacant within the business
- *training* making sure that staff acquire the knowledge and the skills they need to do their jobs properly
- *grading* putting jobs in rank order, depending on the degree of responsibility involved, educational qualifications and skills required
- *agreeing pay scales and conditions of service* hours, holiday entitlements and

arrangements for sick leave and pay
- *dealing with staff problems or disputes* including industrial relations and disciplinary and grievance procedures
- *providing specialist advice and assistance* to managers on personnel matters.

In addition, a personnel department usually has overall responsibility for ensuring that equal opportunities issues and health and safety requirements are met.

Finance

If you want to know more about the work of the finance function, have a look at *Financial and administrative support* in this series.

A finance, or accounts, department is responsible for money flowing into, out of and within the business. Activities carried out within this function include:

- raising invoices and obtaining payment for goods or services supplied to customers
- making sure that invoices from suppliers match the goods or services that were supplied to the organisation
- dealing with payments to suppliers
- paying staff
- analysing the financial performance of the business
- dealing with debts
- providing financial information on performance to managers and shareholders.

Investment in new products is risky – Concorde will probably never recover its investment, Sinclair's C5 never got on the road and Unilever's new soap powder was withdrawn because of customer complaints.

Research and development

This includes both the search for new product ideas and shaping a new idea into a physical product. The same applies to services. The 'prototype' development can take a few months, for example a new coffee flavour, to a few years for such products as aeroplanes or engines. The prototype will be put through a range of scientific, safety, taste, style and consumer tests. It must also be possible to manufacture the product for budgeted costs.

Some examples of production are:
- a factory making castings for car engines where the resources employed are aluminium, electricity, skilled and unskilled labour and capital in the form of machines and buildings
- an advertising agency producing television advertisements where the main resources employed are labour (mostly skilled) and capital in the form of design and computer equipment and office space
- a market garden producing various types of plants where the resources employed are labour (mostly unskilled), seeds and bulbs and capital in the form of machines, buildings and land.

Production

This is the core function of the business – turning raw materials and resources into the outputs that are marketed and sold to provide income for the business. This production process describes service industries as well as those manufacturing goods. A business that provides a service takes as its raw material the expertise and labour of its staff. These may be combined with the resources of specialist equipment to produce the organisation's output.

Sales and marketing

Sales and marketing generate income for the business by offering and selling products and services to customers.

Look at *Consumers and Customers* in this series for more detail on the marketing activities of a business.

The sales aspect of this function is fairly straightforward, and involves selling the products of the business in a variety of ways, including:

- directly to other businesses, using the company's sales force to develop contacts and make sales
- directly to the public, using shops, mail order, teleselling or, increasingly rarely, door-to-door selling.

Marketing includes a wider range of activities. In recent years, the term has come to mean anything to do with making sure that customers (and potential customers) want and are satisfied with the products of the business.

Activities that are part of the marketing function include:

- public relations
- advertising
- market research
- special promotions
- piloting new products.

Marketing might also include the design and development function.

Administration

This function deals with the internal housekeeping of the organisation. Administrative, secretarial and clerical costs can account for a high percentage of business costs, so it is essential that this part of an organisation's operations is run efficiently.

Administration may have to:

- design systems of communication that provide people and departments with the information they require
- deal with enquiries and route them to the appropriate parts of the sales and marketing and other functions
- provide centralised office services such as data processing, word processing, filing, photocopying, dealing with incoming and outgoing mail, switchboard and reception.

Distribution

Distribution or logistics deals with bringing the products of the organisation to their marketplaces, wherever these may be. The function covers:

- packaging and despatching of goods
- warehousing and storage
- organising deliveries
- transport, including export documentation.

The transport function includes the drivers who deliver the goods, mechanics who maintain the vehicles and office staff who are responsible for planning the transport programme. The routes drivers take will often be determined by computer so that deliveries can be made in the most economical manner.

Purchasing

Although buying is sometimes organised so that each department buys its *own* supplies, some large organisations have a centralised purchasing department, which is responsible for buying all raw materials, resources and equipment. Centralised buying brings a number of benefits:

- people in the purchasing department have expert knowledge of the various sources of supply and are better able to select the most suitable products from the vast range available
- because orders tend to be larger, better terms can be obtained from suppliers
- better control over expenditure can be achieved.

Computer (IT) services

Some organisations have a computer services department that specialises in:

- *systems analysis* this is concerned with the design of computerised systems, based primarily on an identification of what their information outputs should be
- *computer programming* this step follows system analysis, and involves writing the detailed instructions the computer needs to carry out the required data processing tasks
- *computer operations* once the system is up and running, these are the day-to-day activities of collecting, inputting, processing and outputting information into and out of computer databases (it may also include *systems support*, providing help and solving problems that anyone in the organisation has using the computer system).

Customer services

This department deals with customers' enquiries and complaints, either in person, by letter or on the telephone. In some organisations customer services staff take orders and process them.

Activity

Decide which of the functions discussed you think would be involved in each of the following areas or activities. There may be one or more functions for each activity:

- administering company health schemes
- designing interdepartmental memos

- redesigning the packaging of one of the company's products
- placing recruitment advertisements
- dealing with a health and safety problem on the factory floor
- producing a profits forecast to present to a shareholders meeting
- changing tax codes in line with instructions from the Inland Revenue
- attending trade fairs
- maintaining vehicles
- organising meetings.

See how your answers match those given below. They may not be identical in some cases, as some of the items could involve more than one function:

- personnel function
- administrative function
- this could involve distribution, production and design and marketing
- personnel function, but the department recruiting may also be involved
- this would be the responsibility of both personnel and production and design
- finance function
- finance function
- mainly marketing, although administration and production and design might also be involved
- distribution or transport
- administration would organise interdepartmental meetings, board meetings and important meetings with customers and suppliers, while other meetings would probably be arranged by the people involved.

The interdependence of departments

The staff of the production department of a biscuit factory are the customers of the purchasing department, which supplies them with the raw materials production needs to do its job. The production department's customers are the distribution department, which receives finished goods from the production department and then sends them on to the external customers – shops and supermarkets.

This last activity has shown that, although organisations are divided up into different departments or functions, these also rely on each other to be able to do their work. The marketing department, for example, could not exist without a product to advertise or sell, without finance to pay for its activities and its resources and without people to do the work. This interdependence is reflected in new thinking about the way that staff in one part of an organisation communicate and relate to staff in other parts.

Some organisations now recognise that customers are not just the people who buy a product or service; they can also be the people within the company who receive work from others. Within a company, therefore, everyone is both supplier *and* customer to other staff.

Organisations have to arrange their structures and procedures so that staff can get the right goods and services to their internal customers at the right time, so that they can do their own jobs properly.

Different ways of working

It is not only organisational structures that have become more flexible during the 1990s; employees' working patterns have also become less rigid. New working arrangements have been brought in that enable organisations to meet customers' demands, while, at the same time, allowing staff to have time to look after their personal commitments.

- *Part-time and shift work* Part-time work or jobs that involve people in working a few shifts every week are becoming more common.
- *Job sharing* This is a way of working where two people share one full-time job between them. All sorts of jobs can be shared – already it's widespread in schools, shops, banks, the National Health Service, community groups, local councils, the BBC and the House of Commons.
- *Flexitime* Under this type of scheme, employees can choose, to a certain extent, how they work a fixed number of hours each month. In most offices, band width (the hours within which you can work) is from 8 am to 6 pm; core time (when you must be working) runs from 9.30 am to 12.30 pm and 2.30 pm to 4 pm.

Marks and Spencer was one of the first companies to introduce flexible hours; they have now been followed by others, such as British Gas, GEC and Shell, as well as organisations in the public sector.

- *Homeworking* Many homeworking jobs are extremely poorly paid, often paying workers piecemeal for manufacturing outwork or producing items such as toys or clothing. With the growth of new technology, homeworkers are writing computer programs, planning business strategies or working from home with their own computers and fax machines. One expanding area is 'telesales' – selling or carrying out market research using the telephone.
- *Contract work* Increasingly work is being contracted out by organisations using short-term contracts for a variety of work, from cleaning and maintenance to clerical work or word processing or large projects requiring specialist skills.

Activity

All of the above ways of working bring both advantages and disadvantages to the people who use them. Suggest at least one advantage and one disadvantage for each one.

You may have thought of some of the following:

- many part-time workers have found that, although working part time allows them to spend more time with their families to study or to pursue their leisure interests, it is often poorly paid and brings few of the benefits of full-time work

- job sharers often find that, although they spend less time at work, they tend to do much more than half a job when they are working
- flexitime is popular with employees because it allows them to plan their day to include looking after children and other activities, but some businesses feel they pay a high price in terms of disruption to the organisation
- in theory, homeworking enables people to fit work in with family life, but the lack of a structured day can often mean that more time is in fact spent at work, plus the pay for homeworking is often poor
- contractors are paid for results rather than the time spent doing the work, which means that they often have a lot of control over the way that they work, but there is often little security and the contract could be terminated without warning.

Teamwork is another new working arrangement that is becoming more important because it allows people more flexibility and brings them closer to the customer. We shall be looking at this in more detail in Section 3.

Structure and change

Sometimes organisational structures are designed complete in every detail before the organisation starts operations. This happens when a new and substantial business is created from scratch – for example, Mercury Communications and Eurotunnel. It is more common, however, for an organisation's structure to grow and change over time. Even an organisation undergoing radical change – for example, British Telecom when it was privatised in the mid 1980s – has to use its *existing* structure as raw material for the new one. The old structure is then adapted to suit the new demands that are going to be made of it.

Organisations are forced to develop or change their working arrangements for a number of reasons, including:

- *customer expectations* businesses are finding that their customers have higher expectations than ever before and they are forced to develop their systems and their procedures to meet these growing demands
- *increased competition* the opening up of the Single Market in Europe in the early 1990s means that businesses in the UK have to compete in a broader marketplace than ever before, but, at the same time, the British market is open to competition from abroad, so businesses are having to find ways of restructuring so that costs are cut and quality is improved
- *advances in technology* the rate of technological change has continued rapidly during the 1990s, so businesses may have to accommodate new technology to keep abreast of the competition or to enhance productivity, and this often involves new working arrangements for employees
- *quality assurance* British companies have been motivated to seek improvements in quality by needing to be more aware of customer

'It's crucial that customers go away feeling positive about the service we provide. If they are not satisfied they will go elsewhere next time, there's plenty of choice for them.'
Manager of a pizza restaurant

'Japanese products are so well made and so competitively priced that we have been forced to reconsider our own processes and our standards.'
Electrical goods manufacturer

'When I started working at the bank, only a few elite specialists were allowed anywhere near the computer system. Now everyone has to know how to key in and retrieve data – it's one of the essential parts of our induction programme.'
High street bank cashier

requirements, to stay competitive and to keep up with advances in technology in order to be successful.

'We were losing so much time and money on faulty goods. Every time items were returned I had to persuade the staff to do overtime – this could not go on.'
Shift manager

The environment in which businesses operate is now so volatile that few organisations can say that change is not a constant factor in their struggle for survival. If a business remains static for long, the likelihood is that it will soon fall prey to one of its more dynamic competitors.

2.2, 2.3, 2.4 C **C**

Assignment

The purpose of this assignment is to compare structures and working arrangements in two different businesses. Your central pieces of evidence for this unit will be organisation charts for the two businesses, one of which must show a traditional hierarchical structure and the other a flat or matrix structure.

Make sure that your organisation charts:

- identify the different departments or functions within the businesses
- identify the differences between the two structures.

In addition to the organisation charts you should supply the following:

- brief explanations of the work of four different departments within the businesses
- notes (and a diagram if possible) that show how the work of one department links to the work of other departments
- short descriptions of different working arrangements (part-time work, flexitime) used within the businesses, noting some advantages and disadvantages of each one
- an explanation of why team working is introduced and how it operates within one business organisation
- an account of some of the structural changes in one of the businesses during the past few years and why these have come about.

If you make visits to organisations, obtain copies of as many of the following as possible:

- health and safety policy
- equal opportunities policy
- grievance and discipline procedures
- job advertisements or descriptions.

If you can, also enquire about the company's policy towards trade unions.
These documents and pieces of information will be used in the rest of this unit.

2 Responsibilities and rights of people in business

The focus of this section is on the relationship between employer and employee and on the laws that govern the actions of both parties at work. Society's idea of what is fair has evolved over the last two centuries and legislation continues to be necessary today in employment. We will discuss the benefits of employer and employee cooperation and look at ways to resolve disagreements.

You will see the main areas where the law has become involved in working practices – health and safety, equal opportunities and the terms and conditions of employment.

Motivation and reward

A leading national food manufacturer has set up a system that involves teams of employees identifying and solving problems in the workplace. The projects tackled by these groups include:

- creating more despatch space
- a cleaning and maintenance system for bakery racks
- prevention of wet floors
- methods for saving ingredients
- setting up a policy for the prevention of back injuries.

Involvement in improving work processes has been taken up enthusiastically by all staff and has been of benefit both to the company as a whole and to individual employees.

Many businesses are working to create an environment in which people feel motivated to work hard. Here we shall briefly comment on ways in which organisations:

- make people feel committed to achieving the organisation's goals, and
- recognise and reward staff when they achieve good results.

Making people feel committed

One of the most important ways of encouraging people to give of their best at work is to involve them in making decisions and taking action outside the normal scope of a particular job. Sometimes team leaders ask members to participate in setting targets for the team, in planning how the team will meet the targets and in making sure that those planned results are achieved. At other times, individuals are asked to participate in special projects where they may be coming up with ideas for improving the working environment, ways of working so they are more efficient or finding solutions to various problems that arise. All these activities make employees feel more involved and that their views are valued by the organisation.

Recognising and rewarding staff

The ways in which staff in business organisations can be rewarded for their achievements are many and various. Here are some examples.

> My firm asks a lot of its managers – total commitment and maximum performance. In return, there are excellent benefits – a

company car, a health insurance scheme and an expense account.

Marketing Manager

If our team does a good job, the boss always comes round straight away and gives us a few words of praise. It's good to know your efforts are noticed and appreciated. At Christmas, we always get a big box of chocolates to share, and, on Fridays, if things have been going well, we go home early.

Assembly Line Supervisor

We have a 'Sales Assistant of the Month' scheme. Every month someone who has done particularly well is chosen and the reward is a small bonus. Their photograph is displayed in the store and it also goes in the newsletter.

Retail Assistant

All employees are presented with shares in the company each year. It's only right that they should share in the profit they helped to make.

Managing Director

Activity

Each of the above quotations is an example of a certain type of reward system. Identify what each one is called from the following list and make notes on a separate piece of paper:

- **performance-related pay**
- **productivity payments**
- bonuses
- job satisfaction
- profitsharing
- incentive schemes
- fringe benefits
- regular praise and encouragement.

See page 97 for the answers.

Ways to resolve disagreements

Grievance and disciplinary procedures The relationship between employer and employee is not always smooth and trouble-free. There will be occasions when one party feels that the other has in some way failed to carry out its responsibilities. Most organisations lay down set procedures to deal with any such disputes. These grievance and disciplinary procedures are usually defined in the contract of employment.

The grievance procedure The **grievance procedure** is a way in which employees can complain to their employers. Problems that are commonly dealt with through grievance procedures are:

- sexual or racial harassment
- changes in hours or working practices
- disputes about grades
- unfair dismissal.

The disciplinary procedure **Disciplinary procedures** enable employers to complain about employee's performance or other work-related problems.

The kinds of problems that might be dealt with by the disciplinary procedure include:

- a pattern of unauthorised absences
- behaviour that endangers the health and safety of other employees
- incompetence
- dishonesty.

Activity

Look at the grievance and disciplinary procedures of the organisation you visited for your assignment in Section 1.

Briefly say why an employer and employees will benefit from having such procedures.

There is no actual law that lays down what *should* and should *not* be contained in grievance and disciplinary procedures. In fact there is no law that says employers have to have such procedures or include them in a contract of employment. However, if an employee can prove that an employer did not give sufficient warning that their job was in danger, an **industrial tribunal** would be likely to find that the employer had acted 'unreasonably' and that the dismissal was unfair.

Similarly, if an employee was forced into a position where they had no alternative but to resign because the employer refused to hear a legitimate grievance, an industrial tribunal would again find that the employer had acted 'unreasonably'. Such a situation, in which a person is backed into a corner and, in effect, forced to leave, is called 'constructive dismissal'.

Industrial tribunals Sometimes the organisation's grievance procedure has failed to resolve a problem satisfactorily. In other instances, an employee may be dismissed and consider that they have been unfairly dealt with. In such cases, where disputes cannot be settled within the organisation, the employee may decide to take the matter to an industrial tribunal.

Industrial tribunals were set up in 1964, and hear evidence and deliver judgments in a similar manner to a court of law. Their findings are also legally enforceable.

If employees fail to obtain a judgment that satisfies them at an industrial tribunal, they may have an option to take their case to the House of Lords and then to the European Court.

A Manchester law firm paid £20 000 to an accounts manager after an industrial tribunal ruled that she was forced to leave after being sexually harassed by a male partner. In papers filed in support of her claim, Ms X said she complained to other partners and the firm's head of personnel about Mr Y's behaviour, but they failed to step in.

Membership of a trade union

Trade union membership has declined sharply since it reached its peak of 13.5 million in 1978. There are two main reasons for this.

- The recessions of the early 1980s and 1990s brought massive job losses in mining, heavy industry and other areas where trade union membership has traditionally been strongest.

- The Conservative government, which came into power in 1979, made no secret of the fact that it believed trade union power had to be curbed. Various governments, therefore, passed a series of acts in the 1980s and 1990s that restricted the power of the unions and limited the actions they were able to take.

It is now no longer legal for unions and employers to operate a **closed shop** – a workplace in which it is compulsory to belong to a trade union. Nevertheless, some organisations still prefer to negotiate with their workforces through one or more recognised trade unions. Some organisations have a 'single union agreement' because it is easier to deal with one union.

When a trade union is recognised by an employer it can bargain collectively on behalf of its members. Representatives of trade unions and employers negotiate and agree pay and other terms and conditions of employment. A recognised trade union also has the right to appoint safety representatives, who can carry out inspections and demand that a safety committee be set up.

Some organisations, however, do not recognise trade unions. In such companies, employees either

- negotiate on an individual basis with their employers, or
- join staff associations with representatives who negotiate on their behalf.

Activity

What is the policy towards trade union membership in the organisation you visited for the assignment in Section 1? (Alternatively, find out about your school or college policy.) Why does the organisation hold such a policy?

The organisation may or may not recognise one or more trade unions. However, whatever the employer's policy, every employee has the right, under law, to choose whether or not to belong to a union.

The right to strike? We now turn to the position that the law takes when relations between the workforce and their employers break down. It is easy to generalise about strikes or other industrial action and say that they are simply about employees wanting more pay. However, in organisations where *good* employee relations exist, employers and unions usually resolve problems without conflict. The **Advisory, Conciliation and Arbitration Service** (**ACAS**) was set up to advise both employers and employees on the legal aspects of disputes involving aspects of employment law.

On the other hand, in businesses where employees habitually have *bad* relations with their employers a simple issue can easily get out of hand and result in strike action. Sometimes the action may be just a way of showing that the workforce is deeply dissatisfied with the current state of affairs.

Industrial action

Some of the most publicised strikes in recent years have been about conditions of work and working practices rather than about pay – the key issue of the strikes in the 1960s and 1970s. Other industrial action, such as the miners' strike, the technicians' dispute at TV-AM and disputes in the newspaper print trades, has been all about people trying, unsuccessfully, to preserve their industries or long-established methods of working. As a result of the failure of such all-out industrial action, trade unions now tend to adopt strategies such as work-to-rules or one-day stoppages when negotiations break down, as did the Railway, Maritime and Transport Union (RMT) in 1994.

Jimmy Knapp, RMT leader

Activity

Think of some reasons for employees deciding to take industrial action. You may have heard about a strike in your area or you may have read about them in the newspapers. Write some ideas on a separate sheet of paper.

Here are some of the main reasons for unions taking industrial action:

- pay
- hours of work
- discipline
- redundancy
- working arrangements.

Rights and responsibilities

Examples of employees' rights are the right to be paid for work done or the right to a safe working environment. For employers, they include the right to expect that their employees will work honestly or act with reasonable care.

As we shall see, both employers and employees have certain rights under law and also certain responsibilities. Rights are things that people or organisations are entitled to. Responsibilities are the other side of the coin – the things that each party must do for the other to enjoy its rights.

The law and the workplace

The idea that it is right for the law to become involved in what happens between people and their employers dates back to the nineteenth century – the peak of the Industrial Revolution in Britain. At that time, the campaigners who demanded basic human rights for people at work were seen as dangerous revolutionaries by many of those who had made their fortunes from exploiting others.

By the second half of the century, laws had been introduced that laid down minimum safety standards in factories and mines and controlled the amount and type of work that children were allowed to do. From then until the early 1980s, the Factories Act and other laws that stated who had to do what in the workplace, developed alongside the growing power of the trade unions.

Now, the emphasis at work is moving back towards individual negotiations between employers and employees. **Acts of Parliament** such as the Employment Acts 1980, 1982 and 1990 and the Trade Union Act 1984 have limited the powers of trade unions in various ways. At the same time, issues such as Sunday opening and the minimum wage (adopted by the rest of Europe, but not by the UK) show how the interests of the organisation and those of its employees can often still be in conflict.

As the power of the unions has waned, however, it has become more and more commonplace for people to take their disputes with their employers to the courts. Laws and directives that come from the European Union

(EU) have helped this process, and you will probably be able to think of at least one recent example of a disgruntled employee being awarded damages against an employer or former employer.

It is easy to think that laws have introduced just to look after employees, but it is also in an employers' interests to protect the people who work for their businesses.

Activity

In a small group discuss the following questions.

- What harm would be done to an organisation if its workers kept on having accidents?
- What would customers think?
- How would workers feel if they believed they were not being looked after?
- What effect would it have on an organisation if employees were not being treated equally?

You may have noted some of the following points in your answers:

- workers who have accidents may have to spend long periods absent from work, which is expensive in lost production and sick pay
- having a poor health and safety record is bad for the company image; this may result in reduced sales and problems in recruiting suitable employees
- people who feel safe and looked after by their company will be more motivated, perform better and produce better results than those who believe they are at risk
- when employment rights are protected, staff are likely to feel secure and are inclined to remain loyal to the company for extended periods
- the organisation is able to make the best use of all the available talent.

To put it simply, failing to provide the necessary protection is bad management practice because it damages the organisation and demoralises or harms employees.

An employer's responsibilities include providing a safe, healthy workplace and paying people for the work they do. Among employees' responsibilities are those of working honestly for their pay and not to endanger themselves or others by their actions.

Many rights and responsibilities are set out in **statute law**, which are specific pieces of legislation that have been passed by Parliament. An example of statute law is the Health and Safety at Work etc. Act 1974. Others are enforceable under what is called **common law**. This body of law has evolved over many centuries and has been created by a combination of tradition and the decisions of the courts.

The following case study illustrates a type of law that comes from neither statute nor common law but from yet another source – the European Union (EU).

Case study

As a result of an EU directive, new regulations have come into force to protect people who use visual display units (VDUs) at work. Since 1993, employers have had to reduce risks to employees' eyesight by ensuring that screens meet certain design requirements. In addition, they have to allow users adequate breaks and make sure they receive appropriate information and training. Employers have to take action to solve posture problems, visual problems, fatigue and stress. People using VDUs are entitled to have eye tests and any glasses required paid for by their employers.

Activity

On a separate sheet of paper:

- list the main rights of employees who use VDUs
- list the main responsibilities of employers.

You will probably have found that employees' rights are usually the other side of the 'employers' responsibilities' coin. Your lists should look something like the following. Employees have the right to:

- be able to use VDU equipment safely
- to receive information and training about how to use VDUs
- have eye tests and any glasses required paid for by their employers.

Health and safety legislation

The right to work in a healthy and safe environment is one of the most important principles in employment law. Even so, many workers can expect to suffer an industrial accident or disease during the course of their working lives. Each year, more than 1400 people in this country die from accidents at work or from occupational illnesses.

Various acts set out the responsibilities of both employers and employees for health and safety at work.

The most important of these laws is the Health and Safety at Work etc. Act 1974 (or HASAW as it is commonly known). The Act states that everyone – employers and employees alike – has an active role to play in maintaining health and safety at work. It also says that any organisation that employs more than five people must publish a health and safety policy.

The main Acts are:

- *the Factories Act 1961* this Act covers health (cleanliness, ventilation, temperatures), safety (guards for machines, fire escapes) and welfare (washing and rest facilities) in factories
- *the Offices Shops and Railway Premises Act 1963* this deals with the same sorts of issues for people who work in places other than factories
- *the Health and Safety at Work etc. Act 1974* this provides the protection of the law for everyone at work and the Act draws together a wide range of previous legislation and enables parliament to introduce or update regulations easily – an important feature when technology often moves much faster than the law.

Duties of employers

Section 2 of HASAW states that employers must:

- provide machinery and systems of work that are safe and without risks to health
- provide all the information, instruction, training and supervision that employees need to remain healthy and safe.

A serious accident occurred when an employee's hand became trapped in a metal press and he lost three fingers. The Shift Manager was prosecuted under the Health and Safety at Work etc. Act because his company's safety policy stated that it was his responsibility to check the machine guards.

A fork-lift truck driver in a docks warehouse in Southampton played a practical joke on one of his workmates. Unfortunately, the victim broke a leg as a result of the incident and spent several days in hospital. The court held that the employee, not the employer, was liable because he had failed to exercise reasonable care in the workplace.

Duties of employees

Employees also have responsibilities under health and safety legislation. HASAW states that they have to take reasonable care of themselves and anyone who may be affected by their work activities. It also says that they must cooperate with their employer in meeting the requirements of the law.

Activity

In what ways could employers provide information about health and safety in the workplace?

Organisations use many methods to encourage employees to look after themselves and their workmates. The ones you thought of may be included in the following list:

- leaflets and handbooks
- poster campaigns
- employee involvement in safety committees and other groups
- stickers on machinery and other appropriate places
- videos
- competitions
- training courses.

Health and safety policies

Activity

In the assignment that ended Section 1, you collected a copy of the health and safety policy of the organisation you visited. Look at this now (or your school or college's policy).

- What are the main features of the organisation's health and safety policy?
- Who is responsible for monitoring the health and safety policy?
- Give two examples of any special arrangements that the organisation has made to ensure that safety standards are upheld.

Every organisation will have its own unique health and safety policy, but the law states that all health and safety policies should cover the following points.

- *General statement of intent* this outlines the company's overall approach to the management of health and safety. It also sets out the main responsibilities of directors, managers and employees.
- *Organisation* This details people's specific duties and responsibilities, and states how and by whom the health and safety policy is to be monitored.
- *Arrangements* Here, the systems and procedures that allow safety standards to be maintained are defined. Arrangements may include aspects such as training, safe operating procedures, procedures for

keeping the workplace clean and tidy, noise control, fire precautions, systems for reporting and investigating accidents.

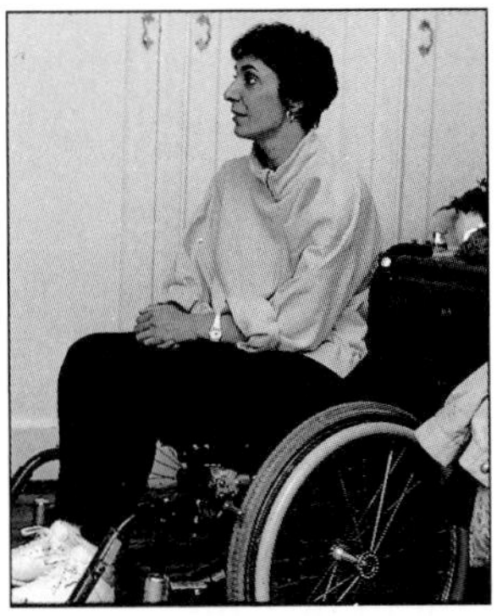

Equal opportunities legislation

Equal opportunities means having respect for all people and treating them fairly and equally. Where choices have to be made between people, it means making those choices purely on the grounds of ability and aptitude.

It is illegal to discriminate unfairly against many groups, both in employment and in situations outside the workplace. In the following activity you have a chance to check your current knowledge of equal opportunities legislation.

Activity

Find out which of the groups listed here have their employment rights protected by law:

- women
- men
- single people
- married people
- old people
- young people
- people belonging to ethnic minorities
- people with disabilities
- gay men
- lesbians
- people with HIV or AIDS.

See if your answers are the same as ours on page 97.

The laws that help to ensure that everyone has equal access to employment, promotion, education and training are as follows.

- *The Sex Discrimination Acts 1975 and 1986* These Acts make it illegal to discriminate against anyone at work on the grounds of sex. They also make **discrimination** against married people illegal.
- *The Equal Pay Acts 1970 and 1983* These state that men and women who do the same job or work of equal value and work for the same employer should receive equal pay.
- *The Race Relations Act 1976* This Act does not just apply in the workplace – it also covers the areas of employment, housing, education and the supply of goods and services. The Act states that it is illegal to discriminate, directly or indirectly, against anyone on the grounds of their colour, race, nationality or ethnic origin.
- *The Disabled Persons (Employment) Acts 1944 and 1958* These Acts were introduced to improve the work prospects of people with disabilities. Their main effect has been to establish the Register of Disabled Persons and to require all organisations with more than 20 employees to employ at least 3 per cent of Registered Disabled Persons.

Many employers now recognise that equal opportunity policies which go beyond the letter of the law can benefit the organisation as well as the individuals concerned. They realise that both sexes, people from diverse origins and those with disabilities have a wealth of talent to offer. Nevertheless, there is still a long way to go in some areas.

Equal opportunities policies

In a major national organisation, women are rarely promoted to operational management posts because managers at this level often have to work unsocial hours and it is assumed that women will not be able to work night shifts.

An equal opportunities policy sets out the organisation's aims and standards about equal opportunities and commits it to doing certain things to achieve or uphold these. The policy is often accompanied by a code of practice that says what the organisation will do to achieve the aims of the policy in practical terms. Without these guidelines it is unlikely that the policy will be enforced within the organisation.

If you have not already done so, you will need to get hold of a copy of an equal opportunities policy to do the following activity. If the organisation that you visited as part of your assignment for Section 1 does not have an equal opportunities policy, you may be able to look at one from another organisation or your school or college may have copies of their own.

Activity

Look through the equal opportunities policy briefly to see whether or not it contains each of the following items:

- responsibilities
- recruitment and selection
- training
- promotion and career development
- grievance and discipline policies and procedures
- harassment
- a named person with responsibility for implementing the policy.

Does the business monitor the success of its equal opportunities policy? (It could do this by, for example, recording the ethnic origins of those who apply for jobs, those who are interviewed and those who are selected.) Make notes on a separate sheet of paper.

What steps, if any, are taken within the business to implement its equal opportunities policy? (For example, special measures to recruit and develop members of ethnic minority groups, courses to prepare women for senior management or arrangements for maternity/paternity leave.) Make a list of some the initiatives that have been taken.

Although policies should try to cover all the areas where discrimination takes place, you probably found that the statement did not include *all* the above items. Most policies cover recruitment and selection, promotion, victimisation, grievances and discipline. For example, Paragraph 1 of the

Royal Mail's equal opportunities policy states:

'Royal Mail is totally committed to providing equality of opportunities. Its mission and values require it to create a positive working environment in which all employees, present and prospective, are respected, and are provided with development and progression opportunities, and can make the most of their abilities within a successful working team.'

If the business monitors the success of its policy, it will be able to find out how much of the workforce is made up of ethnic minority groups, women in senior management posts, disabled people and so on.

You may or may not have found that the business takes steps to implement its equal opportunities policy. However, discrimination at work can only be eradicated when all managers and staff actively support and promote equal opportunities policies.

Terms and conditions of employment

We have now seen how the law deals with the rights and responsibilities of employers and employees in two areas – health and safety and equal opportunities. But, the law is also involved in other aspects of people's working lives: the terms and conditions under which they are employed.

Contracts of employment

A simple contract does not have to be written down to be valid and enforceable in law. It may also take the form of a spoken agreement or be implied by the actions of both parties. However, it can often be difficult to prove that the contract has been made unless it has been written down.

A contract of employment is one of the many **contracts** you are likely to enter into in the course of your life. Some of these, such as buying or renting a house, entering into a hire purchase agreement or getting married, are clearly contracts. Others, such as buying food from a shop, travelling on a bus or taking your clothes to the dry cleaners, though less obvious, are also contracts.

A simple contract is one where two parties enter into an agreement that involves some responsibilities on both sides.

A contract of employment is formed as soon as the employer offers the job and the employee accepts it. Although the Employment Protection (Consolidation) Act 1978 requires employers to provide a written statement of contract within 13 weeks of the beginning of the employment, this statement is not the actual contract.

Activity

Write down three terms and conditions that you might expect to find in a statement of contract of employment.

Virtually every statement of contract will include the following basic elements and most will also specify other details:

- the rate and frequency of pay
- the hours of work

- holiday entitlement and pay
- sick pay
- pensions and pension schemes
- amount of notice required on either side if contract is to be terminated
- grievance procedures
- disciplinary procedures.

While some of the rights and responsibilities of employers and employees are set out in the contract of employment, others do not have to be stated because they are covered in various pieces of legislation or in common law.

	Rights	*Responsibilities*
Employer	to expect employees to comply with the terms of the contract	to provide agreed pay and a safe system of work
	to expect employees to do the job with care and skill	to compensate employees for any expenses incurred at work
	to expect employees to observe health and safety regulations	not to discriminate against employees on the grounds of sex or race
	to expect employees not to damage the firm's property	to consult employees if they wish to change the terms and conditions of the contract of employment
	to take disciplinary action if an employee fails to observe his or her responsibilities	
Employee	the right not to be unfairly dismissed	to comply wth the terms of the contract
	the right to equal pay	to perform tasks personally
	the right to work in a safe environment	to perform the job with care and skill
	the right not to be discriminated against	to act with reasonable care and observe health and safety regulations
	the right to belong (or not to belong) to a trade union	not to damage the firm's property
		to work honestly

The table summarises the rights and responsibilities of employers and employees. In addition to the general responsibilities shown, employers are obliged by law to:

- deduct income tax from employees' pay, called **Pay-As-You-Earn**, or, PAYE
- deduct National Insurance (NI) contributions from employees' pay
- pay a pension to retired employees if this is in the contract.

Activity

Consider each of the cases below and answer the questions, giving reasons for your answers. You may need to do some research.

Case 1

Glyn has worked at Burton's for nearly three months but has not yet received a written statement of contract. Is the firm breaking the law?

Case 2

'I know I agreed to start at Perkins and Mayfield on Monday,' said Tony, 'but then I was offered a better-paid job with the council, so I took that instead.' Can Perkins and Mayfield do anything about this?

Case 3

Maureen was offered a job and agreed to start the following month. Suddenly the company had to make cutbacks and could not take her on. Can Maureen do anything about this?

Look on page 97 to see if you agree with the answers there.

2.1, 2.2, 2.4 C ⓒ **Assignment**

Interview a manager of a local business to find out how the organisation looks after the rights of employees.

Talk to a trade union representative or an employee of the same business to get an alternative perspective.

1 Make brief notes on the rights and responsibilities of the employer and of individual employees of the organisation. Describe some of things that employees can do if they feel that their rights are being infringed or that they are being treated unfairly.
2 Give and explain at least two examples of these rights and responsibilities to demonstrate your understanding that both employers and employees are affected by legislation, especially equal opportunities legislation.
3 Give two or three examples of benefits the organisation has gained from cooperation between employer and employee.
4 Illustrate how this organisation tries to motivate, encourage and reward the workforce and what it would do if employees did not fulfil their responsibilities. Include examples of disagreements and how they were resolved.
5 What role do trade unions or staff associations play in the organisation?

Your report should be illustrated with real documents where appropriate.

3 Job roles in business organisations

In the course of their lives, people assume many roles – for example, student, parent, member of a society or voluntary group and so on. The roles people take on in the workplace are among the most important of these. From the organisation's point of view, well-defined job roles are essential in ensuring that its structure and functions operate smoothly.

In this section, you will be examining the jobs that people do in business organisations, identifying their responsibilities and the tasks they perform.

Identifying job roles

Within organisation structures, people are allocated different responsibilities and tasks depending on:

- the level at which they are working in the organisation
- the function within which they are working.

In some cases, specialist skills or job descriptions will determine individual roles and tasks. For example, the various members of staff of a large hotel kitchen may have distinctive roles such as kitchen porter, commis chef, pastry chef.

In other circumstances roles and tasks may be interchangeable. The workers in the paint shop of a car factory may all be able to operate the machines and carry out the different processes involved. Graphic designers in an advertising agency may all be able to tackle most of the jobs the agency handles.

Activity

Study the job advertisements reproduced overleaf and determine the job role in each case. What are the duties that each applicant would be expected to carry out?

Compare your responses with the following.

- The role of the Sales Engineer is one within the sales function. The advertisement is quite clear about the duties of the job – turning your own sales leads and those found for you by other people into actual sales. Although the job does not appear to include any management duties, it is a position with a lot of responsibility.

Westech Control Systems
Sales Engineer

Westech, an expanding company specialising in the development, manufacture and distribution of electronic access control systems, requires an experienced salesperson to help achieve realistic targets for 1995 and beyond.

With a proven track record of at least two years in the field of electronics, you will be able to demonstrate a sound sales ability and will welcome the opportunity to work under your own intiative with very little supervision. You will be expected to introduce new business through personal endeavour and by the conversion of supplied leads.

Basic salary to reflect experience, plus generous commission. Company car is included.

CV to: Managing Director
Westech Control Systems

Accounts Clerk

DINAS ROADSTONE LTD

A full-time vacancy has occurred in our Cardiff office. In addition to clerical duties, you will be expected to prepare a computerised weekly payroll. Familiarity with this type of system is essential.

Salary: £12000, plus staff benefits

Apply to: Personnel Manager, Dinas Roadstone Ltd

General Manager
Attractive Executive Package
Bristol

Kryptonite is acknowledged throughout the world as a leading manufacturer of precision carbon components for electric motors.

A challenging opportunity has arisen in the Automotive Division of our UK headquarters in Bristol. Reporting to the Managing Director, you will be a senior manger in your mid 30s to early 40s. You will have experience of using information technology systems to measure and enchance performance and will be able to ensure that the BS5750 quality platform secures long-term partnerships with key customers.

The package will reflect the role, and success for the right man or woman will lead to director status.

Please send your CV to: The Personnel Manager, Kryptonite Ltd

Look at *Business Organisations and Employment* in this series for more information about the different types of business ownership there are.

- The second advertisement is looking for an accounts clerk in the finance function. The job involves working accurately with both computer- and paper-based systems. The company is not looking for someone to work on their own personal initiative, but for an individual who is capable of following detailed instructions without making errors.
- The third is for a senior management position, heading the production function and possibly having some responsibility for other functions, such as finance and distribution. A key part of the role is to monitor the performance of the Automotive Division and to make sure that quality standards agreed with customers are met. A place on the Board of Directors is offered as an incentive to achieve success in the role.

Key job roles

The people within most organisations fall into one of following categories:

- directors
- managers
- team members
- supervisors
- production operatives
- support staff.

Directors

Directors are the people appointed to have overall control of limited companies. This type of organisation is the most common in the business world. A limited company is owned by a group of people called shareholders.

A board of directors is responsible for determining the overall direction and objectives of the organisation and deciding on the strategies that will enable the business to achieve those objectives. There are two types of director:

- non-executive directors, who do not participate directly in the running of the company
- **executive directors**, who are actively involved in the company's day-to-day affairs.

Executive directors are senior managers who are brought on to a board of directors to keep it informed about what is happening in the organisation. The **managing director**, as the name implies, is an executive director who is in daily, overall control of the organisation.

Managers

Managers are the people who control the organisation's functions and activities under the overall command of the managing director. Managers are responsible for five main areas of activity:

- decision making
- problem solving
- planning – setting targets that have to be met for the organisation to achieve its objectives
- control – ensuring that those targets are achieved
- organisation – creating a working environment that allows targets to be attained.

Managers are employees of the organisation but may also be shareholders. Many organisations now actively encourage their managers to own a stake in the success of the business by offering options to buy shares at reduced rates or by giving bonuses in the form of shares.

Team members

Team members are the employees of the organisation who actually carry out its operations. The term 'team member' has come into use to reflect the importance of cooperation in achieving the organisation's business objectives. Managers in almost all businesses now recognise that people's motivation and performance can be greatly improved by developing the team as a unit with a strong sense of identity.

Supervisor

A **supervisor** is a 'working leader', responsible for five or six people, sometimes within an individual department or centre. The job should be clearly defined and will probably include a higher level of pay. Often such 'chargehands' will be given a supervisory skills course.

Advantages are

A bricklayer or a carpenter on a building site often works in this way with two or three other people.

- workers know who they are responsible to
- allocation of work tasks is clearer
- increased motivation.

A weakness is that the supervisor may spend too much time on the familiar technical job, and not enough time on leadership.

Production operative

Operatives are involved with tasks which have a direct connection to the core function of the business. Their tasks involve the intake of materials, the processing, production, transport and distribution of products and, often, machinery or equipment used to manufacture them.

Within the NHS a distinction is made between direct patient care, for example midwives, care assistants, GPs, consultants, and support services, which include ambulances, reception staff and the blood transfusion service.

Support staff

These are people who support the internal working of the organisation and who perform support tasks for managers as well as for the production process. Customer services, reception, administration and cleaning come into this category.

Activity

Decide which of the following job titles denotes (a) operative work and (b) support work:

1 lathe operator
2 keyboard operator
3 carpenter
4 nurse
5 bookkeeper
6 baker.

You probably saw that 1, 3, 4 and 6 are operatives and 2 and 5 refer to support functions.

Activity

Look again at the chart showing the organisation structure of Precision Engineering Limited on page 55.

Who do you think would be most likely to carry out the following duties?

- Deciding on a business strategy for the coming year.
- Directing the efforts of teams towards achieving objectives.
- Carrying out the work allocated to them.
- Delivering a report to the Board of Directors on the success of the company's equal opportunities policy.

Now see if your answers match those on page 97.

Levels of staff

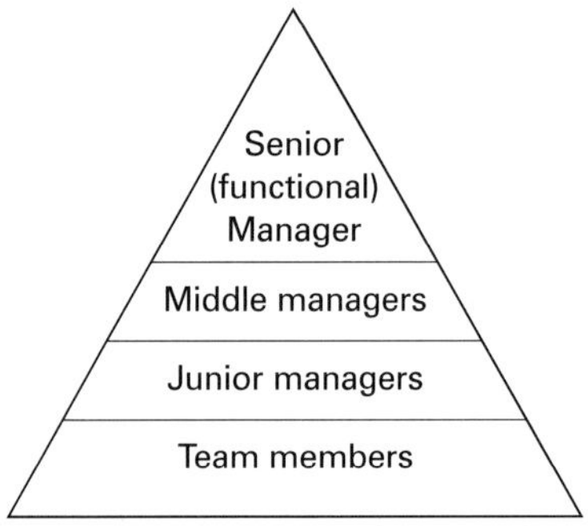

In large organisations, each function or department has its own pyramid structure of senior, middle and junior staff, and each person has a different job title and distinct tasks to perform. Senior managers are likely to be involved in long-term planning and liaising with the wider organisation, middle managers might have responsibility for making sure that policies and plans are implemented on a day-to-day basis, while junior managers tend to be directly in charge of the work carried out by teams and individuals.

Not all organisations would have this number of layers within a single department. As we have seen, it is quite common for businesses to reduce the layers – this is called 'flattening out' the structure.

Activity

Draw a diagram that illustrates the staffing structure of a department in your school or college.

Describe the main responsibilities of the people in the job roles you have identified.

Check that your diagram shows clearly senior, middle and junior managers within a single department and how they relate to each other.

The main responsibilities of the *senior manager* may include making long-term plans, attending meetings, monitoring results, liaising with the wider school or college, planning systems and procedures, identifying long-term trends and solving problems that affect the department as a whole, cascading information and policies down to more junior management levels.

The main responsibilities of *middle managers* (if these exist) may include implementing and monitoring systems and procedures, solving problems on a daily basis, overseeing the work of a particular section, organising timetables, acquiring and looking after resources, reporting to senior management.

The main responsibilities of *junior managers* may include supporting other teachers or tutors, dealing with immediate problems, attending meetings, reporting absences and maintaining health and safety standards.

Changes in the structure of organisations also means that people's job roles have to change. For example, where managers traditionally exercised 'authority' and 'control', we now hear talk of 'influence', 'encouragement' and 'enabling'. Instead of simply 'organising' the work of 'subordinates', the new thinking emphasises the importance of 'communication skills' and 'involving' 'team members'.

Teamwork

Case study

The staff of some Royal Mail delivery offices are now organised as teams of postmen and women. Instead of going out as individuals to deliver mail on single rounds, a number of staff cover one area as a team. The advantage of this is that no one finishes until the whole round has been completed, team members help and support each other and the job gets done more quickly and efficiently than before.

If we are seeing more leaders than traditional managers during the 1990s, the value of treating co-workers as team members has also become more widely recognised in the UK. We have discussed the way that more organisations are flattening out their hierarchical structures and devolving responsibility down to lower levels of the pyramid. This means that managers might relate to other department heads as members of a team. They also lead teams within their own departments. At the same time increasing use is being made of cross-departmental teams. This means that workers from different departments are brought together to pool their ideas and expertise.

This is what some employees have said about the benefits of working in teams.

> Working in teams is like being in a family. People look out for you and give you a hand when you need it.
>
> Francesca Thomas, Sales Assistant

> Sometimes it's hard to see your way round a problem, but when you have a chat with the team, suddenly there seem to be lots of ways of tackling it.
>
> Lhakshmi Patel, Multidisciplinary Healthcare Team

> It would be boring doing the same job over and over again, but you get a bit of variety when you are in a team.
>
> Mark Shaw, worker in a light engineering factory

Activity

Think of different occasions when you have been a member of a team. This may be a sports team, a project team or on an outdoor activity course. Compare your experiences to occasions when you have been working on your own. Give answers to the following questions on a separate sheet of paper.

- What are the advantages of working as a member of a team?
- Compare these advantages to your experience of working as an individual.

There are several advantages to teamwork, for example:

- teamwork helps people to work well together and help each other
- new ideas and ways of solving problems flow more easily when people are working closely in teams
- working in teams makes people feel recognised and appreciated
- teams provide the opportunity for individuals to give of their best.

There are some people who enjoy working on their own and there are definitely occasions when it is better for people to work as individuals rather than in a team. You may feel that you can concentrate harder and work more quickly when you are working alone and that you enjoy the feeling of having accomplished something through your own efforts. However, most people benefit from feeling that they are part of a team, even if that team is not closely gathered around them all the time.

Responsibilities and tasks

Each function in the organisation has to fulfil various responsibilities, allocated to various people working within the function. This will depend on their skills and abilities, their previous experience or their need to develop and gain experience.

Each responsibility is broken down into a number of tasks that a person has to perform as part of the job. For example, the responsibility of purchasing materials can be broken down into the following tasks:

- find out current stock levels
- predict demand for material in question
- identify possible suppliers
- select best supplier on the basis of cost, reliability, quality, etc.
- order materials.

Activity

Note down some of the tasks that you think a manager would perform in order to fulfil the responsibility of recruiting staff.

You may have noted some of the following:

- writing a job description
- writing/designing the advertisement
- identifying possible newspapers or journals or other media for the advertisement
- shortlisting applicants
- interviewing suitable applicants
- making a decision as to who to employ.

Assignment

Ⓒ C 2.1, 2.2, 2.4,

This assignment identifies differences and similarities between three job roles at different levels. You could choose a senior or middle manager, a first-line manager or supervisor and an employee with no managerial responsibility. Interview the three people, using the boxed questions in the margin as a guide. Think of any other questions you may want to ask.

Once you have collected as much information as possible about the job roles, prepare a presentation of the results of your investigation for an audience, using appropriate visual aids (see left for some ideas).

Working towards a presentation, identify one job role and describe the activities and tasks that it entails. This can be an individual job role or one as part of a team.

Include a description of how the person in that job role deals with a routine task, and a non-routine task.

- What are their job roles?
- Which department do they work in (or which function do they perform)?
- What are their main areas of responsibility?
- What tasks do they perform in each of these areas of responsibility? (Consider both routine and non-routine tasks.)
- What skills do they require to perform these tasks? What knowledge and experience do they need?
- What targets are set for them and how do they set about achieving these targets?
- What problems do they face? What sorts of decisions do they have to make?
- Do they work in teams or as individuals? What are the benefits or drawbacks of teamwork or individual work for these people?

You could, for example, draw diagrams to illustrate the structure of the teams or departments within which each job holder works. It would also be useful to show these departments in the context of the structure of the wider organisation.

You may also like to consider using large-scale charts or tables to make it easier to compare the activities of the three different job holders.

4 Preparing for the world of work

Types of employment and self-employment

Organisations are transforming their structures in ways that will help them to fight off the competition and get closer to their customers. People are using different skills in their jobs, the types of jobs that are available are changing and more and more people are looking at alternatives to conventional paid employment – such as starting their own businesses, working flexible hours, doing part-time work and job sharing.

- many organisations employ a flexible labour force of part-time or temporary workers, so if you have commitments and concerns outside work, this way of working could be a choice for you
- the numbers of self-employed have grown dramatically since the early 1980s, so if you are the right sort of person and you have a good business idea, this could be a realistic option for you.

Case study

Since 1990 the Alliance and Leicester Building Society has been providing the same pension scheme and pro rata holiday entitlement for part-time employees. Julian Woodall, the company's human resources manager says: 'Good people are hard to get, so we took the decision to ensure that part-time employees are not any worse off'. In return the building society gained the advantage of being able to operate on flexible working hours which it has identified is crucial to its success.

The Guardian, 21 January 1995

Case study

When Tony was aged 14, his father bought him a dilapidated one-armed bandit which he renovated and swapped for a couple of bubble gum vending machines he managed to site outside local shops. He ploughed the money they earned into buying some more slot machines, and on leaving school aged 16 set up his own business – Windfall Leisure in 1987. Seven years later Tony had over 700 video game, quiz and fruit machines at sites across North Wales. Windfall Leisure now employs 14 staff, has 127 franchisees throughout the UK and achieves a turnover of £2.5 million.

The Link, summer 1994

Working for yourself

The numbers of self-employed people more than doubled between the mid 1980s and the mid 1990s. Certainly this option has its attractions, but it is vital to consider it carefully before rushing into such a large undertaking. First, think about whether you are the right sort of person to be self-employed.

Activity

Think about the following questions and discuss them with a friend.

- Could you cope with pressure?
- Are you self-sufficient?
- Can you keep to deadlines?
- Have you got the determination to succeed?
- Are you prepared to work long hours?
- Can you live on a small income – at least at first?

If the answer to all of these questions is 'Yes', you could consider one of the options for self-employment described below.

- *Your own business* A good idea is vital. Don't just look at your own capabilities, also look at the needs of the market. Look at the area where you live, talk to people you know, do some research. You have to find out what people need but can't get so that you can start a business that is in the right place at the right time.
- *Family business* Joining a business that a member of your family has already established is an easier option than starting up on your own. If you join as an employee, you would have to expect to be treated the same as anyone else in the workforce. If you go in, or 'buy in', as a director or partner you could expect to have some say in making decisions about the future of the business and in planning and implementing changes.
- *Partnership* A **partnership** allows you to share the responsibility whether financially or practically. You share the management of the business as well as the profits, usually in proportion to the amount of money you initially contribute. You have to think carefully before choosing a partner. It is tempting to share with a friend, but in practice this can lead to problems and a broken friendship.
- *Franchise* A **franchise** is a licence to manufacture and/or sell particular brands of goods or provide a trademarked service. Over 100 companies in the UK sell 'business format franchises', which provide a licence, trade name, business know-how and advertising. You have to invest some money in the business and you continue to pay royalties to the company that gave you the franchise. There are franchises for all types of businesses – fast food, drain cleaning, photo processing, computer sales and children's clothes are just a few.

Who can help?

A variety of organisations and schemes have been established to help people who want to start up in business. One of the first hurdles is to find out about these and how they can help.

Activity

Start to compile a personal directory of the names, addresses and telephone numbers of people and organisations offering advice and practical help to prospective entrepreneurs.

As a minimum, make sure that you have notes and printed materials about the services provided by the following:

- Training and Enterprise Councils
- Prince's Youth Business Trust
- Livewire
- banks.

You may have found out some of the following points.

THE PRINCE'S YOUTH BUSINESS TRUST

- *Training and Enterprise Councils* TECs provide a range of services under the Business Start-Up scheme, including help in producing a business plan, advice and guidance, training in business skills and information about enterprise allowances and loans.
- *Prince's Youth Business Trust* This charitable trust helps young people to develop their self-confidence, fulfil their ambitions and achieve economic independence through the medium of self-employment.
- *Livewire* This organisation is sponsored by Shell and aims to encourage any young person to consider the option of self-employment and then to help with common-sense and business skills.
- *Banks* Most high street banks have information sheets, counsellors and packages to help those who want to go, or have gone, into business.

You will be able to use this information for your assignment.

Employment opportunities

A full-time permanent job continues to be the course of action that most people favour. If you think this might be your preferred option, you will find it useful to investigate the job market – both in your local area and further afield.

At the time of writing, the latest information about the types of jobs available comes from the 1991 census. One of the most noticeable employment trends has been the growth in the number of jobs in the service sector. Since 1960 the percentage of employees has risen from 39 to 71 per cent, and the trend is likely to continue.

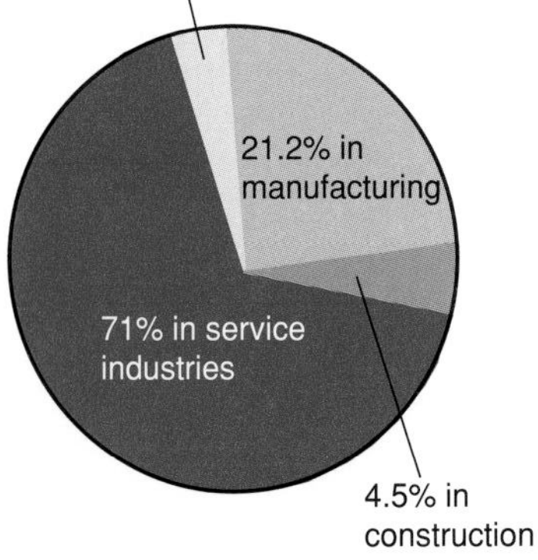

The diagram, left, illustrates the percentages of workers in different sectors of the economy.

Within this overall picture two other major trends have become apparent during the last ten years:

1 the growth in the numbers of women in employment
2 the growth in the numbers of people (mostly women) in part-time work.

UK full- and part-time employment by sex (thousands)

	Males		Females	
	Full-time	Part-time	Full-time	Part-time
1984	13240	570	5422	4343
1985	13336	575	5503	4457
1986	13430	647	5662	4566
1987	13472	750	5795	4696
1988	13881	801	6069	4808
1989	14071	734	6336	4907
1990	14109	789	6479	4928
1991	13686	799	6350	4933
1992	13141	885	6244	5081
1993	12769	886	6165	5045

1 Full/part-time is based on respondents' self-assessment. Excludes those who did not state whether they were full or part time.

2 At Spring each year. Includes employees, self-employed, those on government training schemes and unpaid family workers.

Social Trends 1994. Crown copyright.

The next activity asks you to find out more about the state of the job market and the work opportunities that may be available for you. You can get information from:

- your Training and Enterprise Council (TEC)
- Jobcentres
- careers officers
- newspapers and magazines.

Activity

This activity will help you get a general picture about opportunities for paid employment that may be open to you. After your research, write a brief report that covers as many alternatives as possible.

Collect advertisements, brochures or other printed information about any of the opportunities that particularly interest you.

- Find out about *local* opportunities in as many different types of industry as possible.
- Compare local trends with the picture that has emerged about the UK in general.
- Include a sweep of current appropriate job opportunities in other parts of the UK.
- Investigate suitable opportunities in Europe and further afield.

To get the most out of this activity:

- check that you have referred to both the job market and current opportunities in service organisations, manufacturing and construction industries
- look at a wide variety of careers – those with banks, department stores, The Post Office, the armed forces, the police force and so on
- for job opportunities abroad, contact, for example, Voluntary Services Overseas (VSO) and The British Council, which offer temporary jobs for skilled workers all over the world, and other organisations, which can help less experienced people get work as *au pairs*, holiday couriers or on conservation projects.

Non-paid work is an important aspect of your development and, as such, it features in your National Record of Achievement. You can gain credits for the skills that you develop and for your achievements while you are engaged in non-paid work.

Case study
Martia was keen to get into radio journalism but, at the age of 16, realised that she needed to gain experience and some credibility. She started by pestering the local hospital radio to allow her to go along and help at weekends. Even then it was not easy, as there were plenty of people willing to give up their time to work unpaid as DJs or technicians. After several weeks of watching and learning the ropes, she eventually had a chance to take over a short slot when someone was taken ill. From there she got taken on as a part-time volunteer helper with the local radio station. Two years later, on leaving school, she was offered a full-time post as a trainee radio journalist.

Non-paid work

Many people find that doing voluntary work and other types of non-paid work is a successful step in the direction of finding paid employment. Non-paid work is valuable to our society, to our economy and the people who choose this as a positive option can develop useful skills and reap many other benefits.

The types of non-paid work that you might participate in include:

- *home and family* caring for children or ageing parents, looking after a home
- *study* going to school, university or college, participating in evening classes, doing a distance or open learning course
- *community work* activities with voluntary or community organisations, youth groups, charities like the Red Cross, trade unions, political groups
- *leisure* pursuing sports and hobbies.

Like any other type of work, non-paid work can be full- or part-time, temporary or permanent and it may be an important element in any employer's decision about whether or not to employ you.

Your local volunteer bureau will be able to give you advice about opportunities for non-paid work in your area.

Activity

Find out about opportunities for part-time or full-time non-paid work and write a short report on this.

Back your report up with any printed information or letters that you can obtain from a volunteer bureau or other agency.

Looking at the vacancies in a Jobcentre

Sources of information

Earlier activities have involved you in finding out how different people and organisations can help. You have also researched some of the specialised sources of advice that you can tap into if you are going to start up your own business.

You may, however, still be at a complete loss about what sort of opening you should be looking for. Or you might have *some* idea of the type of work you want, but feel that you have other questions that you need answered. Here is a list of the main sources of advice for job seekers and would-be entrepreneurs.

- *Your teachers or tutors* They may be able advise you about actual vacancies or opportunities, courses, training opportunities or specialist information and advice agencies.
- *Careers service* Careers officers are all professionally trained, they can offer independent and unbiased advice and they know all about the local, national and international employment scene. It's also worth going to talk to them if you are thinking about further or higher education or vocational training.
- *Libraries* Most careers services have libraries where you can go and browse through careers literature, books, college prospectuses and a range of free leaflets and brochures.
- *Jobcentres* These are definitely worth a visit or two – even if they only serve to give you a few ideas. The staff there know about the local and national job situation and new jobs of all types come in every day. Jobcentres also give advice about training courses and special schemes.
- *Private employment agencies* Some act simply as agents – putting employers and recruits in touch with one another – while others give more of a guidance service for job seekers. You will find them listed in the *Yellow Pages* and you can see them on the high streets of most towns and cities.
- *Newspapers* Get into the habit of reading the 'situations vacant' sections of both local and national newspapers. The national press tends to advertise different types of jobs on different days.
- *Trade magazines* If you know which industry you are interested in you can look for information and advertisements that are printed in specialist magazines for catering, engineering, nursing, information technology or whatever it is you are wanting to get into. You may have to order these publications specially from the newsagent or you may find them in your nearest medium to large library.
- *Training and Enterprise Councils* Your TEC will be able to tell you about local arrangements for operating government schemes like Business Start-Up. It will also be able to give you information about enterprise allowances, small business seminars, grants and loans.
- *Charitable trusts* The Prince's Youth Business Trust is the major charitable organisation that gives financial and other types of assistance to young

Trade magazines

businesspeople. Your area organiser will send you an information pack and may also be able to come to talk to a group from your school or college.

Activity

Use this activity to help you plan your strategy for getting more information about jobs or self-employment. Write down what you will do and by when.

- Which people or organisations will you contact for advice and guidance?
- How will you go about getting hold of some literature about your selected area of work, self-employment training or education?
- In which newspapers or magazines will you look for information about suitable vacancies or self-employment? How will you make sure you read them soon after they are published?
- How could you find out which employers it could be worth writing to 'on spec'?

Identifying your strengths and weaknesses

By now you should have some ideas about employment and self-employment opportunities and which of these two paths you may decide to take. But, you cannot go far in making decisions about the future or taking action until you know a little more about yourself – your skills and the areas that you need to develop if you are to make a success your working life.

Where are you now?

Whenever you have to make a decision about your career, it is a good idea to review the skills and qualities you have to offer. You can do this informally (either on your own or with a friend to help) or formally (in consultation with a teacher, tutor or counsellor). Aim to get constructive feedback about your strengths and weaknesses.

If you are involved in a youth club you may have developed the skills of organising, being a team member, communicating and so on. In a part-time job you may have learned a number of occupational skills, such as how to manage your time and get on with other people.

Activity

Look at each skill in the checklist that follows and assess yourself. Copy the list onto a separate piece of paper. Say for each whether or not you feel that you can do this well, do it adequately or don't do it.

- Behavioural skills
  - work as part of a team
  - work independently
  - can get on with people.
- Core skills
  - communicate in writing and images
  - communicate verbally
  - apply numerical techniques to interpret and present data

- Organisational skills
  - manage time effectively
  - make difficult decisions
  - use imagination to solve problems
  - know where to get information
  - use information to make decisions
  - use information technology to input, process and present information.

Once you have done that, assess yourself in relation to the occupational skills that you know you will need in your future career.

You will find it useful to discuss your assessment with a friend, a teacher or a tutor. You might need particular help in identifying relevant occupational skills and assessing your abilities in relation to these.

You have now assessed yourself doing or doing well a fair number of different things. All these skills are essential in both employment and self-employment and the knowledge of your strengths and weaknesses will help you towards your plan for future action.

Personal qualities

It is easy to focus on skills to the exclusion of the personal qualities individuals bring to their work and life. Yet, these are often the factor that makes the difference between average performance and excellent performance. They are particularly important in work where technical expertise is less significant than attitudes towards people, patience or integrity.

Our personal experiences often develop these qualities rather than our academic studies or the jobs that we do. You will have developed your strengths through your experiences of family life, community work or leisure activities. Both positive *and* negative experiences can help you to develop these attributes.

Activity

Reflect on your own experiences. On a separate sheet of paper, copy down *five* words from the list below that you feel apply to you. For each one, say how you developed that quality *or* give an example of how you use it.

If you wish, give examples and illustrations of any other important personal qualities that you feel you possess.

- Self-reliant
- Conscientious
- Responsible
- Honest
- Determined
- Persistent
- Enthusiastic
- Confident
- Loyal
- Creative

Activity

First, write down your three greatest strengths (these can be either skills or personal qualities).

What do you think are your three main weaknesses?

Now, look at these weaknesses and decide whether they matter or not – you don't have to be perfect! If they *do* matter, decide which skills or areas you want to improve.

2.2 C, 2.1, 2.2, 2.3 IT C **Assignment**

This assignment is in three main parts.

1 Interview people in three different types of employment:
- paid
- voluntary
- own business or self-employed.

Write a report, identifying who you interviewed, how they came to be in their current position and summarising the skills the interviewees and you decide are required for the type of employment as well as the particular job. (This will be useful for part 3 of the assignment.)

2 Use the information you have gained from the interviews and from the activities you have done in this unit to describe three local, national and international employment or self-employment opportunities. Check that you include supporting information from relevant sources, a variety of career and job opportunities and paid as well as voluntary employment.

3 Now design a chart on a word processor, if possible, showing the skills needed for employment and self-employment, which you have identified in part 1, on the vertical axis. The boxes of the chart are used to indicate how your own skills and achievements match those required *or* how they could be improved and developed.

Your chart may look something like this one.

Type of employment / Skills needed	Paid employment	Voluntary employment	Own business/ self-employed
Work as part of a team			
Decision making			

Finally, record a discussion about these strengths and weaknesses, stating when it took place, who was involved and brief notes about the content and outcome. Keep in mind that some of this discussion can have taken place as part of your interviews in part 1 of the assignment.

Summary

In this unit you have investigated the ways in which organisations try to achieve their business objectives.

In the first section, you saw how the structure of an organisation influences how decisions are made and implemented. You looked at the main business functions and the different ways in which they can be organised. You explored the activities each function is responsible for and how each department relates to other parts of the organisation. In the assignment you visited an organisation to study its structure and functions.

The second section focused on how employers and employees can arrive at a fair and productive relationship in the workplace. The laws that govern the actions of both parties in the areas of health and safety, equal opportunities and the terms and conditions of employment were discussed. You also looked at the role of trade unions in the workplace.

The third section explored job roles in organisations, examining the broad roles of directors, managers and team members.

Relating these to responsibilities and tasks linked you to the final section where employment opportunities and requirements were looked at in relation to your own strengths and weaknesses. The final assignment should have helped you to draw up an action plan that sets out the steps that you will need to take to prepare yourself for employment or self-employment.

Review activity

You have now completed your work on this study unit and should spend some time reviewing what you have achieved.

1 Grading themes

For Intermediate GNVQs, you can achieve a higher grade depending on how much initiative and independent action you take in the areas of:

- planning
- information gathering
- evaluation
- quality of outcomes.

Action planning

Look over the assignments you worked on for this unit.

- Did you complete detailed action plans for each assignment?
- How much support did you need from your teacher/tutor to complete the plans?
- Did you regularly review and update your plans?
- How successful were you in achieving your plans and targets?
- What would you have done differently?

Information gathering

Look over all the assignments you worked on for this unit.

- Did you successfully identify the sorts of information you needed to complete activities and assignments?
- Did you succesfully gather the information you needed? How did you do this?
- How would you assess the quality of information you gathered? Was it:
  - useful and relevant
  - appropriate for your needs
  - accurate and complete?
- Were there any areas where you were not able to gather the information you needed?
- Why was this?
- What would you have done differently?

Evaluation

Evaluation is an important part of your GNVQ. It is one of the grading themes that will enable you to obtain a Merit or Distinction. As part of your evaluation, you should consider the following questions.

- Have I completed all the performance criteria for each element?
- What have I learned from this unit?
- How do my achievements compare with my Action Plan?
- What sources of information did I use and how did I access them?
- Is there anything I would do differently if I had to do it again?

Outcomes

- Did you present complete assignments that covered all of the areas mentioned in them?
- Did your assignment work show that you identified and selected only the appropriate parts from all the information you collected?
- Did you use business language and vocabulary accurately in your work to put information and points across clearly to your target audience?

2 Performance criteria and range

Look at the standards for this GNVQ unit. Work through the performance criteria for each element and check that you have done work to help you meet each one. Do this by noting down the relevant performance criteria number against the work.

Finally, check through the information given under the range.

3 Core skills

This unit has covered the following core skills:

- Communication level 2 : 2.1, 2.2, 2.3, 2.4
- Information technology level 2: 2.1, 2.2, 2.3.

Answers to activities

page 54

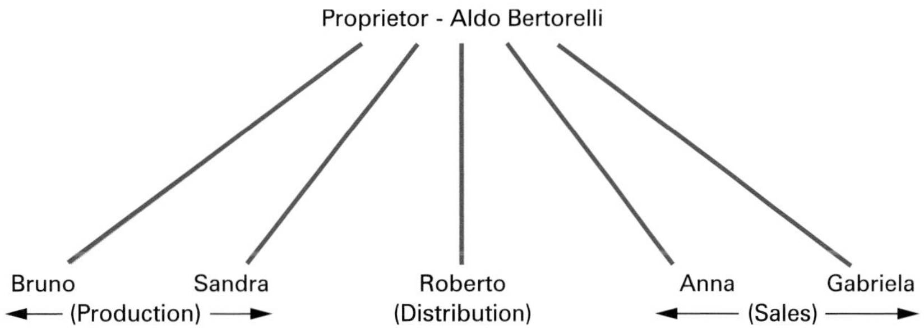

page 57 The correct categorisation of the organisations is as follows:
1 flat 2 hierarchical 3 hierarchical 4 flat 5 hierarchical 6 flat.

page 67 Fringe benefits, regular praise and encouragement, bonuses, profit sharing.

page 74 At present there is no legislation to prevent discrimination in employment against: Old or young people, single people, homosexual men and women and people who are HIV positive or have AIDS.

Case 1 The firm could be breaking the law because Glyn has already been in the job for three months. Employers are supposed to provide a written statement of contract within 13 weeks of an employee starting work.

Case 2 In theory, Tony is breaking the contract he made with Perkins and Mayfield when he agreed to take the job. However, the firm would be unlikely to go to the trouble and expense of taking any action against Tony.

Case 3 In this case, Maureen has been laid off before she has even started work. The firm is breaking its contract with her, but could argue that it had no option but to take this course of action. You may have found out that employees are not protected from being made redundant until they have been in full-time employment for more than two years.

page 78 The duties would be carried out by the following people or groups of people: The Board of Directors would decide on a business strategy for the coming year. Senior managers – the Production Manager, the Sales Manager, the Finance/adminstration Director and the Personnel Manager – would direct the efforts of teams towards achieving objectives. Team members – machine operators, apprentices, clerks and secretaries – carry out the work allocated to them. The Personnel Manager would deliver a report to the Board of Directors on the success of the company's equal opportunities policy.

Glossary

Act of Parliament a law that has been put before Parliament and approved by a majority vote of MPs

Advisory, Conciliation and Arbitration Service (ACAS) an independent body charged with the duty of improving relations between employers and employees. Its approach is both impartial and confidential

closed shop a workplace in which it is compulsory to belong to a trade union

common law laws that have evolved over many centuries and been created by a combination of tradition and the decisions of the courts

contract a legally enforceable spoken or written agreement between two parties, but it can often be difficult to prove that a contract has been made unless it has been written down

delegate some managers delegate certain tasks to their subordinates, which means that they hand over responsibility for carrying out these tasks but retain authority for them

directors the people appointed to have overall control of limited companies

disciplinary procedure the process by which an employer can complain about an employee's performance or other work-related problems

discrimination acting more or less favourably towards one person or group of people than to others

equal opportunities the name given to laws, policies and activities that try to ensure that all people are treated fairly in employment and in other areas of life, regardless of their colour, race, gender, religion or disability

executive directors senior managers of limited companies who are brought on to a board of directors to keep them informed about what is happening in the organisation

franchise a license to manufacture and/or sell particular brands of goods or provide a trademarked service

functions the specialised activities (personnel, production, etc.) that combine to ensure that the purpose of the business is achieved

grievance procedure a way in which employees can complain to their employers

hierarchy in a business context, this refers to the way that most organisations are structured. The layers of the hierarchy are usually arranged in a pyramid structure

industrial tribunals hear evidence and deliver judgments on employment law in a similar manner to an ordinary court of law

managers the people who control the organisation's functions, people and activities under the overall command of the managing director

managing director an executive director who is in daily overall control of the organisation

matrix structure a structure in which a parallel system of management runs alongside the traditional vertical chain of command. For example, a company manufacturing several main products would have a manager responsible for each product in addition to a manager for each function

organisation chart a diagram that illustrates the structure of an organisation and how the different parts relate to each other

partnership an arrangement where two or more people share financial and/or practical responsibility for a particular business. The partners share the management of the business as well as the profits

Pay-As-You-Earn (PAYE) income tax deducted from employees' wages and salaries

performance-related pay a system that rewards employees for good performance with pay rises

productivity payments special payments or bonuses paid for achieving or exceeding work targets

proprietor the owner of a small- or medium-sized business

sole trader the ownership and management of the business is vested in one person

span of control the number of people who directly report to a particular manager

statute law specific pieces of legislation that have been passed by Parliament

supervisors first-line managers who form the level of management that directs the activities of team members

Intermediate Level: Unit 3

Consumers and customers

G N V Q

Contents

Introduction	**100**
1 **The importance of consumers and customers**	**101**
2 **Promotional materials**	**111**
3 **Providing customer service**	**125**
4 **Improving customer services**	**137**
Summary	**144**
Glossary	**146**

LONGMAN

Introduction

Since the early eighties the attitudes and values of business organisations all over the world have changed dramatically. Good customer relations and the production of goods and services that customers want to buy are now matters of prime importance. Without customers there would be no sales; without sales there would be no jobs nor the money to run the business. A focus on customer services underpins the success of many business organisations.

In the first part of this unit you will consider the importance of consumers and customers to a business and you will be asked to investigate consumer demand for goods and services. Some of the characteristics of consumers and trends in demand are introduced as well as the causes of demand. Section 2 looks at promotion materials and marketing and examines the various types of promotion and their objectives. In Section 3 you will consider the needs of customers and see how these can be identified and met by providing customer services. Finally, Section 4 looks at the way in which customer services, as provided by business organisations, can be improved.

By the end of this unit, you will be able to link your personal experience of being a consumer and a customer to the effect all consumers and customers have on a business. You should understand how the demand for products and services stimulates jobs and you will have gained some practical experience of providing customer service in a business organisation.

1 The importance of consumers and customers

To establish, and plan for, **consumer** demand for goods and services requires knowledge of at least some of the characteristics of consumers. Consumer **demand** can change, both in general terms and in relation to a particular product or service and this section identifies some of the causes of change. The section also identifies sources of information about trends in consumer demand.

All **business organisations** must be aware of:

- who their **customers** are
- what their customers want.

Unless an organisation knows who its customers are (their special characteristics and what motivates them to buy the organisation's goods or services), has identified what those customers want, and has set out specifically to satisfy those **wants**, those customers will go to another organisation that does.

Organisations which put their customers first are called customer-led. They are more likely to be successful than organisations which are not customer-led.

Case study

A local public library began to close at 4.00 p.m. on Fridays, rather than at 7.00 p.m., as on every other weekday, as the result of a decision taken at County Hall 20 miles away, without consulting either the staff or the customers of the library.

The number of library users dropped dramatically. What had not been realised was that most of the people who used the library on Friday evening did so because no other time was as convenient. The assumption at County Hall had been that people did their shopping at the local supermarket at that time.

Activity

Read the case study in the margin and discuss the implications of the library's experience for:

1. **a doctor's surgery deciding to open a clinic for mothers and toddlers on one morning each week**
2. **a museum in a small country town deciding to offer school education facilities.**

The principal implication is the importance of knowing about your customers and their needs. The mothers and toddlers clinic will not attract many customers if the surgery is situated in an area lived in mainly by retired people. Money spent by the museum on educational facilities will be wasted if there is only one small primary school in the town. The museum might see its facilities put to better use if it focused on local adult groups instead.

Consumers and the supply of goods and services

Business organisations provide **goods** (things you can touch and use, such as yoghurt, televisions and textbooks) and **services** (things that are done to you or for you).

People who use the goods and services of business organisations are called consumers. Everybody is a consumer because everybody uses some goods and services – food, electricity and health services, for example.

However, not everybody is a consumer of *specific* goods or services. For example, while everybody is a consumer of food, not everybody is a consumer of particular foods, such as fish fingers, tinned soup or even meat.

We are consumers of goods and services because we:

- need them to sustain our life and well-being; for example food, housing, heating, clothes
- want them; for example CD players, computer games, sweets.

Need or want?

Consumer or customer?
Someone who buys and pays for a product or service supplied by an organisation is called a customer. He or she is a customer of the organisation. This is so regardless of whether the thing bought is for their own use or for someone else. If you go into a shop and buy a T-shirt, you are a customer of that shop. If you then give the T-shirt to your friend, perhaps as a birthday present, you are still the customer but it is your friend, who will wear the T-shirt, who is now the consumer.

When we need something, such as food, what we actually choose to satisfy that **need** is often influenced by what we want or desire. For example, you may *need* food, but you buy a Big Mac or fish and chips on the way home because that is what you *want*.

When consumers want something enough to be willing to pay for it, they create a consumer demand. For example, if consumers want chocolate-flavoured yoghurt, and are willing to pay a shopkeeper or supermarket for supplying it, a consumer demand has been created for chocolate-flavoured yoghurt. If there is a large enough consumer demand (there are enough consumers willing to pay for what they want) business organisations may be prepared to meet that demand as long as the cost of meeting it (for example, the cost of producing chocolate-flavoured yoghurt, packaging it, distributing it to shops and supermarkets and selling it) is less than the price consumers are prepared to pay, directly or indirectly.

As well as individuals, organisations and groups can also be customers.

- Hospitals are customers of drug companies, although their patients are the consumers.
- A car manufacturer is a customer of other organisations which produce and supply the raw materials (such as steel) and parts (such as batteries and brake shoes) out of which cars are made.

Consumer characteristics

Although we are all consumers in general, and there are some things that we all buy or use, different people want different types of goods and services and buy them for different reasons.

Consumers can be described by looking at the following characteristics:

- demography – gender (sex), age, wealth, whether they are employed or unemployed, family circumstances, where they live
- lifestyle – likes and dislikes, hobbies, how they dress.

Although everybody is unique in some ways, it is possible to identify a range of characteristics that are shared by several people and so group them together.

Activity

Using the categories given above, subdivide them into narrower ranges or groups.

You might have suggested:

- for gender, male or female
- for age, under 21, 21–35, 35–50, over 50
- for wealth, income less than £15 000 per year; £15–25 000; £25–35 000; and over £35 000
- for likes and dislikes, whether they prefer tea or coffee, eat meat or are vegetarian.

It is important for an organisation to know the characteristics that are shared by consumers of its goods and services. By identifying these characteristics, an organisation can also identify *potential*, future consumers of its goods or services. It can then direct its **marketing** and sales efforts at these consumers as you will see later in the unit.

Activity

From the list of products below, suggest those most likely to be purchased by the list of consumers that follows.

1 **A savings scheme offering a high return after 15 years.**

2 **A supermarket's own-label economy washing powder.**

3 **An all-in-one shampoo and hair conditioner.**

4 ***The Sun* daily newspaper.**

5 **A ticket for the National Lottery.**

Consumer characteristics

a Mary Parkin, a 27-year-old marketing executive. She lives on her own in a flat in town and has a busy lifestyle. She plays sports and likes going to parties.

b Ben Freeman, a 42-year-old male nurse at the local general hospital. He is a homeowner who lives with his wife and two teenage daughters. There are another 10 years to go on the 25-year mortgage on his semi-detached house. Most of his spare time is spent making improvements to the house or working in the garden.

c Amina Hussein retired last year from the factory where she did assembly work. She is 61 and has a married daughter who visits her regularly. She has always been active in local politics, but now that she has retired she feels she wants to spend more time with her husband who will retire later this year.

d Julie Pileggi is 18. She is at college, studying beauty therapy and business studies and shares a room on campus with another student. When qualified, she wants to start her own business. She is ambitious and most of her time is taken up with her studies. She has a weekend job to help to make ends meet.

There are no right or wrong answers to this activity. In matching the **products** with the likely consumers, however, you probably wrote that Mary would buy the all-in-one shampoo and conditioner as this would suit her busy lifestyle. Ben may take out the 15-year savings scheme, although Mary might be interested in this too. Julie is likely to buy the economy washing powder, as is Ben. Amina might also buy this, especially if her income became reduced on retirement. Ben is the one most likely to be a *Sun* reader and he, Mary and Amina might also buy a ticket for the National Lottery just for a bit of fun.

Activity

1 Choose two television advertisements for different models of cars. View the advertisements carefully. It will help you if you can record the advertisements on video and watch them several times.

2 Write short descriptions of the type of consumer each advertisement is aimed at. Base your descriptions on demography and lifestyle. If you have recorded the advertisements, keep the video tape with your portfolio.

The characteristics of consumers influence the types of goods and services they want and are prepared to pay for, and therefore also influence consumer demand. Remember that, as consumers, it is the combination of several of our characteristics that determines what we buy, not just one characteristic in isolation.

- Age – people of different ages want different things for different reasons.
- Gender – our gender (whether we are male or female) also influences the kinds of goods we buy and services we use. Some items are specifically designed to be used by one sex. These include clothing and accessories, perfume and aftershave, special interest and hobby magazines.

However, some goods that were traditionally thought of as being bought by one sex are increasingly being bought by both. More and more women are now making a significant contribution to the family income or may even be the main breadwinner. Consequently, women are becoming major purchasers of things such as cars or holidays.

- Where people live – products are also aimed specifically at people who live in villages or rural areas, or are city dwellers.
- Whether people are employed or unemployed – people's economic circumstances influence their consumer behaviour simply through what they can or cannot afford to buy.

Activity

The following is a selection of items commonly bought by both men and women:

- computers
- sports shoes or trainers
- bikes
- personal stereos.

1 **Use a matrix to write down the factors that you would consider if you were buying them. Think of things like technical specifications, style, colour, power, economy and so on. Rank the factors in order of importance to you.**

2 **Now write down the factors which you think someone of the opposite sex would consider. Again, rank them in order of importance.**

3 **As a group, discuss your answers. Individually, write up your findings and conclusions.**

A person's lifestyle is their way of life. The different lifestyles adopted by consumers have a major impact on consumer demand.

Some people adopt a particular lifestyle because it is 'in', or the current fashion. Advertising and the media can have a considerable influence on the lifestyle people adopt, by making some lifestyles appear attractive and desirable.

Some cars are targeted at high-powered executives living in the fast lane. Others are targeted at busy parents, more concerned with shopping or family holidays.

Many organisations develop and target their products and services with particular lifestyles in mind.

Activity

In a few paragraphs, describe your own current lifestyle. What do you spend your money on in order to maintain your lifestyle? What kind of lifestyle would you like to lead in five years' time? How would this affect the way you spend your money?

Taste is your personal preference for certain types of things. For example, you may prefer

- tea to coffee
- pop music to classical music
- one make of trainer rather than another.

Your taste influences everything you buy. It is the reason you choose one item rather than another, even when they are identical in every other respect.

Activity

As a group, discuss your individual tastes in things like clothes, music, food and books. Try to identify factors, such as age, gender, fashion and upbringing, which have influenced the tastes of group members. Are there any cases where the same factors seem to have influenced people's tastes in different ways? If so, can you identify other factors which could have caused this? Individually, write up your findings.

Trends in consumer demand

An important aspect of consumer demand is that it changes. Consumers' wants, as well as fashions, can change. What was in demand last year may not be what consumers want this year. A **trend** in consumer demand can be identified when consumer demand in general, or in relation to a particular product or service, increases or decreases over a period of time.

Trends in consumer demand can be long-term – continuing for many years or even permanently – or short-term, lasting for only a little while before demand returns to its original level.

Some of these trends in consumer demand may be caused by changes in consumer characteristics already identified, such as the following.

Advertising
The main objective of advertising is to influence demand – to make people want the item enough to go out and buy it. Sometimes advertising will create a demand for a new product by making it seem attractive and desirable. When GNVQs were first launched as a vocational alternative to GCSEs and A levels, the government advertised the new qualifications. There is now a considerable demand among students for courses leading to GNVQs. The qualification is widely accepted by both employers and higher education.

Gender – The traditionally defined roles of men and women as parents, earners and carers are changing. Many household tasks are now decided on and performed by both men and women. More women are now earners and responsible for, or have influence on, major household purchases. Producers of all types of goods, from washing powders to yachts, are now having to appeal to both sexes in their attempts to attract customers.

Many insurance companies offer special rates for people over 50. Others, such as Saga Holidays, design their product or services specifically for older people.

Age – The increasing average age of people in the UK is resulting in an increase in demand for health care and other services for the elderly.

Lifestyle – You will be aware of the trend towards exercise and keep fit as part of a general movement towards a healthier lifestyle – fewer people smoke; foods contain fewer additives, fat and calories; people eat more fresh fruit and vegetables.

Other changes are brought about by changes in society as a whole or by technological developments.

New technology – It seems that every month now brings major new developments in technology which affect the way we live and the things we want. Personal computers and computer game consoles have created their own demand. Compact discs have replaced other products.

Satellite and cable TV – These enable us to choose from a greater variety of television programmes. Other developments in information technology are creating a so-called 'IT super highway', where two-way information can be transmitted at the touch of a button or shown on a visual display screen.

Consumer confidence – Consumer demand largely relies on the confidence of consumers to spend rather than save their money. In times of recession or high inflation, consumers may be unsure of their future spending power and save their money against a rainy day. There may be a threat of unemployment. If food prices are rising sharply, a larger proportion of people's income may be spent on food, leaving less for other things.

2.3 AN Ⓒ **Activity**

Year	Sales £000s
1987	20
1988	21
1989	24
1990	23
1991	27
1992	30
1993	28
1994	30

Sales of videos by Savoy Videos

1 As a group, identify ten products which are popular now but were not popular five years ago. Can you suggest reasons for this?

2 The table shows sales of videos by Savoy Videos between 1987 and 1994. Construct a line graph of these figures, with the years along the horizontal axis, and the sales against the vertical axis. Does your graph show a trend in consumer demand for videos? If so, is the trend upwards (increasing sales) or downwards (falling sales)?

Information about consumer demand

An organisation needs to know what the current consumer demand for its products and services is, and also to be aware of trends in demand. Knowing about and understanding trends enables the organisation to predict, with some degree of accuracy, what consumer demand will be in the future.

Refer back to the graph you drew for the activity above. As you can see, the line of the graph is irregular, which means that while it shows an overall upward trend in consumer demand, the increase in demand has not been constant throughout the period covered by the graph. Despite this, it is still possible to predict what demand will be at some point in the future, providing the average trend remains the same.

The first step is to construct a line which shows the average trend for the period covered by the graph. To do this, divide the data in two, each half containing a complete number of years. Add up the data in each half and divide each total by the number of years in each half. This produces two averages. Plot each average against the middle year in each half and join the two points. This produces a trend line. The trend line can now be extended to any future year to show what demand can be expected, providing the average trend remains the same.

Activity 2.2, 2.3 AN Ⓒ

1 Add a trend line to the graph you constructed for the activity above by following the steps outlined in the margin.

2 Assuming the average trend in demand remains constant, forecast what the demand for Savoy videos will be in the year 2000.

Information about customers

Market research usually uncovers trends in consumer demand for a particular product or service. This may involve:

- carrying out a survey of the organisation's existing and potential customers
- analysing information already held by the organisation (such as sales records, records of enquiries).

If the organisation is just starting out in business it may not yet have the skills or resources to undertake market research in sufficient depth. Alternatively, an organisation may be considering expanding into new **markets**, either by supplying new products (for example, a washing machine manufacturer considering producing microwave ovens as well) or by selling its existing products in new areas (such as a British furniture maker considering selling to other countries in the European Union). In situations like these, published sources of information about trends in consumer demand are useful.

Information about consumer behaviour and demand is regularly collected and analysed by government departments and other bodies, such as employers' federations, professional institutes, trade associations and private firms. Much of this information is then published in the form of statistics and made available to interested organisations and individuals. The main published sources of information are:

Crown copyright, 1995

Social Trends – containing information and statistics on things like population changes, income and spending patterns

Family Expenditure Survey – analysing family income and expenditure, identifying the type of goods being bought

Economic Trends – a monthly publication giving the background to trends in the UK economy

British Business – a weekly compilation of statistics, with commentary, published by the Department of Trade and Industry

Population Trends – providing data on population in total and by region, including information on births, marriages and deaths.

General Household Survey – giving information on households, including gender and ages

Department of Employment Gazette – containing statistics on retail prices, employment, unemployment and wage rates

Information and statistics useful to business can often be found in articles and reports in the business and financial pages of newspapers and magazines, especially trade or professional publications. The following bar charts were taken from a recent survey of the computer industry published in *The Economist*. The charts show:

- yearly sales in millions of CD-ROM drives between 1990 and 1993
- the numbers of CD-ROM titles in print between 1988 and 1993 (in thousands)
- forecasts for 1994 and for the number of titles in print in 1995.

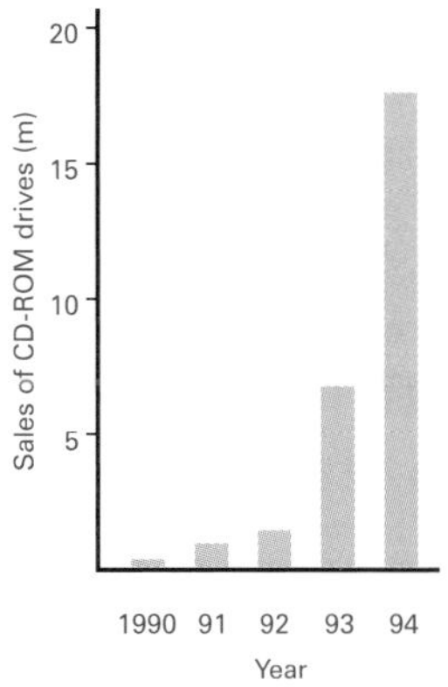

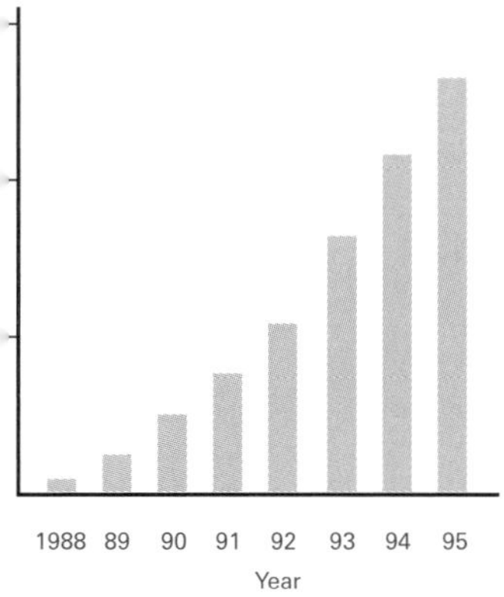

Sources: Dataquest; Info Tech

Activity

Study the charts carefully and:

1. **compare the actual and forecast trends in sales of CD-ROM drives with the numbers of CD-ROM titles in print in the years 1990–94**
2. **decide how a book publisher who is considering expanding into new markets might use this information.**

Sales of CD-ROM drives are shown as rapidly increasing. The number of titles also shows an increasing trend, but one which is steadier and does not match the rise in sales of drives. This could mean that consumer demand for CD-ROM titles (based on the number of drives sold) is not being fully met.

A publisher considering expansion should carry out further research – for example into the types of CD-ROM titles that consumers want. These might be games, education, business-related, etc. From the information in these bar charts, it appears that the demand for CD-ROM titles is growing, looks set to grow at an even greater rate in the future and is certainly an area for possible expansion by a book publisher.

2.1, 2.2, 2.3, 2.4 C
2.1, 2.3, AN
2.1, 2.2, 2.3 IT

Ⓒ Assignment

1. **Think of three consumers, individuals, clubs or companies you know, whose buying habits have changed over the last two or three years. Describe the consumers' characteristics in each case, and suggest why their buying habits may have changed.**
2. **Using any of the published sources of information given in this section, identify three products and look at trends in demand for them. For each, describe the product, illustrate past trends in demand and suggest reasons why demand has changed. Predict how the consumer demand for each product might change over the next two to three years.**

People who sell the product would be able to give you the reasons for any changes in demand, and by talking to people that buy the product you might get a different viewpoint.

You will get further information from the published sources to back up your reasons. For example, have the numbers of expensive holidays sold each year changed over the last five years? Are people tending to spend less on their holidays or not to go on holiday at all?

3 Write a summary of how consumers created the demand for the products you chose. How have consumers caused changes in the demand and supply for the products?

4 Write notes on why customers are important as a source of income, repeat business and information. Include business examples that reinforce your points.

5 Present your findings in the form of a written report which is supported by information and statistics obtained from any of the published sources of information, wherever possible.

Word process your report and, if possible, use graphics packages to produce tables, charts and spread sheets.

All sources of information must be acknowledged.

Your report should contain graphs, tables and other charts where appropriate, to illustrate information such as trends in consumer demand.

2 Promotional materials

Promotional materials are all the leaflets and advertisements that aim to tell you about a particular product or product range. Different types of promotional material – in print, on television and film – are all around us. Here you will look at the main purposes of promotional materials and the planning and resources needed to produce them. Approaches to **promotion** are identified and the potential of different media to produce and present promotional materials is explained.

You will consider the objectives of different forms of promotional materials and discuss the constraints or restrictions on their content. You will be introduced to appropriate resources for producing promotional materials for a product or event, will design and produce some of these and will then evaluate how successful the promotion was in achieving its purpose.

Marketing and promotion

By marketing, we refer to the identification of, planning for and satisfying of customer requirements while at the same time meeting organisational objectives. This requires customer and market knowledge, clear business objectives and a marketing process which is used to:

- make potential customers aware of the goods and services provided
- inform existing customers of developments in the organisation and its products
- present a favourable image of the organisation and its products.

In doing this, the objectives of promotion are to:

- create a demand for the product
- generate sales of that product
- influence consumer perception of the organisation and the product.

While all organisations must market their goods and services, the way in which they do this will depend upon:

- the type of organisation and the image it wants to convey
- the goods or services it provides
- the type of customer it wants to attract.

The marketing mix includes activities covering the so-called four Ps: the product, its price, promotion and the place where the product is available.

Promotion is one element of the marketing mix – the approach that a company takes to marketing each of its products.

Types of promotion

There are four main types of promotion:

- advertising
- direct marketing
- personal selling
- **public relations**

Most organisations use a combination of these.

Advertisements

Every day we see advertisements all around us – on hoardings, when we watch TV and in the newspapers and magazines we read. Advertising is probably the most obvious way of promoting a product and can range from multi-million-pound national campaigns to less costly local activities.

This is the most expensive method – a 30-second advertisement at peak viewing times can cost around £35 000 to broadcast, in addition to the costs of producing the advertisement. Each advertisement is short so the message must be kept brief and clear.

Commercial television – At peak viewing time, a television advertisement can reach millions of viewers. It is the form of advertising that is most easily remembered as it consists of both sound and visual images.

Television advertisements can also be screened regionally. In view of the cost and the fact that it reaches such a wide audience, television advertising is used principally for products with wide consumer appeal, such as cars and other consumer durables, food and household goods.

The listener profile is a fairly detailed idea of the sort of person who listens to that radio programme. The advertiser can select programmes with listener profiles which match the type of customer it is seeking to attract.

Commercial radio – Radio advertising can be more selective in the audience it reaches. It is also cheaper, both in terms of producing the promotion and the cost of 'air-time'. There are currently two national commercial radio stations, Classic FM and Virgin. There are also many local commercial radio stations which means that local organisations can often afford to advertise on these stations. Advertising on commercial radio can be more specifically targeted towards a particular audience, especially when the **listener profile** of different programmes can be taken into account.

Sound and image can be used to create more impact in the same way as television commercials. For lower budget advertisements, just sound and static images can be used.

Cinema – Cinema advertising reaches only a small audience – the audience who are in the cinema at the time the advertisement is shown. Some national organisations, such as banks, increase the size of audience reached by advertising in many cinemas throughout the country. However, the advertiser usually has little control over the type of audience it will reach. Cinema advertisements, therefore, tend to be for local services or products with general appeal.

These advertisements can include reply coupons and money-off offers to encourage response.

Newspapers and magazines – One of the advantages of advertising in newspapers and magazines is that the advertisement is relatively longlasting. It is therefore possible to include more – and more complex – information in a newspaper or magazine advertisement than on television or radio. It is also cheaper than television, although prices vary depending on the newspaper – a full-page advertisement in one of the 'quality' Sunday papers can cost around £40 000. National dailies and Sunday papers reach a wide audience. An advertiser can target a more specific audience by advertising in local newspapers (including free papers), national or local general interest magazines such as *ID Magazine* or *Lincolnshire Life* or even the in-flight magazines of airlines. Special interest magazines, such as *PC User*, or trade and professional magazines, such as *Management Today* and *Commercial Motor*, reach even more specifically targeted audiences.

Many people do not bother to read advertisements in print. The style (size, design and colour) and position are often vital to attract the attention of the reader.

Activity

Visit your local library or branch of a large newsagents, such as W H Smith, and look carefully at the range of magazines on display and the type of advertisements they carry.

1 **Identify magazines which you would select to place an advertisement for:**

a bedroom furniture
b a book on gardening
c a new banking service for students.

2 **Which magazines might you choose if you wanted to reach:**

a mothers with young children
b students
c as many consumers of all types as possible?

Point-of-sale advertising

As you walk around various shops, you will often see different products being promoted. This is called 'point-of-sale' advertising because it is done in the place where the product is sold. Types of point-of-sale advertising are posters, eye-catching packaging and special display stands such as those used to promote new novels in bookshops, cosmetics in chemists, or the latest Disney video in the supermarket. Point-of-sale advertising is sometimes called merchandising. Its purpose is often to encourage people to buy on impulse.

Sales promotions – Sales promotions are often coupled with point-of-sale advertising. Special offers, such as giving an extra percentage of a product free, cut-price trial packs, introductory money-off offers and coupons, free gifts and competitions are all examples of sales promotion.

Competitions

These are often added attractions and aim to invite an immmediate response from the recipient. Part of the prize can be a second competition or draw.

Other types of advertising

In addition to the types of advertising described above there are many other ways of promoting products through advertising. These include posters on hoardings, bus shelters and in underground stations, in buses and trains, electronic message boards and neon signs. Trade exhibitions, such as the Ideal Home Exhibition and the Motor Show, are opportunities for organisations to advertise their products to potential customers who have shown a real interest in their type of product by attending the exhibition.

Direct marketing

Many organisations contact potential customers directly. The most common method of doing this is by direct mail – sending letters (often personally addressed) and other promotional literature to the homes or workplaces of potential customers.

The aim of their promotional material is to make direct, personal contact with prospective customers and to encourage them to respond by returning a coupon, sometimes placing an order but usually asking for further information about a product or service. There is often an incentive to do this, in the form of a free gift, a competition or a prize draw.

Names and addresses of potential customers are often obtained from the organisation's own records. These may be records of enquiries received or of customers of other products of the organisation. Alternatively, or in addition, organisations can purchase lists containing the names, addresses and other details of consumers from firms which specialise in putting together such lists. The organisation usually specifies certain characteristics of the type of consumer about whom they want details and addresses, for example only people in certain professions, such as doctors, sales managers or the self-employed, or they might require details of consumers in specified age groups or with particular interests.

These lists are called mailing lists because the organisation generally uses them to send out promotional material.

Many magazines contain advertisements inviting interested readers to order a product direct. This is a form of promotion known as **direct response advertising**. It is common in business and industry, where some specialist magazines are made up entirely of advertisements inviting enquiries about products from readers.

Activity

Study the advertisements in the colour supplement of a daily or Sunday newspaper carefully. Cut out all the direct response advertisements you can find and answer the following questions.

1 **What products is each advertisement promoting?**

2 **How are readers invited to respond to the advertisement (for example, by telephone, by letter enclosing a cheque)?**

3 **What is the advertiser offering in return for the reader's response (for example, further information, the product advertised, a prize)?**

4 **Are readers offered any incentive for responding to the advertisement (such as a free gift or entry to a prize draw)?**

Construct a table of your answers as follows

Product	Method of response	Offer	Incentive

Sponsorship

The organisation generally aims to sponsor an event, competition or personality that reflects the image the organisation is trying to convey, or an event or competition which appeals to the same consumers as the organisation or product.

One way of promoting or raising awareness of a product or organisation is through **sponsorship**. This generally involves the organisation in giving money or other support to an event (often a sporting event or an exhibition) in return for the display of the product or organisation name and logo on promotional material for the event.

Sponsorship can take place at a local level, for example a local company sponsoring the local flower festival or a programme on local radio. Or it can take place at a national or international level, with major sporting events or art exhibitions, which may have support from several sponsors.

Motor racing is largely (though by no means exclusively) sponsored by car manufacturers, while many top tennis players are sponsored by manufacturers of tennis equipment and sports clothing. This is not always the case, however, as with events such as the Natwest Trophy in cricket.

Public relations

Sponsorship of an event is a form of public relations (PR) by the company – aiming to establish and promote a good reputation for the organisation and its products and to make potential customers more aware of it.

The PR department will also send out **press releases** (short, topical reports about the organisation or its products) to the press. The purpose is to get free publicity and promotion by having a favourable story published.

Opportunities for other PR activities include:

- in-house newspapers and magazines which are circulated among employees and customers
- open days when potential customers are invited into an organisation to see how it operates (promotional materials are usually given out during the visit).

Activity

1 **Make a list of as many sponsored sporting and artistic events, with their sponsors, as you can. You will find reference to these in the sporting and arts pages of newspapers, sports magazines and programmes of past and forthcoming events, including performances at theatres and concert halls. Posters for events usually carry the names of sponsors.**

2 **Collect visual promotional material with information about the sponsors (newspaper advertisements, leaflets and posters). How obvious are the sponsors' names on the material? How frequently do their names appear?**

3 **Identify those sponsoring organisations whose business is closely connected with the event they are sponsoring (for example, Slazenger supply the Wimbledon Lawn Tennis Club with tennis balls).**

4 **Of those organisations which are not connected with the event they are sponsoring, that is, there is no clear link with the product, what benefit do you think they gain from their sponsorship?**

5 **What image is the sponsoring organisation trying to convey, and to whom?**

Promotional materials and their purpose

An organisation must take several factors into consideration when deciding on the type of promotion and promotional materials it should produce.

Lucozade used popular and successful athletes in television and magazine advertisements to promote a new image as a high-energy health drink, in order to move away from its previous image of a drink given to people who were ill or convalescing. This made it an acceptable drink for teenagers and young adults, which gave SmithKline Beecham, its producers, a new market and a consequent boost in sales.

Target

The target for the promotion – that is the consumers at whom the promotional activity is aimed. For example, it is a waste of money and effort to mount a national television advertising campaign (which is very expensive) if your product is only purchased by a limited number of buyers in the steel industry. Such a specific target can be more effectively reached by advertising in a trade journal, for example.

Image

The organisation must decide what image of itself and its products it wishes to convey. Customers have an image of certain organisations and types of product and expect this to be confirmed by the organisation's promotional activities. The promotional material must reflect that image.

Integration

If an organisation uses more than one method of promotion, the methods used should be carefully co-ordinated so that they work together, each reinforcing the others. Many organisations use the same images for advertisements on television and on hoardings. Homepride uses the popular and well-known image of the bowler-hatted flour graders in advertisements on television and on hoardings, packaging and delivery vehicles. In this way they create and reinforce an immediately identifiable image. This increases the impact of the advertisements and makes consumers more likely to remember them.

Cost

All promotional activity costs money. In deciding which methods to use an organisation must take into consideration the financial resources (amount of money) it has available and is prepared to spend on promotion.

Objectives

These are what the organisation has decided it wishes to achieve in terms of increased sales, larger profits, a greater share of the market or an improved image for the organisation by means of the promotion. It is important to monitor the actual outcomes of the promotion against the anticipated outcomes by comparing what is achieved with the original objectives. In this way the organisation can check both the achievements and the cost-effectiveness of the promotion and change their plans if necessary.

Activity

Study the advertisement below for *Encyclopaedia Britannica* and answer questions 1 and 2 in the margin.

Write short descriptions of:

1. **the consumer group at whom the advertisement is aimed**
2. **the image of itself that the organisation wishes to convey.**

The advertisement is broadly aimed at middle-class customers who feel education is important, those who are most likely to be able to afford it and prepared to buy it. It seeks to attract fairly intelligent consumers who probably have teenage children whose education is important to them as parents and whom they are keen to help.

The image the organisation wants to convey is one of tradition and quality, of confidence in the product and familiarity.

Medium and message

There are two elements in all promotional activity:

- the medium
- the message.

The medium is the material used for the promotion. It is the actual method used to get the promotional message across to customers and potential customers. Promotional materials may be:

- paper-based – such as advertisements in newspapers and on hoardings, leaflets, brochures and other literature, and point-of-sale materials, including packaging
- lens-based – such as advertising on television and in the cinema; photographs can also be incorporated as part of paper-based promotional materials
- computer-based – such as desktop publishing packages, computer graphics and so on; computer-based promotional materials may be incorporated as part of paper-based or lens-based promotional materials.

The message of the promotional material and the medium used must be carefully developed to:

- grab the attention of the target audience
- hold their interest while the message is being put across or read
- create a desire for the product or service being promoted
- stimulate action to buy that product or service.

High Street Cred
VISA
BARCLAYCARD
Apply today and a choice of FREE gifts could be yours

In marketing, these four objectives of promotion are known by the acronym AIDA – Attention, Interest, Desire, Action.

The message of promotional materials must also influence consumer perception by creating a favourable impression of the organisation and the goods or services it offers, such as that it is environmentally aware or friendly.

Activity

Study the advertisement for Barclaycard carefully. What is the message of the advertisement? Is the message designed to influence consumer perception? If so, how does it do this? Do

you think it is successful? How does the advertisement fulfil the objectives of AIDA? Write out your analysis.

Each method of promotion has its advantages and disadvantages. Some methods are more suitable for a specific promotional campaign than others. In particular, an organisation must consider carefully the objectives of the promotion – the image of itself and its products that it wants to convey and the type of customer it hopes to reach and attract. The design and use of promotional materials and activities should be part of a well-thought-out and integrated strategy.

Constraints on promotions

While the message of any promotional material must inform, it must not be misleading nor offend people. Certain restrictions or constraints are placed on what can actually be said or included in promotional material. Some constraints are voluntarily imposed by the advertising industry itself. A magazine, for example, will refuse to publish an advertisement that makes claims for a product which cannot be backed up. A television company will not transmit an advertisement which might offend viewers.

Constraints such as these are set out in codes of practice. These are rules drawn up by the broadcasting companies, newspaper and magazine publishers, advertising agencies and the advertisers themselves, who all agree to abide by the them. The main codes of practice that apply to promotional activities are:

- the British Code of Advertising Practice
- the British Code of Sales Promotion Practice
- the codes of practice of the Independent Television Commission and The Radio Authority.

Complaints about the content of advertisements can be made to the Advertising Standards Authority. It is their aim that advertising is 'legal, decent, honest and truthful'. The Advertising Standards Authority is an independent body. It publishes the results of its investigations and will ask for an advertisement to be withdrawn if this is felt to be appropriate.

A separate code of practice, The Code of Practice for Traders on Price Indication, which is not enforceable in law, states that where there is a price reduction, the price shown as being previously charged should have been charged for a period of not less than 28 days in the previous 6 months. Organisations can get around this by displaying a disclaimer to the effect that this is not the case.

The content of promotional materials is also covered by the following legislation.

- The Control of Misleading Advertising Regulations 1988 reinforces the codes of practice.
- The Trades Descriptions Act 1968 makes it illegal to misrepresent a product by describing it as something other than it is, for example describing a table as oak when, in fact, it is beech stained to look like oak.
- The Sale of Goods Act 1979 states that all goods sold must be as described, of saleable quality and suitable for the purpose for which they have been sold.

- The Consumer Protection Act 1987 covers sales of goods and sales promotions, stating that where there is an advertised price reduction, the price shown as previously charged must be a real price, so that an organisation cannot put up the price of an article in order simply to reduce it again and show a price reduction.

Activity

Obtain copies of 'Advertising under Control', a leaflet which summarises the contents of the British Codes of Advertising and Sales Promotion, from the Advertising Standards Authority. As a group, discuss implications of the codes for:

1. **a supermarket considering trying to attract pre-Christmas shoppers with the promise of 'unbeatable' special offers**
2. **an advertising agency which is approached by a new client to handle a special promotion on jeans, aimed at young people and portraying wearing jeans as stylish and 'cool', implying that the image the person wearing the jeans can convey to the opposite sex is worth far more than the price of the jeans, which can therefore be considered value for money.**

Individually, write up your conclusions and keep them, together with copies of the relevant parts of the codes of practice, in your portfolio.

Planning promotional materials

Producing effective promotional materials, such as advertisements in the press and on TV, posters, brochures and point-of-sale materials, requires the careful selection and use of appropriate resources. These must be identified and planned for in advance so that they are available when needed.

Promotional materials and campaigns can either be produced by an organisation in house – that is by its own staff – or by an outside advertising agency. If the materials are to be produced by an outside agency, much of the planning and selection of resources will be left to the agency.

Planning

Planning promotional materials and campaigns involves considering factors such as:

- the objectives of the promotion – what is to be achieved (for example, increased sales, the launch of a new product, entry into a new market, improved image)

- the methods to be used – advertising, direct marketing, personal selling or public relations, and the types of promotional material to be used (for example, TV advertisements, brochures, point-of-sale display stands, competitions, sponsorship)
- available resources – in terms of money, people, time and physical resources (materials and equipment)
- any additional resources that will be required or jobs that will have to be contracted out.

Human and physical resources might not be available:

- in a small company
- through policy decision
- for a new product
- through cost.

Once the objectives of the promotion and the methods to be used have been agreed, the necessary resources must be identified and made available. Resources are basically of four types.

Time – How long is needed or available to plan the promotion, produce the materials, carry out and evaluate the campaign. For example, the promotion may be intended to boost flagging sales, in which case time might be of the essence. Where demand is regular, it may be possible to plan a campaign many months ahead. For example, promotional activities for Christmas are planned several months ahead.

If people with these skills are not found within the organisation, the promotion should be handled by an agency – the skills have to be 'bought in'.

People – What people are available and what skills do they have in designing advertisements, writing copy, photography, draughtsmanship and so on.

Physical – Producing a brochure requires a computer with a desktop publishing package, printer, paper, camera and film for photographs – and maybe pens and pencils to draft the whole thing out in the first place. Designing an advertisement for the press or a billboard requires paints, brushes, paper or board, dry transfers, masking tape and so on. Producing a promotional film or video requires a camera, film or tape and editing equipment. If these resources are unavailable, then, once again, the promotion should be handled by an agency.

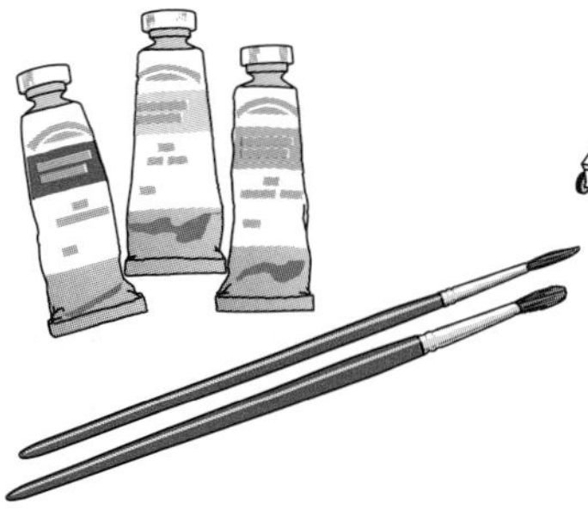

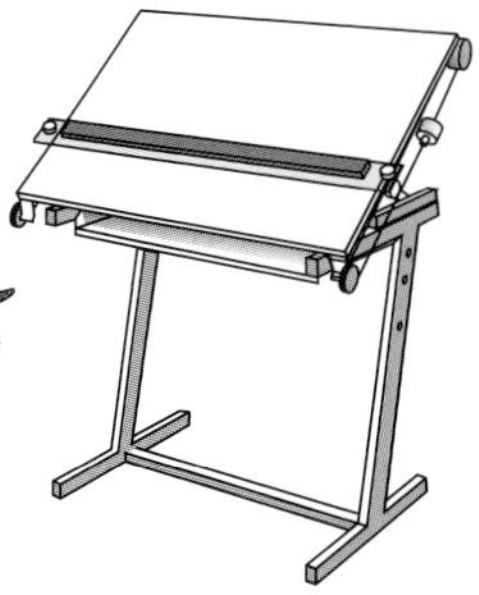

Financial – Money will be needed to purchase resources which are not already available, to pay for the services of an agency if the promotional materials are not to be prepared in-house by the organisation, and to pay for other expenses, such as postage for mail shots, advertising space on television or in the press, and so on. These financial costs have to be accurately estimated and budgeted for.

Evaluating promotional materials

All promotional activity costs money and needs to be evaluated. The criteria for success will depend on the stated purpose of the promotion.

- How well was the intended message communicated?
- Was the information provided accurate?
- Was the promotion suitable?
- Did the promotion lead to increased interest or increased sales?

In direct marketing, the percentage of return enquiries is used as a measure of success, followed by conversion into sales. With point-of-sale advertising, increased sales are an immediate measure of success. However, relying on sales figures or enquiries alone can be misleading as these can be due to other causes, such as fashion or seasonal variation.

Activity

Collect three different types of promotional material, for example point-of-sale, direct marketing and a magazine advertisement. Determine the following.

- How well does the message come across?
- Is the information of the right amount and accurate?
- Is it suitable for its purpose?

2.2 C, 2.1, 2.2, 2.3 IT Ⓒ **Activity**

You are an assistant in the Marketing Department of Fischer and Company Limited, a small cosmetics manufacturer. Jane Hollis, the Marketing Director, is thinking about a forthcoming promotion of the company's products in time to catch Christmas sales. She has sent you the following memo.

Memorandum

From: Jane Hollis

To: Marketing Assistant

Christmas promotion

Christmas is now only four months away, and this year I would like us to make a special effort in promoting our range of cosmetics to retailers. Obviously, our resources are limited and it is essential that we make full and effective use of them.

It seems to me that we have a choice of producing: (a) a full-colour brochure, including photographs; (b) a promotional video aimed at the retailers themselves; or (c) point-of-sale advertising, including packaging, posters and display stands.

In order that I can consider which type of promotional material we should develop, please identify the resources needed for each type of promotion I have listed above. Don't forget the time factor - the material must be with the retailers within ten weeks.

Reply to the Marketing Director, giving the information asked for. Remember to include in 'resources needed' time, people and finance. You should produce your reply in the form of a memo, using a word processing package.

Your memo could look like this.

Memorandum

To: Jane Hollis, Marketing Director   Date:

From: Marketing Assistant   Subject: Christmas promotions

In response to your memo of yesterday, I have identified the resources required to be as follows.

a Full-colour brochure requires: photographic studio, models, desktop publishing, typesetting and printing facilities. We will need a copy writer and I would suggest that we contact a specialist agency.

b Promotional video requires: camcorder and tape and studio facilities for editing and copying. A scriptwriter and producer will be required. Perhaps also professional actors, models or, alternatively, a presenter. Here again, professional outside help will be needed.

c Point-of-sale advertising requires: design and manufacture of display stands, design and production of posters which will need similar resources to (a).

Any special packaging can be done by our regular supplier, with enough notice.

Cost factors: a video will be more expensive to produce than printed material. As a large part of point-of-sale advertising is the product displayed, this may prove the most cost-effective method.

Production and distribution: to produce, copy and distribute the video will take longer, without control over whether it will be watched. A brochure is easiest to produce and distribute. We should also be able to meet the ten-week limit with the point-of-sale advertising.

2.1, 2.2, 2.3, 2.4 C ©
2.1, 2.2, 2.3 IT

Assignment

Collect at least three examples of promotion. You could use some of those you looked at in the activity on page 122, but make sure you include an example of sponsorship.

Write a brief report or give a presentation which describes the product being promoted, and the information and claims it contains. Identify any areas that you think the promotion is barred from covering because of the Consumer Protection Act and the codes of the Advertising Standards Authority.

Estimate the amount of time, people, materials, equipment and costs that would be needed to produce each of the materials you have selected. Remember to include all the stages, such as writing of copy (text), design, laying out the pages, taking photographs, checking the materials and printing.

Draw up a plan for each of your examples. The plan should cover identifying the objectives of the promotional material and estimating which resources would be needed to produce it. These factors were identified under the headings of time, people, physical and financial in this section.

Plan, design and produce one of the following:

a an advertisement promoting an exhibition which will take place near you in the next few months. Think of a suitable company or companies that might be interested in sponsoring The exhibition, and include dates, opening times and admission prices

b a leaflet advertising a new supermarket which is opening in your area

c point-of-sale material for a new computer game (it should include a competition for which purchasers of the game are automatically entered).

You can produce **a**, **b**, or **c** by hand or with the aid of a computer package, using graphics or photographic images. You should include video or audio tapes as well.

File the materials. You may wish to keep photographs of the point-of-sale material. You should also include your plan for each item, together with a description of the purpose of the promotion and a list of the resources used. Evaluate the promotion against the following criteria.

- Did it reach the target audience?
- What was their response?
- Was the information provided accurate?
- Was the promotion suitable for the purpose?
- Did it achieve its purpose?

Write notes on your conclusions, including how you found out the answers to the above, and keep these in your portfolio.

3 Providing customer service

In this section you will look at the needs of customers and the reasons organisations strive to meet those needs. This does not just include the customer's need for the goods or services that the organisation produces but other needs such as effective communication, prompt service and efficient handling of queries and complaints. These can sometimes be more important to the customer than the product itself. The legal requirements of providing satisfactory service to customers are also identified.

You will see in this section how organisations deal with customer queries and complaints according to agreed procedures.

Customer needs

You might go to a business organisation not only because you want to buy their product or service, but also to find out more about a product, any after-sales service and the policy on refunds. These factors may all influence your decision whether or not to buy the product.

For example, you might go to:

- a hairdresser to have your hair done
- a clothes shop to buy a new jacket or to return one that does not fit
- your local college if you want a qualification in business or to find out about careers in general.

Customer needs include

If you are buying a pair of trainers, you may need information and advice from the sports shop about the comparative performance of different types. If you receive sound information and knowledgeable advice you are more likely to buy your trainers from that shop.

Information – about the organisation and its goods or services, prices, suitability and alternatives. Such information can help you to choose one type of product rather than another, or a particular supplier.

Some organisations provide more general information about the products they sell and their policies towards such things as environmental issues. They provide this information both as a service to consumers and in the hope that they will attract and retain customers who are in agreement with their policies.

Assistance – Assistance in choosing a particular product or service that is appropriate to customers' needs, in getting it delivered and in paying for it. When you first approach a college wishing to do a course in business, you need help and guidance from the college in choosing the course that best suits your needs.

Care – All customers expect, and are entitled to be treated with, care and consideration. If you go into a shop, you want to be served promptly and efficiently. However, if you wish to spend time browsing, you do not want to be hurried or feel that the sales assistant is hovering.

British Telecom has a scale of financial compensation whereby they will pay up to £1000 in respect of private telephone lines and up to £5000 in respect of business telephone lines if there is a 'failure of service'. 'Failure of service' includes being late in carrying out repairs to the line or equipment rented from them, not keeping appointments, and disconnecting a telephone by mistake. This is part of British Telecom's 'Customer Service Guarantee'.

Refunds or replacements – If the product or service is faulty, not as promised or unsatisfactory, the customer is entitled to a refund, or to have it replaced without quibble.

Customers are not only those paying for goods and making enquiries from outside the organisation. They may also be other staff from within the organisation or people wanting help and advice. By meeting customers' needs, an organisation is providing more than just its product or service; it is providing additional service to its customers. This additional service is called customer service.

When an organisation satisfies its customers' needs by providing good customer service, the following usually happens.

- The organisation is likely to benefit from satisfied customers who are likely to return and purchase more goods or services. This can result in the organisation gaining a good reputation and attracting new customers, leading to improved business performance and increased sales and profits. The organisation can benefit from increased production, more cost-effective use of resources and other economies of scale.
- The staff of the organisation benefit from working for a successful and respected organisation.
- The customers benefit from having their needs met in a satisfactory manner. They will be satisfied with the service they have received and their morale will be improved by being made to feel valued as customers by the organisation and its staff.

Communications

The different needs of customers must be identified promptly and accurately, so that the separate needs of each individual customer can be met quickly and efficiently. A customer's needs can only be identified through effective communication, and this is the responsibility of the person in the organisation who has first contact with the customer, whether face to face, by telephone or by letter.

There are two basic forms of business communication:

- oral – speaking and listening
- written – letters, memoranda, customer and product information.

Oral communications

You use oral communications when you speak to somebody either face to face or on the telephone. It is the most commonly used form of communication.

Although we all talk every day, being a 'good' oral or verbal communicator takes skill and experience. Some of the techniques you can practise to help you become a good communicator are the following.

- Always speak clearly and at a speed your listener can follow easily.
- If you are speaking to someone face to face, watch for feedback to show you that what you are saying is understood – either by facial expression or verbal response.
- Choose your words with care. They should be appropriate to your listener and to your relationship with him or her.
- As with the words you use, you must also use an appropriate tone. If you are talking to friends your tone will be informal and friendly, but when speaking to customers your tone should be more polite and formal, while also trying to put the customer at ease.
- Allow the other person time to speak, and listen carefully to what he or she says to you. This will enable you to answer confidently and in a way which satisfies the other person's needs.

Activity

In groups of two or three, act out a business situation with which you are familiar or can identify and which demonstrates business communications. This may, for example, be in a shop, restaurant, hairdresser, the reception of a hotel or other organisation. One of your group should take the part of an employee of the organisation, while the second takes the part of a customer who is complaining about the service. If there are three in your group, the third may take the part of the manager of the organisation.

When you have decided on the situation and the role each group member is to take, each group member should make a few notes, responding to the others. It is the role of the employee to identify the customer's problem, what is needed to solve it, and to satisfy the customer with the help of the manager if appropriate. The whole role play should last for three or four minutes.

Now write out enough of the script to answer the following questions.

1 **What did it feel like to be the customer who had received poor service? Did you feel the employee and manager did enough to put matters right? Were you satisfied with the way they spoke to you and with their reactions to what you had to say? What comments would you make?**

2 **What did it feel like to be the employee, faced with a customer making a complaint? Were you able to find out easily what they were complaining about? Did you think they were being unreasonable, and that it wasn't really your fault? Did you satisfy the customer so that they went away happy, or should you have done something differently?**

Indicate on your copy of the script which part you played, and keep it with your notes in your portfolio of evidence.

Non-verbal communication

If you are speaking to someone face to face, you can get additional clues as to how they are feeling from their non-verbal communication.

Non-verbal communications include facial expressions, gestures, postures and so on. They can tell you as much about what a person is thinking, their attitude and how they are receiving what you are saying to them as their verbal responses. Being able to read and interpret non-verbal communications is a skill which you should cultivate.

Activity

Look carefully at the drawings below. Identify the message that each person is conveying through non-verbal communication.

Telephone

Many people find using the telephone more difficult than speaking to someone face to face. This is quite natural because you cannot then see the person you are speaking to, and therefore cannot pick up any non-verbal communications. When using the telephone, it is important to listen carefully to what the other person is saying – and the way they speak. Their tone of voice – cold and distant or warm and friendly – can help you to understand their feelings and needs. Bear in mind that they may dislike using the telephone too and may find it difficult to communicate their needs. Points to remember when using the telephone are:

- always answer the telephone promptly when it rings
- be enthusiastic, friendly, polite and helpful
- have a pen and paper handy so that you can write down any messages.

- if you cannot deal with the call yourself, pass it promptly to somebody who can
- make sure you know how the telephone system works so that you can transfer a call to someone else's extension when you need to without cutting off the caller off
- if necessary, take down the caller's telephone number and arrange that either you or someone else will call them back when you have found the answer to the query
- if you arrange to call somebody back, make sure that you do.

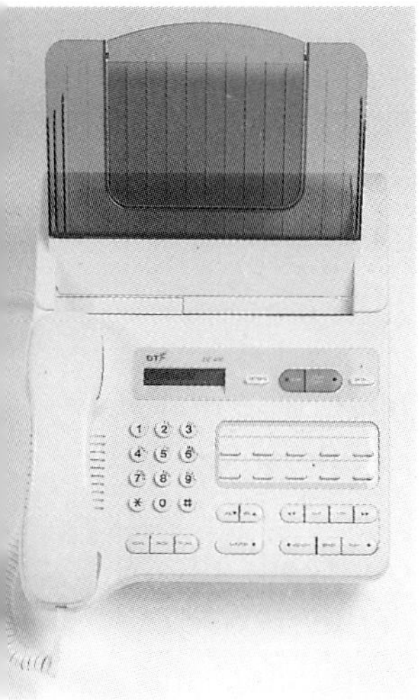

A combined phone, fax and digital answering machine

Written communications

Although the quickest and easiest form of communication, whether face to face or at a distance, is verbal, written communications are common, and often essential, especially in business. Written communications can take many forms including:

- letters
- memoranda (memos)
- reports
- minutes (records) of meetings
- forms.

Written communications can also be sent or transmitted in a variety of ways including:

- post
- electronic methods such as telex, facsimile and electronic mail
- an internal distribution system for written communications between people within an organisation (many large organisations have an internal mail system for letters, memos and other documents).

A statement of account is another form of written communication between a business and its customers. It is a record of what the customer has bought and spent, how much they have paid the business, and notes any orders or payments still outstanding. Look at *Financial and administrative support* for further information.

Written communications are permanent, slower, call for less immediate or spontaneous response than when speaking or using the telephone, and give more time for thought. In writing a letter, memo or report, it is possible to take more time to investigate facts and check the accuracy of information. In addition, more complex information, such as statistics, can be included as the person reading the written communication will be able to spend longer digesting and understanding the information given. Written communications can also include other types of visual information such as graphs and diagrams.

Customer information, such as product information, prices, guarantees and safety notices are provided in written format. They are designed to look attractive and may include photographs or drawings.

Types of customers

While every customer is unique and has his or her own specific needs, some general types of customers who require special attention can be identified.

Children often need help in expressing themselves and in deciding exactly what it is they want. They may need help in understanding things and in dealing with money.

Elderly people are sometimes unsure of themselves. They may also have difficulty dealing with money. Some will need physical assistance, perhaps with steps. They may need a chair to sit on.

Other people with special needs include:

- the disabled, who may require physical or other assistance
- those with learning difficulties, who may need help in expressing themselves or in understanding and dealing with money
- customers who are particularly shy or nervous
- foreign people, for whom English is a second language, who may have difficulty in understanding and making themselves understood.

All customers deserve, and should receive, prompt, courteous and efficient service. Some customers will be satisfied with the service they receive, but others will be dissatisfied and may have complaints and grievances.

Dealing with dissatisfied customers calls for courtesy and tact. Nobody should have to put up with rudeness, but all customers should be treated with the same care and attention. Most organisations have established procedures for dealing with queries and complaints, and staff who come into contact with customers should know these procedures. Queries or complaints should be referred to the appropriate department and person so that they can be dealt with without delay and according to established procedures.

Activity

You work at the Customer Services desk of Hogarth and Son, a large family owned department store. The departments and managers are:

Household Goods: Manager Miss J. Fish
Furnishings and Fabrics: Manager Mr A. Amin
Stationery and Gifts: Manager Mrs E. Mistry
Furniture: Manager Ms L. Keddell
Books: Manager Mr Z. Patel
Toys: Manager Ms B. Amritrage

In addition, there is an Accounts Department, managed by Ms Rider, and an Administration Department.

The procedure for dealing with customer queries and complaints is that if you cannot help a customer yourself, you should immediately telephone the manager of the appropriate department on the internal telephone system, who will then come and see the customer personally.

You receive the following customer queries. Write notes on how you would deal with each customer.

09.00: Mr Zainab telephones. He is very angry that he has received a statement of his account this morning which does not show a payment he made in cash last week. He wants this matter dealt with straight away.

09.45: Mrs Kennedy, a young mother, comes to you very distraught. She has lost her little boy. She tells you that she was looking at jackets in the Ladies' wear Department and when she turned round her little boy was no longer with her.

10.18: Miss Ashton comes up to the Customer Services desk and says she bought a new washing machine last week and is still waiting for it to be delivered. She is quite polite but you can see that her patience is wearing thin.

10.25: Another annoyed customer. Mr Simonson had a wardrobe delivered last Friday. On examining it he found that there was an unsightly scratch on one of the doors. You offer to call the Furniture Department, but Mr Simonson says he has already spoken to a 'young man who was quite rude'.

12.29: It is nearly lunchtime when an elderly lady, Mrs Hassan, arrives at the Customer Services desk. She has difficulty in speaking English and is quite flustered. This makes her nervous and she talks quickly so that you find her hard to understand. As she talks, she keeps shifting her weight from one leg to the other, as though her legs are tired.

Activity

Find out how complaints are dealt with in your local sports centre. Be sure to include an example incident, the recording of it, the process of dealing with it and its resolution.

Customer protection

As well as prompt, courteous service, customers have a right to expect an organisation to behave fairly and honestly and to supply products or carry out services which meet the legal requirements of health and safety. In law, an organisation can be held liable for:

- injury or loss to a customer which is caused through negligence – whether intentional or not – on the part of the organisation or its employees
- injury to a customer or harm to a customer's belongings, caused by a faulty product or service supplied by the organisation or its employees
- any financial loss suffered by a customer due to the negligence or faulty workmanship of the organisation or its employees.

Activity

Consider the following case studies carefully and identify who is liable. Give your reasons.

1 Mary Hoskins wants a refill for the new fountain pen she was given for her birthday. As she is not sure what type of refill she requires, she takes her pen to a local stationer where the assistant gives her the correct one. Mary asks the assistant to fit the refill for her. The assistant readily agrees but, in doing so, some ink is splashed onto Mary's coat. The assistant says he is not responsible as Mary asked him to fit the refill and he only did this as a favour. Mary, however, insists that the shop is liable.

2 Bob Roberts has just bought a new spreadsheet package for his computer. When he gets it home, he finds that not only will it not run on his computer (although it is supposed to be compatible) but it corrupts some of the information already contained on the hard disk. Bob takes the spreadsheet package back to the shop. The assistant apologises and offers to send the software back to the manufacturer who will send a replacement to Bob. The assistant says there is nothing that he can do about the information that has been lost. Bob thinks that it is the shop's responsibility to replace the software and compensate him for financial loss caused by the information being corrupted.

3 Jill Thompson has always been a bit of a gambler – but she doesn't like losing! Recently, her bank wrote to her about an investment scheme linked to the stock market, which, if past performance was anything to go by, would produce a good return over the next ten years. Jill decided to invest £5000 in the scheme, although the bank pointed out that share values can go down as well as up, and that past performance is not necessarily a guide to future performance. After six months, Jill's original investment was worth £4200. She immediately went to the bank and demanded her original investment back, saying that when she invested her money it was on the understanding that the scheme was a good investment, and losing £800 in six months cannot be considered good. The bank said that she could only get £4200 back as that was what her investment was currently worth.

The organisation is liable in case studies 1 and 2. In case study 3, the bank is not liable, as it was clearly explained to Jill that the value of her investment could go down as well as up, and that past performance is not necessarily a guide to future performance.

An organisaion can take out various forms of insurance to protect itself against claims for loss or injury, which, in some cases, can be substantial. The most common types of insurance policy are:

- public liability, which covers claims for personal injury or loss caused by negligence or faulty equipment on the organisation's premises
- product liability, which covers claims for personal injury or loss caused by faulty goods supplied by the organisation
- professional indemnity, which is a special form of insurance for professional people such as accountants, management consultants, architects, solicitors and so on, covering claims for damages or loss caused by professional negligence or faulty service.

When a customer makes a payment in exchange for goods or services, they enter into a legal contract with the provider of the goods or services. If the goods or services supplied in exchange for the payment are faulty or unsatisfactory and do not match up with the description of the goods or services offered, this forms a breach of contract. Under the Unfair Contract Terms Act 1977, it is illegal for suppliers to try to remove the statutory rights of consumers by including exclusion clauses in this contract.

Consumer law

Other examples of Consumer law are the Trades Descriptions Act and the Sale of Goods Act, which you can find on page 119.

There are several laws whose purpose is to protect customers from unsatisfactory products or service. These include:

- the Supply of Goods and Services Act 1982, which requires suppliers of goods and services, in particular services such as home maintenance and improvements, to provide work which is satisfactory, at a reasonable price and within a reasonable period of time
- the Consumer Protection Act 1987, which makes manufacturers responsible for damage or injury caused by defective products; the Government has the power to prevent the sale of goods which are considered potentially dangerous, and also to set standards of production.

Activity

In each of the following cases, identify which, if any, of the Acts described above apply. Give your reasons.

1 Lazarus Dube has recently had a new kitchen installed in his flat. Lazarus moved back to stay with his parents for a few days while the workmen were in. On returning to his flat, Lazarus found the kitchen flooded from a leak in the new sink tap. He telephoned the firm who installed the kitchen only to be told, 'Sorry, we're too busy to do anything about it at the moment. You'll have to call out a plumber. Anyway, faulty plumbing isn't our responsibility'.

2 Judy Trewartha saw an advertisement for an oak coffee table in a magazine. She sent for the table, enclosing payment for it. When the table arrived, however, she was surprised to see that the label on the carton described it as 'beech, stained dark oak'. 'You'll have to come and collect it,' Judy told the manufacturer's salesman who answered her telephone call. 'I wanted an oak coffee table, not one that just looks like oak.'

3 David took the teddy bear back to the shop. He showed the sales assistant how the head could be pulled off, leaving a long length of sharp wire. 'I bought this for my three-year-old daughter,' David explained, 'but it's too dangerous for a child to play with.'

'This is one of our best-selling toys,' the assistant replied. 'We've not had any other complaints. Anyway, you're not supposed to pull the head off. You can't hold the shop responsible for your little girl misusing the toy.'

You probably identified that, in the case of Lazarus's kitchen, the Supply of Goods and Services Act 1982 applies. The firm who installed the kitchen have a duty to ensure that it is installed correctly. They should certainly not have told Lazarus to call out a plumber unless they really were unable to attend to it themselves and had taken full responsibility for payment and workmanship.

Judy bought the table on the understanding that it was actually made of oak and the Trades Descriptions Act 1968 applies. The manufacturer must therefore collect the table and refund Judy's payment.

The dangerous teddy bear comes under the Consumer Protection Act 1987. The manufacturer is responsible for any damage or injury caused, but the shop is responsible for selling the item and could be prosecuted for this.

Communicating consumer protection

Protection for consumers is of little use unless consumers are made aware of the forms of protection they have and know how to go about making a complaint.

Many organisations have their own codes of practice by which they operate. These often include procedures for informing consumers of their rights. In the public sector, citizen's charters are widely available to consumers. By these methods, consumers are made aware of their rights, the standards of service they should expect and how to obtain redress if they don't get it. Organisations and their staff are made aware of their responsibilities and the standards of service they should provide. As a result, complaints and dissatisfaction can be avoided to the benefit of the customers, the organisation and the staff.

2.1, 2.2, 2.4 C ©
2.1, 2.2, 2.3 IT

Assignment

This assignment is in three parts.

1 Write a report identifying customer services provided by one of the following:

- a high street department store, such as Marks and Spencer or Debenhams
- a private utility, such as British Gas or British Telecom
- your local hospital or GP practice.

What are the main categories of customers and how does the organisation meet their customer service needs? Include examples of business communications which take place and show how enquiries and complaints are dealt with.

2 In groups of four, act out one of the following scenarios. Each group member will take the role of a customer, and each member in turn must play the role of the employee serving each of the other three customers. (The combination of customer needs will thus be different for each member taking the part of the employee). If possible, record the role plays on video; alternatively arrange for an observer to take notes.

The scenarios

Scenario 1: the counter of a main Post Office. The employee is serving behind the counter.

***Customer 1*: requires information on sending a parcel to India.**

***Customer 2*: requires help in completing a form for a visitor's passport.**

***Customer 3*: requires a refund on three months' unexpired portion of a vehicle licence disc.**

***Customer 4*: requires a replacement for a first day cover of a new stamp issue which has a badly smudged postmark.**

Scenario 2: The Customer Services Department of an Electricity Board showroom. The employee is serving in the department.

***Customer 1*: has very limited eyesight and would like information on special aids to cope with setting the thermostat on her central heating.**

***Customer 2*: wants to buy a suitable fan heater for a small office.**

***Customer 3*: requires a refund on an electricity bill just received They moved house three months ago, giving the Electricity Board sufficient notice, but the bill refers to the period after the move.**

Customer 4: **requires replacement of a new cooker which was delivered this morning in a damaged condition.**

Write a short piece (no more than 500 words) about the legal requirements of providing service to customers. Explain the main purpose of legislation to protect customers and identify the four Acts which protect customers.

4 Improving customer services

Organisations monitor customer satisfaction and use this as a basis for improving services. In this section you will not only consider the importance of customer services, but also suggest improvements.

Businesses are expected to be well informed about customer protection and to give information about this to customers.

Customer services – a matter of survival

You have already seen that many customers want more from an organisation than just a good product. They also want appropriate customer services.

We live in a competitive world where business organisations compete for customers. To attract new customers and keep existing ones, a business organisation must provide what customers want. This includes a high level and quality of customer services.

Activity

You work in a high street camera shop. Realising the number of customers that there are for photographic goods, another photographic dealer has decided to open a shop at the other end of the high street. Obviously, the new shop will be competing for your customers.

As a group, discuss how you can make sure that you keep your customers by providing good customer service. What kinds of service do you think your customers require? What forms of customer service would you provide? Give your reasons.

Some of the ways in which your shop can ensure that it is providing the service your customers need are:

- making sure that all members of staff know about the goods the shop sells and the services it provides, so that they can provide any information a customer requires – for example, one customer may want to know about the specifications and prices of different cameras, while another may want advice on the suitability of different colour films for night or sports photography

Our radically new policy on Q's is a 1st. It means there shouldn't B more than A single person in front of U at the .
At Tesco, if there's ever more than one person in front of you at the checkout we'll do our level best to open another checkout A.S.A.P., until all our tills are open. We hope you'll feel like a V.I.P.
TESCO Every little helps.
EXCLUDES Wm LOW STORES. AT OUR EXPRESS CHECKOUTS THERE MAY BE MORE THAN ONE PERSON IN FRONT OF YOU. BUT WE AIM TO SERVE YOU JUST AS FAST.

Realising the importance of not keeping customers waiting in queues at their checkouts, Tesco ran full-page advertisements in local papers, promising that if there are ever more than two people at a checkout, they will open another until all the checkouts in the store are open. In this way Tesco is trying to attract customers by promoting customer service, rather than just products or prices.

- being helpful when needed – for example, if your camera shop is known to be helpful over the delivery of fragile items, dealing promptly and efficiently with enquiries and complaints and sorting out queries, it is likely to retain satisfied customers and attract new ones
- ensuring that all customers are treated with care and respect – politeness costs nothing, yet customers appreciate a friendly smile and polite, enthusiastic service as it makes them feel valued. A customer who feels valued is more likely to come back next time; care and respect should be afforded to everybody who contacts your shop, either in person or by telephone, whether with an enquiry, a problem or complaint
- making sure customers are served promptly – most customers appreciate prompt service and see this as an important factor when choosing where to shop.

It goes without saying that the goods sold and the services provided by your shop must be reliable, of an appropriate quality and represent value for money. When something does go wrong, however, and a camera you sold develops a fault, or a customer has a complaint, your shop can help to keep the customer by providing prompt, efficient after-sales service. This includes repairs and maintenance. Faulty goods should be put right or replaced, or the customer's money refunded without delay. Customers with complaints that are dealt with quickly and efficiently may well become satisfied customers, happy to deal with your shop again.

Customer-led organisations

Business organisations which put their customers at the centre of their operations and strive to provide what their customers want are customer-led or customer-driven. This means that they try to find out exactly what their customers want, in terms of services, products and customer services, and strive to provide this.

On the other hand, an organisation which is product-led is more concerned with the goods it produces than with trying to find customers for them. The customer-led organisation is more likely to be successful at attracting and keeping customers.

Putting the customer first is essential for private-sector organisations such as ICI or Marks and Spencer – or a high street camera shop! However, it is also essential for public-sector organisations such as hospitals and schools.

They also have to attract and keep customers. If a school does not provide the expected level of customer service, its customers – parents and their children – will choose another school. The drive for public-sector organisations to become customer-led has an added impact, for example when hospitals are funded according to the number of patients they treat.

If you go into a large store, such as Marks and Spencer, you will probably see a 'customer service' counter where staff deal with customer queries and complaints, requests for information or help, exchanges and refunds. If you phone British Telecom on one of their free numbers, you will be answered by their customer service staff who will either deal with your enquiry or else put you through to the right person or department.

One of the most important forms of customer service provided by organisations is information. Customers want information about the organisation itself, its policies and procedures, its products or services, where to get help or advice and so on.

Activity

Visit:

1 **a private-sector organisation, such as a supermarket, or**

2 **a public-sector organisation, such as a hospital.**

It could be an organisation where you have done work experience or Saturday work. Find out, with examples, what kinds of information they provide for their customers. Write up your findings, using a word processor if possible. Keep this in your portfolio of evidence, together with any examples of information provided, such as leaflets which the organisations make available for their customers.

Monitoring customer satisfaction

The customer services provided by a business organisation are only effective if they result in satisfied customers. Through careful monitoring of customer satisfaction, an organisation will obtain accurate and up-to-date information on which to base future decisions. Customer satisfaction can be monitored in several ways.

Monitoring sales performance

By monitoring the trend of sales over time, an organisation can judge the overall satisfaction of its customers. Customer service is, however, only one factor which can influence sales performance. Other factors include price competitiveness (whether prices are higher or lower than competitors' prices), product quality and whether the product is currently in fashion. These factors must all be taken into consideration when deciding on courses of action based on the results of monitoring sales. Sales performance will also cover repeat business generated by initial sales. This will indicate customer satisfaction more clearly.

Monitoring feedback and complaints

All organisations occasionally receive complaints about the services they provide. By monitoring the number of complaints it receives over time, an organisation will obtain a good indication of how satisfied (or dissatisfied!) its customers are.

It is important for an organisation to record all the feedback and complaints it receives, for whatever reason. An increase in the number of complaints is a cause for concern, and the factors which have given rise to the complaints should be analysed. Based on this information, decisions can then be taken which will address and seek to correct those factors. Monitoring the positive feedback will also give useful information on what customers feel is working well.

Market research

Market research is concerned with finding out what types of goods and services consumers want and are prepared to pay for. It is also concerned with discovering the characteristics of consumers of particular goods and services and why they want them. Market research is a highly specialised function and is normally carried out by personnel in the marketing department of an organisation, who have the appropriate skills, or by an outside, professional marketing firm.

Monitoring feedback from customers – actually obtaining and listening to their views – is a more accurate way of monitoring customer satisfaction. There are several ways of obtaining feedback, using similar methods to those used in market research.

Renault UK is one motor car supplier which telephones customers who have bought new cars to check that they are satisfied with the service provided by the dealer who sold the car.

- Interviewing and asking customers for their views. This can be done:
  - at the point of customer service provision (for example in a supermarket or a hospital waiting room)
  - later, perhaps by telephone to the customer's home or place of work.
- Customer surveys – many organisations carry out surveys of all their customers from time to time, to find out how satisfied they are with the level of customer services provided. This is normally done with the aid of a questionnaire, and may be conducted face to face, by telephone or by post.
- 'Undercover customers' – these are employees of the organisation or others acting on behalf of the organisation, who pose as customers in order to assess the level of customer service provided by the organisation.
- Panels of customers and consumers which meet regularly to discuss the quality of the organisation's products and customer service and ways in which they may be improved.
- Inviting customers' comments. Many organisations in both the public and private sectors ask for customers' comments on the service they have received. The customer may be asked to fill in a short questionnaire at the time they receive the service. Holiday companies, for example, often give their clients a questionnaire to complete on their flight home.

Similarly, some banks and insurance companies regularly seek their customers' views on the services they provide. Under the new inspection regulations, schools have to send a questionnaire to all parents, asking them to comment on how satisfied they are with the school.

2.1, 2.2, 2.4 C
2.1, 2.2, 2.3, IT
2.1, AN

Activity

As a group, design a questionnaire to find out how satisfied the students at your college are with the services provided by one of the facilities of your college, such as the refectory, college shop or library. Try to be objective and think of as many relevant questions as you can. When you have designed your questionnaire, it should be produced on a computer and copies made for each member of the group. The questionnaire should be used as follows.

1. **Acting as an 'undercover' customer', visit the facility you have chosen to investigate and rate it against the questions on your questionnaire. *Note:* you should complete the questionnaire after you have visited the facility.**
2. **Interview other college students with the aid of your questionnaire and obtain their views on the service provided by the facility.**

Keep the completed questionnaires in your portfolio of evidence. You will need the results for the activity on page 142.

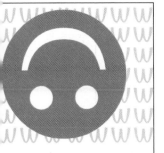

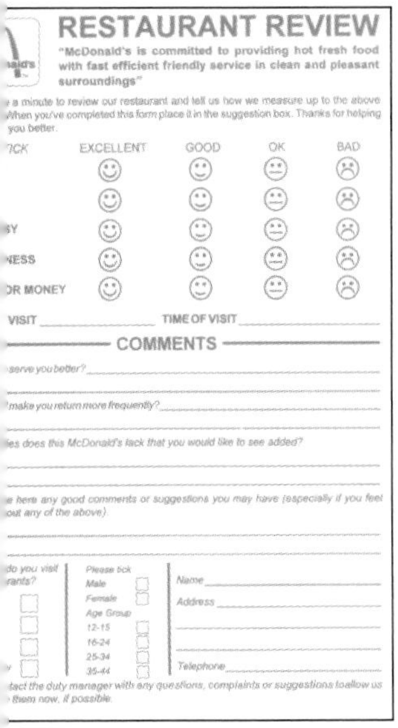
RESTAURANT REVIEW
"McDonald's is committed to providing hot fresh food with fast efficient friendly service in clean and pleasant surroundings"
...a minute to review our restaurant and tell us how we measure up to the above. When you've completed this form place it in the suggestion box. Thanks for helping ... you better.

...ICK	EXCELLENT	GOOD	OK	BAD
	☺	☺	☺	☹
	☺	☺	☺	☹
...Y	☺	☺	☺	☹
...NESS	☺	☺	☺	☹
...OR MONEY	☺	☺	☺	☹

...VISIT ______ TIME OF VISIT ______

COMMENTS

...serve you better? ______
...make you return more frequently? ______
...es does this McDonald's lack that you would like to see added? ______
...e here any good comments or suggestions you may have (especially if you feel ...out any of the above) ______

...do you visit ...rants? | Please tick: Male / Female / Age Group: 12-15 / 16-24 / 25-34 / 35-44 | Name ______ Address ______ Telephone ______

...tact the duty manager with any questions, complaints or suggestions to allow us ... them now, if possible.

McDonald's encourage their customers to comment on the quality of service and meals. Here is a form that can be completed at any McDonald's restaurant

Improvements to customer services

In today's competitive world, organisations are always striving to improve their customer services in order to retain existing customers and attract new ones.

Recommendations for improvements should be based on information obtained by monitoring customer satisfaction in one or more of the ways described above. It is important that recommendations for improvements to an organisation's customer services are both realistic and relevant to the type of organisation and the goods or services it supplies.

Helen Pearson, a chain of hairdressers with salons in seven towns in the West Midlands, recently carried out a survey of existing customers. This was done by asking customers who visited the salons to complete a short questionnaire.

Most customers were pleased to be asked for their opinions, and completed the questionnaire before they left the salon. The responses were carefully analysed and, as a result, customers are now served tea or coffee while waiting in the reception area, or for their hair to dry. Each salon now also employs a full-time manicurist and beauty adviser.

No additional charge is made for these services, which are more than paid for by more frequent visits by satisfied customers as well as an increase in the number of customers attracted by the services the salons offer. One suggestion resulting from the survey – for each salon to have a crèche – has not been put into effect, as it was felt that they could not offer sufficient facilities for this. There was also concern that having a crèche might disturb more customers than it satisfied. An experiment with a crèche on one morning a week is, however, being undertaken at one salon for a trial period.

Other areas where customer services can be improved may be:

- the availability of goods and speed of delivery
- a 'no quibble' exchange or refund
- access to buildings, particuarly for disabled people and people with pushchairs and small children
- signposting around buildings
- aspects of safety in products
- care for the environment in the manufacturing of the product or in its packaging.

2.1 C, 2.2, 2.3 AN Ⓒ

Activity

As a group, analyse the results of the survey you carried out for the activity on page 141.

1 **Add together the results of all the questionnaires obtained by everyone in your group and calculate what percentage of students surveyed (including 'undercover' customers) were satisfied by the service provided by the facility chosen. What percentage were dissatisfied? Did your survey produce any other significant findings, such as student needs that are not catered for? Produce the results of the questionnaire in table form, with a line for each question and a column for each type of response.**

2 **Discuss the findings of your survey as a group. Think carefully about your conclusions and make recommendations for improvements to the facility's service where appropriate. Make sure the recommendations you suggest are realistic and objective, and are based *only* on the results of the questionnaire.**

You should keep a copy of the questionnaire and the table of results, together with your recommendations for improvements to service, in your portfolio of evidence.

2.2, 2.3, 2.4 C Ⓒ
2.1, 2.2, 2.3 AN
2.1, 2.2, 2.3, IT

Assignment

For this assignment you will need to prepare a presentation proposing improvements to customer services in a business organisation.

1 **Using one or more of the methods for monitoring customer satisfaction described in this chapter:**

a identify the types of customer service that customers want from the organisation you have chosen
b measure the extent to which each organisation satisfies these wants.

2 On the basis of your findings, suggest improvements to customer services which the organisation could make in order to respond more fully to their customers' needs. The improvements should cover three of the following:

- friendliness
- availability of goods or services
- speed of delivery
- policies for exchanges or refunds
- access to buildings
- care for the environment
- customer safety.

3 Write up your findings and recommendations in the form of a report for each organisation you have investigated. Include details of your methods of investigation, with a copy of any questionnaire you used and any material (leaflets etc.) which you obtained from the organisation. Show all of the data and statistics on which you based your recommendations and suggestions, in both table and chart form (for example, bar charts or pie charts). Your reports should be produced using a computer word processing or desktop publishing package.

4 To a group, present your proposals for improvements to customer services for your selected organisation. The presentation should show how improvements

- could help attract customers
- secure customer satisfaction and loyalty
- enhance the organisation's image.

Prepare visual aids to go with your talk, which show what customer services the organisation offers and how customer satisfaction is currently monitored. Include the current level of customer satisfaction (for example, the bar charts or pie charts you have prepared).

Outline your proposed improvements to the customer services in the three areas you looked at. Summarise how you think these will improve customer satisfaction.

Summary

In this unit you have investigated the importance of consumers and customers and their effect on business. Consumer demand – the willingness of people to pay for what they want – stimulates businesses to make products to sell. Consumer demand is influenced by a range of factors and changes over time.

Promotion is a vital communications link between a business and its customers and you should have developed some promotional approaches of yor own.

You will now also understand what customer service is intended to provide and have had some practical experience in this.

Such services can always be improved and you will have identified approaches in this respect in the last part of this unit.

Review activity

You have now completed your work on this study unit and should spend some time reviewing what you have achieved.

1 Grading themes

For Intermediate GNVQs, you can achieve a higher grade depending on how much initiative and independent action you take in the areas of:

- planning
- information gathering
- evaluation
- quality of outcomes.

Action planning
Look over the assignments you worked on for this unit.

- Did you complete detailed action plans for each assignment?
- How much support did you need from your teacher/tutor to complete the plans?
- Did you regularly review and update your plans?
- How successful were you in achieving your plans and targets?
- What would you have done differently?

Information gathering
Look over all the assignments you worked on for this unit.

- Did you successfully identify the sorts of information you needed to complete activities and assignments?
- Did you succesfully gather the information you needed? How did you do this?

- How would you assess the quality of information you gathered? Was it:
  - useful and relevant
  - appropriate for your needs
  - accurate and complete?
- Were there any areas where you were not able to gather the information you needed?
- Why was this?
- What would you have done differently?

Evaluation

Evaluation is an important part of your GNVQ. It is one of the grading themes that will enable you to obtain a Merit or Distinction. As part of your evaluation, you should consider the following questions.

- Have I completed all the performance criteria for each element?
- What have I learned from this unit?
- How do my achievements compare with my Action Plan?
- What sources of information did I use and how did I access them?
- Is there anything I would do differently if I had to do it again?

Outcomes

- Did you present complete assignments that covered all of the areas mentioned in them?
- Did your assignment work show that you identified and selected only the appropriate parts from all the information you collected?
- Did you use business language and vocabulary accurately in your work to put information and points across clearly to your target audience?

2 Performance criteria and range

Look at the standards for this GNVQ unit. Work through the performance criteria for each element and check that you have done work to help you meet each one. Do this by noting down the relevant performance criteria number against the work.

Finally, check through the information given under the range.

3 Core skills

This unit has covered the following core skills:

- Communication Level 2 : 2.1, 2.2, 2.3, 2.4
- Application of number Level 2: 2.1, 2.2, 2.3
- Information technology Level 2: 2.1, 2.2, 2.3

Glossary

business organisation any organisation in the private or public sector whose activities involve providing goods or services

consumer any person who uses the goods or services of business organisations

customer a person who receives the goods or services of a particular business organisation. A potential customer is somebody who, in certain circumstances, may become a customer for a particular product or of a particular organisation

demand the demand, or consumer demand, for a product is the level of pressure from consumers for goods or services to be supplied by business organisations, and for which the consumer is willing to pay

direct response advertising advertising, usually in magazines or newspapers, which encourages the reader to order a product direct from the manufacturer

goods products manufactured or supplied by business organisations. Goods are tangible and are used by consumers

listener profile a description of the main characteristics of the sort of people who listen to a particular type of radio programme

market the total number of actual and potential customers for a product or group of products

marketing the activities involved with identifying, planning for and satisfying customer requirements in a way which also meets organisational objectives

market research a specific exercise aimed at gathering, processing and analysing data on a particular sales topic, product or customer group

needs the requirements of consumers for goods and services essential to sustain life and an acceptable level of comfort

products the goods and services produced and supplied by business organisations

press release a piece of information about a company's achievements which is issued to the media

promotion the activities involved in marketing an organisation or its goods and services. Organisations frequently have special promotions on particular goods and services in order to attract customers and generate sales

public relations a company's efforts to establish a good reputation and image in the eyes of consumers

services activities which business organisations do to or for consumers

sponsorship when a company contributes money or some form of support to a person or event. In return, the event or person will display the company logo and name and thus give the company good publicity

trends a general move by consumers, either in favour of a product or against it

wants the requirements of consumers for goods and services to enhance their lives and lifestyles

Financial and administrative support

GNVQ

Contents

Introduction 148

1 Financial transactions and documents 149

2 Completing financial documents 161

3 Business documents 175

Summary 188

Answers to activities 190

Glossary 194

LONGMAN

Introduction

Every business is concerned with buying and selling goods or services. All businesses, regardless of size, must keep accurate records of every transaction – sales and purchases. This rule applies to very big companies, such as Virgin, Burger King and The Body Shop, as well as much smaller organisations, such as newsagents, greengrocers, garages, dentists and solicitors, and those of all sizes in between.

In this study unit you will look at business and financial transactions, and see the financial documentation businesses must produce so that they can keep a record of their sales and purchases. You will gain experience of the financial and administrative skills that help businesses to run smoothly and effectively. Routine documents, such as letters and memos are also included, and you will see the ways in which business documentation can be created, stored and transferred between businesses and their customers.

Purchase Order

Order No. 27182 | **Date:** 17 May 1995

From:	**To:**
Luigi's Pizzeria 17 Castle Lane Edinburgh EH9 3TP	Kitchen Kraft Unit 8 Leazes Industrial Estate Leeds LS17 5PA
Deliver to: As above	**Special Instructions:** None

Reference	Quantity	Details	Unit Price	Total Price
Catalogue No: AJN332	12	9" wooden spoons	48p	5.76
Catalogue No: GHY980	1	2 Lt. Glass casserole dish	4.75	4.75
Catalogue No: KLI432	72	Bistro wine glasses	37p	26.64
Catalogue No: OSP21	24	Oval serving plates	2.20	52.80
Catalogue No: WEQ771	1	12" non-stick frying pan	5.20	5.20

Authorised by: Caroline Robson

This is an example of a purchase order.
Purchase documents are covered on pages 150–2.

1 Financial transactions and documents

Financial transactions (sales and purchases) take place between:

- *a business and a personal customer* – for example, Boots the Chemist sells cosmetics and pharmaceutical products, petrol stations sell petrol, and their customers are generally members of the public who make their purchases in person, pay by cash, cheque or credit card and take the goods away with them, there and then
- *a business and a business customer* – for example, Boots the Chemist purchases cosmetics from a manufacturer, and petrol stations purchase petrol from an oil refinery. Transactions between businesses often involve very large quantities of goods that are delivered some time after the order has been placed, and payment may be made by cheque, credit card or electronic transfer of funds.

The purpose of records of financial transactions

Regardless of whether a business is dealing with the general public or another business, it is necessary to keep a strict record of every sale and every purchase that is made. This information enables businesses to:

- monitor how well or how badly the business is doing
- make any changes that might be necessary, such as saving money by cutting back on spending or increasing prices
- plan for the future.

Records of financial transactions:

- give businesses details of their sales figures and **turnover figures**
- show businesses which customers have not paid their bills (although the sales figures may appear to show that the business is doing well, if customers do not pay their bills, then debts to the company can increase alongside sales)
- provide businesses with information about how much they are spending and how much they are earning
- help businesses to monitor their business performance (this means checking earnings over a year in comparison with those of previous years to see whether profits are staying the same, increasing or decreasing)
- enable businesses to put all the figures together to produce annual accounts

The information given in annual accounts includes how much money the business has earned and spent over a 12-month period, how much money is owed to the business (by people who have not yet paid their bills) and how much profit or loss the company has made.

- allow businesses to calculate how much VAT and income tax they must pay
- provide written evidence that transactions have taken place.

Accurate records must therefore be kept of both inward and outward financial transactions.

Inward transactions

An **inward transaction** is a financial transaction that brings money into the business. This could be:

- money from customers (either individuals or other businesses) for goods or services they have bought
- money from a bank or building society that is:
  - a loan to the business
  - interest on money the business has deposited with a bank or building society
- money paid into the business as:
  - a refund
  - a repayment on a loan the business has made to an individual or to another business.

Outward transactions

An **outward transaction** is a payment of money out of the business and includes:

- staff pay
- payments for any kind of goods or services
- refunds to customers who have overpaid or who return faulty or damaged goods.

Purchases and purchase documents

All businesses need to buy goods, services and utilities, such as electricity and gas. Documentation for each purchase proves that the transaction has taken place and shows how much money has been spent.

Purchases

Activity

Working on your own, think about a business you are familiar with – perhaps you are a regular customer of a particular business. Make a list of the kinds of purchases your chosen business might make.

Consumables are so called because they are items that are used and then replaced with fresh stocks.

Your list of purchases will, of course, depend on the business you have chosen, but here are some you may well have put on your list:

- products
- consumables (such as stationery, petrol, stamps)
- parts (a manufacturing company may purchase parts)
- raw materials (to manufacture anything from sandwiches to socks, raw materials are needed)
- vehicles and equipment (most businesses need to buy cars or vans, computers, fax machines and other types of equipment and machinery)
- services (for example the services of the staff who work for the business, garage repairs photocopying and printing services, legal services, maintenance and transport)
- utilities (every business needs gas, electricity, water and telephone facilities).

Petty cash

The word 'petty' means small, and so petty cash is the money used by companies to pay for small purchases. In most offices there is a **petty cash** box containing a small amount of money – usually between £25 and £100, depending on the size of the company.

Purchase documents

Every time a business makes a purchase, there are a number of documents that must be carefully and accurately completed.

The information Caroline gives on the order form includes:

- her order number
- date
- the name and address of the company ordering the goods
- the name and address of the company selling the goods
- the address where the goods are to be delivered
- Kitchen Kraft's reference (the number shown beside the product in the 'Special Offer Catalogue')
- the quantity of each item ordered
- a description of each item ordered
- the price of each item ordered
- the total cost of the order
- her name.

Purchase orders

Purchase orders, sometimes called order forms, give details of the goods or services a business wants to buy.

> Caroline is Head Chef at Luigi's Pizzeria in Edinburgh. She needs some items of kitchen equipment and decides to place her order with Kitchen Kraft, a company she has dealt with before. She makes a list of what she needs and she also looks through the Kitchen Kraft 'Special Offer Catalogue'. Caroline telephones the company to check that they have everything in stock and places a verbal order.
>
> She then completes her purchase order form, and sends it to the supplier, Kitchen Kraft. Caroline's completed order form is on page 148.

Goods received notes

When the ordered goods arrive, the person who actually takes delivery should compare the goods delivered with the purchase order to make sure that the delivery is correct. They may then have to complete a **goods received note**. Many companies use the goods received note system to keep a record of what has been delivered.

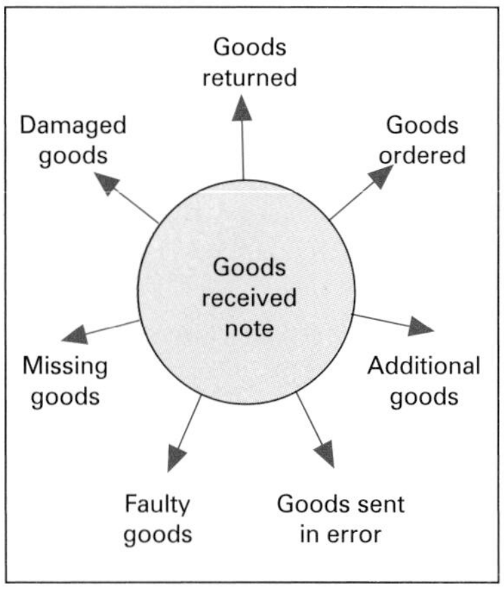

The system also allows a business to identify and record damaged, faulty or missing goods and goods sent in error. It also serves as a security check, helping to ensure that suppliers are dealing honestly, and that the staff receiving the goods are working honestly.

Goods Received Note		Number 9378
Date received: 3 June 1995		Received by: Shanaz Sareeta
Received from: Pearsons Stationery Park House Camberley Surrey		
Quantity	Description	Entered into stock
12 boxes	60 reams copy paper	3 June 1995
1 packet	24 ballpoint pens	3 June 1995
3 boxes	5000 white window envelopes	3 June 1995
1 box	Typewriter ribbons	Not ordered. Returned to supplier

Activity

Find out from your work placement or from a local business what system they use to make sure that:

- the goods delivered by a supplier match up with their order
- additional, damaged or faulty goods are returned to the supplier.

Purchase invoices

Once goods or services have been ordered, the purchaser can expect to receive a **purchase invoice**. This document details the items ordered and is used to inform the purchaser how much they have to pay and the date when the bill should be settled. Businesses must make sure that every invoice is carefully checked against the matching purchase order to confirm that the details are correct. They need to do this so that they can be sure, when they pay their bills, they are paying the right amount.

'E & O E' means 'errors and omissions excepted'. Some companies put this on their invoices so that, if they send an invoice for an incorrect amount, they can simply send a replacement showing the correct figures.

Activity

You work in the Accounts Department of Save & Spend, a large supermarket. Part of your job is to check the invoices received by Save & Spend against the purchase orders that have been sent out.

Look at the purchase invoice on the next page received from Rowley Foods and check the details on this invoice against the purchase order shown. Note down any errors you find.

Check your answers against those given at the end of this study unit.

INVOICE

Rowley Foods
Belmont Industrial Park
Leicester LS34 8BY

Date: 12 March 1995

Invoice No.	Your Account No.	Your Order No.	Date of Your Order
22176098	01576883	98100217	4 March 1995
Quantity	**Description**	**Unit price**	**Total price**
48	Black Forest Gâteaux	1.20 each	77.70
72	Fudge Delight	78p each	54.72
72	Deep-dish Apple Pie	60p each	43.20
130	Toffee Crunch	1.12 each	143.00
125	Raspberry Pavlova	1.08 each	135.00
		Total amount	435.62
		VAT at 17.5%	Zero rated
		Total amount due	435.62

E & O E Terms: 30 days

PURCHASE ORDER

ORDER NO. 98000217 DATE: 4 March 1995

FROM:	TO:
Save & Spend Supermarket Cox Lodge Shopping Centre Manchester MR5 4FB	Rowley Foods Belmont Industrial Park Leicester LS34 8BY
DELIVER TO: As above	SPECIAL INSTRUCTIONS: None

REFERENCE	QUANTITY	DETAILS	PRICE	TOTAL PRICE
	48	Black Forest Gâteaux	1.20 each	57.60
	72	Fudge Delight	76p each	54.72
	72	Deep-dish Apple Pie	60p each	43.20
	130	Toffee Crunch	1.10 each	143.00
	25	Raspberry Pavlova	1.08 each	27.00

Authorised by: Sylvia Wilson, Frozen Food Manager

Sales transactions and documents

All businesses – retail, manufacturing and service – aim to generate sufficient sales for the company to make a profit. To keep track of sales, documentation is required.

Sales documents

Businesses must make sure that there is documentation to support every sale they make. This documentation must cover:

- sales made to individual personal customers and to other businesses
- sales of goods (products and raw materials) and services.

Advice notes

When the supplier (the company that is selling) receives a purchase order for goods and services, they often send the purchaser an advice note. The purpose of an advice note is to confirm that the order has been received and to let the purchaser know the date when they can expect the goods or services to arrive.

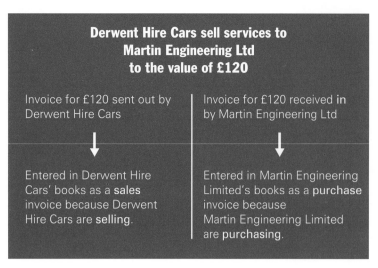

Derwent Hire Cars sell services to Martin Engineering Ltd to the value of £120

Invoice for £120 sent out by Derwent Hire Cars	Invoice for £120 received **in** by Martin Engineering Ltd
↓	↓
Entered in Derwent Hire Cars' books as a **sales** invoice because Derwent Hire Cars are **selling**.	Entered in Martin Engineering Limited's books as a **purchase** invoice because Martin Engineering Limited are **purchasing**.

Delivery notes

If the goods are sent by post or by the seller's own delivery van, then the company making the sale also sends a **delivery note**, which details the items being sent. Most suppliers expect the purchaser to sign and keep the top copy of the delivery note, while the driver keeps a carbon copy for the supplier's records.

The customer receiving the goods should check the delivery note against the purchase order and the goods themselves. This should be done to make sure that everything ordered has been sent and is in good condition.

A consignment note is similar to a delivery note except that it is sent with the goods when the seller uses a specialist transport company to deliver them to the customer.

Sales invoices

As mentioned in the discussion about purchases, once the purchaser has received the goods, then a **sales invoice** is sent by the seller, requesting payment.

Credit notes

A credit note credits a customer with one of the following:

- the amount for the goods they have not received
- the amount for the goods they have returned
- the amount they have overpaid.

Credit notes are given to customers for various reasons. Sometimes, for one reason or another, the seller is not able to supply everything that has been ordered. Customers may decide to wait for the ordered items or to buy from another company.

Sometimes goods are damaged or faulty when they arrive, and customers return the goods. They may ask for a replacement, a refund of the money they have paid or a credit note.

Sometimes customers do not check their invoices properly and then later discover that they have overpaid.

Statements of account

Because it is important for suppliers and their customers to keep track of outstanding invoices, most companies send their regular customers a monthly **statement of account**. By checking the statements they send and receive, companies can see:

- how much they are owed by other companies
- how much they owe to other companies.

STATEMENT

Number: 27155
From: Dawson Vinters
14 Long Street
London EC2V 8YT

Date: 28 July 1995
To: JJ's Wine Bar
Short's Yard
London WC2 9TG

Date	Details	Debit £	VAT £	Credit £	Balance £
2/7/95	Balance				3,407.00
9/7/95	Invoice 76998	1,299.27	227.38		4,933.65
13/7/95	Cheque			4,933.65	
17/7/95	Invoice 77371	2,931.48	513.01		3,444.49
18/7/95	Credit note 8776	72.00	12.60		3,359.89
26/7/95	Invoice 78135	420.00	73.50		3,853.39

Payments made after the 26th of the month will be shown on the next statement
VAT Reg. Number 0271 65332

Payment methods and receipt documents

Whenever a purchase is made, a payment must also be made. There are many ways to pay for goods and several different forms of receipt.

Payment methods

Activity

On your own, read through the following description, then make a list of the ways in which payment might be made for the goods purchased.

> Surinder works for J. G. Accountancy Services and is responsible for ordering all the stationery the business uses. He regularly orders from a mail-order stationery supplier, which delivers orders by van within 24 hours. Surinder telephones the company and places a large order for supplies. The purchase invoice comes to a total of £422.36, plus VAT.

How could Surinder, on behalf of his employer, pay the supplier? Make a list of at least four payment methods.

When making purchases, businesses usually do not pay with cash (except for small items), but, instead, use the following payment methods:

- cheque
- credit card
- charge card
- debit card
- hire purchase
- electronic data interchange (EDI).

Paying by cheque

Anyone who opens a current bank or building society account will also be issued with a chequebook and **cheque guarantee card**. There are a number of reasons that businesses, in particular, prefer to pay by cheque.

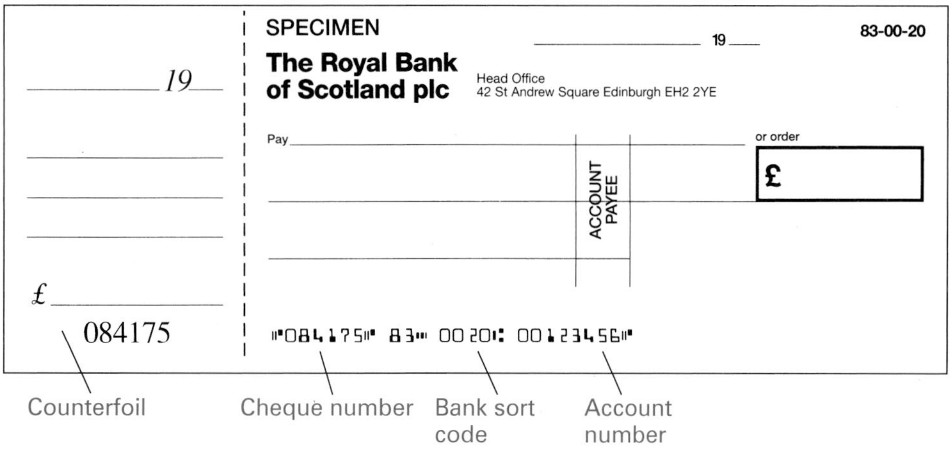
SPECIMEN
19
83-00-20
19
The Royal Bank of Scotland plc
Head Office
42 St Andrew Square Edinburgh EH2 2YE
Pay
or order
£
ACCOUNT PAYEE
£
084175
⑈084175⑈ 83⑆ 00 201⑆ 00123456⑈

Activity

In a small group, identify five reasons for businesses preferring to pay for their purchases by cheque rather than cash.

You could have suggested the following:

- businesses can pay for goods, services and utilities without having to go to the trouble of withdrawing cash from the bank
- a chequebook is much safer than holding large amounts of cash – if a chequebook is stolen, the bank can be informed and all of the cheques can be stopped, so that money cannot be withdrawn from the bank account
- businesses can settle their invoices quickly and easily by post
- in every chequebook, alongside the cheque itself, there is a **cheque counterfoil** that is stamped with the same number and **bank sort code** as the cheque alongside and, when completed correctly, the counterfoils provide a record of the payment:
  - its date, the name of the payee (the person or firm to whom the cheque is made out) and the amount of money being paid by the cheque
  - by comparing cheque counterfoils with bank statements, businesses can:
    - check to see that payments have been made out of the bank account
    - check that the transactions shown on the bank statement match the transactions detailed on the counterfoil.

Paying by credit card

Credit cards, such as Visa and Access, can be used to pay for goods or services, providing the seller accepts the cards.

The owner of the credit card is given an agreed spending limit and may choose to either:

- clear the outstanding debt with one payment on an agreed date or
- make an agreed payment to the credit company by an agreed date (usually monthly).

Interest is charged on the amount left unpaid each month.

EFTPOS is a quick and easy way to pay. Because the money is electronically transferred from the purchaser's account to the seller's account:

- there is no need to write a cheque
- there is no £50 or £100 limit.

Paying by debit card

Debit cards can be used in many retail outlets, such as shops and petrol stations. These cards are presented to the cashier who 'swipes' them through a special electronic funds transfer at point of sale (EFTPOS) machine.

Hire purchase

Sometimes individuals and businesses use hire purchase when buying expensive items. They choose this method of payment because the hire purchase repayments can be spread over a fairly long period of time, usually from one to five years.

Hire purchase can be an expensive way to buy something because you may be charged interest at an **annual percentage rate (APR)**. Sometimes large stores and car dealers offer '0 per cent finance'. This means that customers can buy expensive items, such as furniture or cars, on hire purchase over the agreed time period without having to pay any additional interest.

Electronic data interchange (EDI)

Computers can now be used to transfer money between accounts. You have seen how EFTPOS does this when debit cards are used.

Businesses and banks also use **EDI** to transfer money between accounts. For example, businesses can pay supplier's invoices by the **BACS (bureau automated clearing system)**. The supplier provides an invoice for goods or services, together with details of the bank account into which the money should be paid. The purchaser then instructs his or her bank to transfer the money by computer from one account to another.

If a business in the UK purchased products from a supplier in Japan, it could use SWIFT to transfer money from its bank account in England to the supplier's bank account in Japan.

Businesses can pay their suppliers abroad by **SWIFT (Society of Worldwide Interbank Telecommunications)**.Using this system, organisations can transfer messages and money between countries.

Some employers prefer to pay their staff by transferring money electronically, rather than issuing individual cheques or cash payments.

Regular payments of prearranged amounts for goods, services or utilities can also be made electronically. For example, to settle:

- telephone accounts
- hire purchase payments.

These payments can be made by **standing order** or **direct debit** from one account to another.

In these cases the purchaser agrees the amount to be paid (usually on a monthly basis) and provides the supplier with details of the account (bank or building society) to be debited. On the agreed date, money is transferred from the purchaser's account to the supplier's account

Receipts

Receipts can be:

- till rolls
- credit and debit card vouchers, signed by the purchaser
- bank, building society, credit company statements
- cheque counterfoils
- paying-in slips
- invoices.

Purchasers expect to receive a **receipt** when a financial transaction has taken place. This differs from a statement, which is a record of financial transactions over, say, a month.

Receipts are evidence that money has been paid and they are used to:

- show that a business has spent money on goods and services
- show that pay has been given to staff (payslips)
- provide proof of ownership, for instance, if you bought a CD that you found was faulty when you got it home, you could return it to the shop, with your receipt, to prove that you bought it there
- allow individuals to claim money back from their employer for petty cash items, for instance, if you spent 40p on a pint of milk for work,

providing you have the till receipt from the shop, you could complete a **petty cash voucher** and reclaim the money
- prove that money has been paid into banks and building societies.

Activity

Look at the list of receipts given below. Your task is to match up the receipt with the transaction.

	Type of receipt	Type of transaction
1	bank statement	purchase of items costing £5
2	petty cash voucher	purchase of parts costing £620 from Midvale Engineering Co.
3	credit agreement	deposit of £3,200 in cash and cheques
4	credit card statement	purchase of goods over the telephone
5	cheque counterfoil	purchase of a car costing £8,200

The answers to this activity are given at the end of this study unit.

Statements

Statements, which act as both a receipt and a record of inward and outward transactions, are usually issued by:

- banks and building societies
- charge card, credit card and hire purchase companies
- businesses that allow their regular customers to make a number of purchases over a period of time (say a month) and then settle part or all of the outstanding debt with a regular payment (say once a month).

Businesses and individuals must check statements very carefully to make sure that:

- all payments made have been recorded on the statement
- all the purchases shown on the statement are accurate and match other documentation, such as purchase orders, invoices and cheque counterfoils.

Security

Business documents and financial records must always be safely and securely stored. In addition, as already mentioned, businesses need to make regular checks to make sure that all of their financial transactions are honestly and carefully carried out and that every transaction is properly and accurately recorded.

Activity

In a small group, discuss why security is so important.

Businesses need to take security measures to make sure that they:

- prevent dishonest dealings (fraud) and theft
- do not lose money as a result of errors and mistakes, such as paying incorrect invoices or paying the same supplier twice
- promote high standards of honesty among staff.

How to ensure security

Every business has a list of **authorised cheque signatories** – people authorised to sign cheques. The bank holds the names and sample signatures of these people, and the bank will refuse to honour cheques that have been signed by anyone else.

All invoices should be checked against:

- quotations (if these have obtained)
- purchase orders
- delivery notes or consignment notes.

By cross-referencing these documents, a business can be sure that it is paying the correct price for the goods that have been received. In addition, all invoices should be checked for numerical accuracy.

Whenever a delivery is received, the incoming goods should be:

- counted and checked
- compared with the purchase order.

The goods should be noted on a goods received form, together with details of any items that:

- are missing or damaged
- have been returned to the supplier by the carrier
- have been delivered, but were not actually ordered.

All businesses allow only certain, authorised members of staff to place orders on behalf of the business. Every purchase order should show the name (and sometimes the signature) of the person placing the order.

2.2, 2.3, 2.4 C ⓒ
2.4, IT

Assignment

For this assignment you will need to visit businesses, banks and building societies in your local area.

Your task is in three parts.

1 **Obtain examples of the following financial documents:**

- purchase orders
- sales invoices
- purchase invoices
- delivery notes
- credit notes
- goods received notes
- till receipts
- bank statements
- cheque counterfoils.

2 **Write a short description of the purpose of each of the documents you have gathered together.**

3 **Describe two ways in which an individual customer might pay for something that has been bought over the counter from a shop or service business.**

Describe two ways in which a business might pay for goods or services that have been bought from another business.

List security checks a business might carry out and explain the importance of security to a business.

2 Completing financial documents

All the documentation to do with financial transactions needs to be completed carefully and accurately. This is because, when put together, these documents help businesses to:

- prepare their **annual accounts**
- set **budgets**
- monitor incoming and outgoing payments.

This section focuses on completing the documents used to process and record financial transactions. You will also see how budgets are set and monitored, and how information technology is used to record and monitor financial information.

Purchase and sales documents

When businesses are either buying or selling, they need to take value added tax (VAT) into consideration.

VAT

Businesses that have a turnover of over £46,000 per year (as at 1995) must, by law, charge VAT on their sales. This means that they become a VAT-registered business and are issued with a VAT number. The law states that this number must be shown on their invoices. You may also see this number on receipts.

VAT is a tax on a range of goods and services, which businesses collect on behalf of the Government.

VAT is charged on most goods and services, but not on:

- food (with a few exceptions)
- children's clothing and footwear
- books and newspapers
- medicines.

Here is an example of how it works.

G. N. Electricals sells electrical goods and also repairs damaged electrical items, such as video recorders, televisions, washing machines and so on. The business is registered for VAT.

If G. N. Electricals sells:

1 television at £100, plus VAT at 17.5 per cent (£17.50), the total price is £117.50

1 hi-fi system at £160, plus VAT at 17.5 per cent (£28.00), the total price is £188.00.

If the company buys:

stationery at £80, plus VAT at 17.5 per cent (£14.00), the total price is £94.00
petrol at £40, plus VAT at 17.5 per cent (£7.00), the total price is £47.00.

So far, then, G. N. Electricals has collected from customers:

£260.00 from sales (£100 + £160)
£45.50 VAT (£17.50 + £28)

and has paid out:

£120 on purchases (£80 + £40)
£21 VAT (£14 +£7).

Every three months, G. N. Electricals has to complete a VAT return form and send HM Customs and Excise the amount of VAT the company has collected in, less the amount of VAT it has paid out, which, in this example, is £24.50 (£45.50 – £21).

Purchase documents

Purchase orders

As you saw in Section 1, a purchase order must always be completed whenever a business buys goods or services.

2.2 C, 2.2, 2.3 AN **C** **Activity**

You work in the Accounts Department of the Superfit Gym and Health Centre.

On 11 July, 1995, your Manager, Tina King, gives you the information shown below. She asks you to use this information to prepare purchase orders. Refer back to the example of a purchase order shown on page 148 and use a similar layout for your purchase order.

Please order the following items from:
Prestige Office Stationery
14 Holly Court
Manchester M26 3ED

20 reams of copier paper at £2.20 per ream, plus VAT at 17.5 per cent
1 angled desklamp at £32, plus VAT at 17.5 per cent
12 roller-ball pens at 65p each, plus VAT at 17.5 per cent
2 rolls sticky tape at 70p each, plus VAT at 17.5 per cent
24 telephone message pads at 60p each, plus VAT at 17.5 per cent.

The completed purchase order is on page 192.

Purchase invoices

As you saw in Section 1, purchase invoices are the bills for payment received by businesses.

2.1, 2.2, AN Ⓒ **Activity**

You work in the Accounts Department of Offbeat Records. Your task is to consider the following set of financial documents and calculate the value of the cheque that should be sent to the supplier, Swift Supplies.

Complete a cheque for Swift Supplies to clear the correct outstanding balance.

For the answer, see the end of this study unit.

INVOICE

Swift Supplies
Grosvenor Business Park
Nottingham NG21 32DD

To: Offbeat Records, Head Office,
Ellsway Centre, Walthamstow, London E17 2GV

Date: 21 September 1995

Invoice No.	Your Account No.	Your Order No.	Date of Your Order	
78511290	DR-350082	51432	13/9/95	
Quantity	**Description**	**Unit price**	**VAT**	**Total price**
21	1996 Diaries	5.99	1.01	157.00
5 boxes	Manila folders – green	2.75	0.49	16.20
20 boxes	3.5 DD diskettes	7.99	1.40	187.80
5 packs	A4 refill pads	6.49	1.14	38.15
24	Lever arch files	3.99	0.69	112.32
		Total amount	437.55	
		VAT at 17.5%	73.92	
		Total amount due	511.47	

E & O E Terms: 30 days *VAT Reg. No. 421 544 112*

CREDIT NOTE

FROM:	TO:
Swift Supplies Grosvenor Business Park Nottingham NG21 32DD	Offbeat Records Head Office Ellsway Centre Walthamstow, London E17 2GV
Number: 215489 Date: 29 August 1995	Your account: DR-350082
1 Lotus facsimile machine £350.00	

Sales documents

Sales invoices

Sales invoices are the bills for payment sent out by businesses.

Goods Received Note: No. 769		
Date received: 17 August 1995		Received by: Jasmine Wong
Received from: Swift Supplies Grosvenor Business Park Nottingham NG21 32DD		
Quantity	Description	Entered into stock
50	Suspension files	17 August 1995
1	Lotus fax machine	damaged – returned to supplier
4 boxes	Large padded envelopes	17 August 1995

STATEMENT

No. 9981 Date: 23 September 1995

From: Swift Supplies
Grosvenor Business Park
Nottingham NG21 32DD

To: Offbeat Records
Head Office, Ellsway Centre
Walthamstow
London E17 2GV

Date	Details	Debit £	VAT £	Credit £	Balance £
5/9/95	Balance				125.00
9/9/95	Invoice 78501367	318.00	55.65		498.65
10/9/95	Cheque			125.00	498.65
16/9/95	Invoice 78509428	17.69	3.01		519.35
21/9/95	Invoice 78511290	437.55	76.58		1033.48

Payments made after the 29th of the month will be shown on the next statement
VAT Reg. No. 421 544 112

2.2 C, 2.2, 2.3 AN **C** **Activity**

You are again working at the Superfit Gym and Health Centre. On 17 July 1995, your Manager, Tina King, gives you the information shown below. She asks you to use this information to prepare the sales invoices. Look back to page 163, refer to the invoice there and use this to design your own for the following.

1 To: Mrs J. Bennett
238 Alderson Avenue
Manchester M33 8BG
For: 3 months' club membership at £48, plus VAT at 17.5 per cent, 2 suncradle sessions at £7 each, plus VAT at 17.5 per cent.
Mrs Bennett's account number is 879931.
She does not have an order number.
The invoice number is 27755.

2 To: Mr J. Johnstone
Kimberley, Clark & Wilson
West House
87 West Road
Manchester M34 8H
For: 1 years' company club membership at £592, plus VAT at 17.5 per cent, 12 pairs of running shoes at £7 per pair, zero rated for VAT, 12 tracksuits at £22.50 each, zero rated for VAT.
Mr Johnstone's account number is 880026.
Mr Johnstone's order number is 45661, dated 10 July.
The invoice number is 27756.
Mr Johnstone would like the running shoes and tracksuits delivered to: Kimberley, Clark & Wilson
Sycamore House
Colne Avenue
Manchester M2710NN.

Now compare your completed invoices with the ones on page 193.

Discounts

Businesses offer discounts because they want to encourage customers to:

- do business with them – this is usually referred to as a **trade discount**
- settle their outstanding invoices quickly – this is usually referred to as a **cash discount** or **prompt payment discount**.

VAT is calculated on the amount that is charged after the discount has been deducted.

Trade discounts are offered by the seller to the purchaser to encourage the purchaser to place large orders or to buy on a regular basis. For example, regular customers who place an order every month or customers who spend, say, over £5000, might get a 5 per cent discount on every order.

Cash and prompt payment discounts are often offered to encourage buyers to pay their bills quickly. For example, a business might offer, say, 2 per cent discount if the invoice is paid within 30 days of the invoice date.

Payment and receipt documents

Whan paying for goods and services, it is important to know how to complete the necessary documents clearly and accurately.

Payment documents

Petty cash vouchers

Petty cash items are usually quite small purchases. Even so, the total amount of petty cash expenditure in a business over a year can be considerable. This is particularly true for large companies with many employees. For every petty cash purchase, a petty cash voucher must be completed. Even for very small purchases (say, of 50p or less), on each petty cash voucher a note should be made as to whether or not the price paid included VAT.

Receipt documents

There are a number of documents that act as receipts to show that money has been paid for goods or services.

Invoices

Sales invoices can be matched to cheque counterfoils to confirm that payment has been made.

Payslips

Most employees receive a payslip from their employer when they are paid. Staff usually receive their pay either weekly or monthly, in cash, by cheque or by transfer between the employer's bank account and the employee's bank account. The payslip is a record:

- for the employer, of the amount that has been paid
- for the employee, of the amount that has been received.

Activity

List up to five items of information that appear on most payslips.

The information that usually appears on a payslip is the:

- employee's name, National Insurance number, income tax code and reference or payroll number
- date on which the payment is being made and the period it covers
- amount of National Insurance that has been deducted for the payment period and the total amount deducted to date
- amount of income tax that has been deducted for the payment period and the total amount deducted to date
- amount deducted for the employee's contribution to the pension scheme.

Receipts given to customers

Businesses may provide customers with any of the following.

Hand-written receipts are always made out in duplicate so that both the buyer and the seller have a copy.

Delivery notes, consignment notes, cheque counterfoils, credit notes, credit card payment vouchers and hire purchase agreements are also receipts.

Hand-written receipts
These are often offered by small businesses that do not have a cash register capable of printing receipts.

Printed receipts
These are usually printed out by a cash register and are offered to customers by businesses such as petrol stations, restaurants, department stores and supermarkets.

SPECIMEN ONLY
Issued by Banking Information Service
Date
Code No
bank giro credit
40-76-20
Notes over £20
£20 Notes
£10 Notes
£5 Notes
£1 Coins
Other Coin
Teller's stamp and initials
Any bank
Any where
Total Cash
Cheques etc
(See over)
Total £
Paid in by
Credit
Account holders name/s
Items Fee Deferment
Please do not write or mark below this line
000151 40 76 20 15516696 77

Bank statements, which show a list of financial transactions (money paid into and out of the account) are receipts. The counterfoils of banks' paying-in slips are also receipts. Whenever money is paid into a bank, a paying-in slip must be completed, showing the date, the name of the account, the name of the person making the deposit, the amount of money being paid in and whether it is cash, cheques or a combination of both.

Recording financial information

Large companies usually have an accounts department, which is responsible for making sure that:

In small companies, all of these tasks may be carried out by the owner of the business or by just one member of staff.

- all financial transactions are recorded
- every sale and purchase is properly checked and authorised
- all the financial documentation leaving the company is correct
- the outstanding invoices owed by the company are paid
- the outstanding money owed to the company is collected
- staff are paid on time
- expenditure is carefully monitored to make sure that spending does not exceed the limits set by the budget.

Sales documents	Purchase documents	Receipt documents
• Sales invoices • Credit notes that have been issued	• Purchase orders • Purchase invoices • Credit notes that have been received • Goods received notes • Petty cash vouchers with receipts attached • Copy payslips for when staff are paid	• Receipts including: – till receipts – hand-written receipts – credit card vouchers – cheque counterfoils – bank and building society paying-in slip counterfoils – bank and building society statements – statements from suppliers

If financial records are inaccurate, then mistakes can be made when calculating the amount of VAT that must be paid to HM Customs and Excise, or the amount of income tax to be paid to the Inland Revenue.

Business accounts show whether or not the business is making a profit. These accounts are prepared after careful examination of a company's financial documentation. On the left you can see examples of the purchase, sales and receipt documents used to prepare business accounts.

Annual accounts are prepared for both internal and external use.

Internal accounts

All businesses regularly need to make important financial decisions and plan for the future. For example, they need to know the answers to questions such as the following.

- Can we afford to move to new premises?
- Can we increase staff pay?
- Can we employ more staff?
- Can we buy new vehicles or equipment?
- Can we spend more money on advertising?

A simple example of profit and loss would be if a company earned £5,000 from sales, but spent £6,500 on pay and other purchases. In this case, the business would have made a *loss* of £1,500. If, though, a company earned £5,000 from sales, but only spent £4,000 on pay and other purchases, there would be a taxable profit of £1,000.

These questions can only be answered if the business has a clear understanding of how much or how little profit it is making. Accurate accounts (based on accurate financial documentation) will show how much money is being spent on purchases and how much money is being earned from sales. The difference between sales and purchases is the profit, or the loss.

External accounts

Sole traders or partnerships
They need to prepare annual accounts to present to the Inland Revenue in order to be assessed for tax.

Limited companies
A copy of the annual accounts must be sent every year to the Registrar of Companies.

Public limited companies
Public limited companies are required, by law, to publish an annual company report and accounts.

A business may be one of several kinds and the requirements regarding accounts will vary accordingly.

What annual accounts consist of

The annual accounts, when completed, consist of:

- the **profit and loss account**
- the **balance sheet**.

The profit and loss account

This is the master document produced as a result of inspecting and calculating all the other financial documents, such as those of:

- sales
- payments
- receipts

that the business has generated over the year.

The profit and loss account consists of all the items generating income and all of the expenses, plus information about the total income and expenses.

The Inland Revenue and HM Customs and Excise may have access at any time to a business' accounts if they wish to investigate a company's financial transactions.

Activity

Examine the profit and loss account shown below and then answer the questions that follow.

1 **What was the total turnover of this business?**

2 **How much was spent on staff pay and other expenses?**

3 **How much profit or loss was made?**

HAIR WORLD HAIRDRESSING SALON

Profit and loss account to the year ended October 1995

	£	£	£
Sales			42,000
Cost of sales			
Purchases		10,500	
Less: Closing stock		1,000	
			11,500
Gross trading profit			30,500
Expenses			
Salaries	19,000		
Motor expenses	1,220		
Light and heat	1,600		
Telephone	900		
Repairs and renewals	620		
Insurance	500		
General expenses	1,300		
Furniture and fittings	580		
Advertising	3,000	28,720	
Total expenses			28,720
Profit			1,780

See if your answers are correct by checking them against those at the end of this study unit.

The balance sheet

Once the profit and loss account has been prepared, the figures are transferred to the balance sheet. The balance sheet lists all of a company's **assets** and **liabilities**.

Assets are things owned by the company, for example, money in the bank, desks, computers, stationery, cars and vans, raw materials used to make the products the company sells and so on.

Liabilities are the outstanding amounts of money owed by the company, such as unpaid bills, bank loans and any overdraft.

Monitoring financial information

Every business must keep a careful eye on the money coming into the business from customers, and the money going out of the business on staff pay, expenses and payments to other businesses. Monitoring allows businesses to make adjustments. For example, if sales are down, a business may decide to cut back on spending or spend more on advertising to, hopefully, achieve more sales.

If financial monitoring shows that problems are likely to occur, most businesses will cut back on spending, make determined efforts to gather in any money owed by debtors, seek to increase sales and may, if the situation is really serious, borrow money. This may take the form of a business loan or an overdraft.

Budgets

Most people find that the most sensible way to manage their money is to set some kind of budget. The budget takes into account the money they expect to receive (income) and the purchases they expect to make (expenditure) over a period of time.

Businesses need to set budgets to make sure that spending is controlled and does not exceed expected income. At the beginning of every financial year, most businesses set a budget for the next 12 months. They do this by:

- calculating the amount of income they can expect from sales over the coming 12 months
- looking at how much they spent during the previous 12 months on items such as staff pay, raw materials, stationery, rent, petrol and so on
- considering very carefully how much they will need to spend on these items over the next 12 months.

For example, if a business spent £2,000 on petrol in the preceding year, providing petrol prices and mileage are expected to be approximately the same, the company would most probably allocate £2,000 to be spent on petrol in the next year. Of course, things can – and often do – change, and it could be that:

- the price of petrol has increased
- the business plans to buy an additional vehicle
- the business plans to use the existing vehicle for more journeys.

In any of these circumstances, the business would have to increase the budget allocation for petrol to cover the expected additional costs. So, instead of £2,000, the budget figure for petrol might be £3,000 for the next year.

Depending on the size of the business, a number of people may be involved in setting the budget. It is usually the job of a senior person within the company – perhaps the owner or the accountant – to monitor the amount of money actually being spent against the amount of money allocated in the budget. Businesses aim to keep their spending within the budget they have set. Careful monitoring of the budget on a daily, weekly or monthly basis, enables businesses to identify problems and see if there is underspending or overspending.

2.1, 2.4 C, 2.2, 2.3 AN **C** **Activity**

In a small group, examine the budget below.

Budget: 1 June 1995 to 1 June 1996 THE AMAZING T-SHIRT COMPANY												
Allocation	**Expenditure**											
Item & amount	**Jan.**	**Feb.**	**Mar.**	**Apr.**	**May**	**Jun.**	**Jul.**	**Aug.**	**Sep.**	**Oct.**	**Nov.**	**Dec.**
Pay £6,0000	£5,000	£5,000	£5,000									
Stationery £2,500	£1,000	£1,500	£750									
Petrol £5,000	£800	£750	£2,000									
Telephone £2,000	£100	£100	£100									
Petty cash £1,000	£350	£400	£350									
Raw materials £20,000	£1,500	£2,000	£2,000									
Heat & light £1,500	£100	£100	£100									
Rent £3,000	£250	£250	£250									
Insurances £800	£66	£66	£66									
Advertising £5,000	£1,300	£1,500	£2,50									

- The left-hand column headed 'Item & amount' shows the amount that has been allocated for a 12-month period
E.g., pay of £60,000 is divided by 12 months = £5,000 to spend per month.
- The Jan. Feb. and Mar. columns show the amount of money that has actually been spent
E.g. pay in Jan. is £5,000 + Feb. £5,000 + Mar. £5,000 = £15,000 spent

Look at the expenditure for January, February and March and compare the amounts of money that have been spent against what was allocated for the items. Then answer the following questions.

1 **The allocation for stationery for the whole year is £2,500.**
Is the spending on stationery so far on target with the budget allocation or is the company overspending? Give the reasons for your answer.
Do the same for petty cash and advertising.

2 **If the company has overspent regarding any of these allocations, what can it do, if anything, to put matters right?**

In the first three months of the financial year, this company has spent £3,250 on stationery. This is £750 more than the amount that was allocated for the *whole* of the year.

In the first three months of the financial year, the company has spent £1,100 on petty cash. This is £100 more than the amount allocated for the *whole* of the year.

In the first three months of the financial year, this company has spent £5,150 on advertising. This is £150 more than the amount allocated for the *whole* of the year.

So far, the company has overspent on stationery, petty cash and advertising by a total of £1,000. The company could find that it is spending more than it is actually earning. There are three possible solutions to the problem:

- make sure that there is no more spending for the rest of the year on stationery, petty cash and advertising – this is not a very practical solution because all businesses regularly use stationery and need petty cash items
- increase the allocations and simply make some more money available to be spent on these items
- look at all the allocations in the budget and think about whether or not money can be saved anywhere else to make up for the overspending.

Certain items are fixed costs. For instance, the rent that has been agreed with the landlord of the premises is £3,000 for the year. Insurances are also fixed costs. However, savings can be made on some of the other items because they are what is known as variable costs. For example, £5,000 has been allocated to petrol, but the amount of money spent on petrol really depends on the number of journeys and the distances travelled. So, with careful route planning, some economies could be made on petrol. The money saved on petrol could then be used to compensate for some of the overspending on the other budget areas such as stationery.

Monitoring methods

The best way to monitor *actual* expenditure against *budgeted* allocations is to check the documentation that provides proof of purchases made and money spent. This **monitoring** can only be done accurately if all the documentation and calculations relating to financial transactions are:

- available – all the documentation must be carefully and secured filed and available for inspection and nothing should be missing
- accurate – the figures on, for example, invoices must be correctly calculated and accurately entered into the books as mistakes will give a false picture of sales and expenditure
- up to date – all the figures relating to money coming into and going out of the business must be logged on a daily basis; if this is not done, then checks between expenditure and budgeted allocations will be misleading.

Using information technology to record and monitor financial information

Some small businesses still record their financial transactions by hand in the ledgers often referred to as 'the books'. The majority of companies, though, prefer to use information technology to help them to run their businesses more efficiently. This is because computers can:

- store more information
- transfer information between departments
- perform complicated tasks and calculations, swiftly and accurately.

The important thing to remember is that a computer, no matter how sophisticated, is only a tool and it relies on the operator for the information entered. When incorrect data is keyed in, incorrect data will come out of it.

Computer software (the programs that give computers their instructions) is available for a wide range of applications. Many companies now use computers to:

- compile **databases** of the names, addresses and other details of their customers, suppliers and staff
- control stock – by using the appropriate software, companies can have instant access to details of the amount of stock they have, the items they need to re-order, the cost of items, the location of items and the transfer of items between locations
- produce accounts, VAT reports and prepare staff pay
- do calculations – providing the correct figures are keyed in, there is software available that will produce detailed and accurate figures at the touch of a key – such calculations are performed using **spreadsheets**
- monitor budgets – providing the software is given the correct budget allocations and every item of expenditure is accurately keyed in, there are programs that can give immediate access to budget figures, so companies can monitor their actual spending against what has been budgeted on an hourly, daily or weekly basis
- send electronic mail
- produce graphics – sophisticated desktop publishing software can be used to both copy and create pictures and decorative text, and they are used by many types of businesses, including book, newspaper and magazine publishers, advertising and graphic design companies and printers (for example, many commercial printers who produce letterheads for business stationery will use desktop publishing software to create eye-catching and distinctive lettering for the company name and address).

Many products now have a bar code printed on the label. In most large stores, this electronic system is also used to control stock.

3 141728 701355

Activity

For this activity, you will be using the budget for the Amazing T-Shirt Company on page 170.

On a spreadsheet, enter the text for each column and row heading, as shown top right.

Enter the expenditure figures given in the budget for January, February and March.

Enter the figures shown top right for the months April to December.

Using the spreadsheet, calculate the totals for the columns so you have the total monthly expenditure for all the items, such as the pay, stationery, petrol and so on. Also calculate the total expenditure for the year.

Item	April	May	June	July	Aug.	Sep.	Oct.	Nov.	Dec.
Pay	5,000	5,000	5,300	5,300	5,300	5,300	5,300	5,700	5,700
Stationery	800.91	163.02	290.17	576.10	971.28	376.22	148.09	77.25	68.34
Petrol	900.76	520.98	615.25	779.19	276.44	689.33	763.70	700.00	1,021.89
Telephone	127.00	145.39	100.00	167.56	100.00	177.28	220.40	316.90	397.27
Petty cash	220.17	189.10	77.56	83.12	74.90	213.65	340.76	229.15	87.60
Raw materials	2,300.00	2,470.67	2,580.00	2,500.15	1,089.20	221.39	2,570.98	3,130.40	2,071.63
Heat & light	98.26	101.42	78.14	61.22	55.18	61.00	78.44	97.12	120.33
Rent	250.00	250.00	250.00	250.00	250.00	250.00	250.00	250.00	250.00
Insurances	66.00	66.00	66.00	66.00	66.00	66.00	66.00	66.00	66.00
Advertising	1,700.00	1,602.57	1,898.33	2,133.98	789.00	1,900.00	2,109.65	2,604.76	1,438.77

SALES	
y	21,079.13
ary	17,216.28
	28,031.19
	18,433.76
	19,773.20
	24,531.75
	26,387.90
t	12,230.77
nber	19,881.00
er	22,008.16
nber	23,128.99
nber	20,761.45

Disadvantages of using computers include:

- lack of security – data can be lost when computers **crash**, floppy disks are stolen or damaged, and if unauthorised people have access to the hardware, software and password
- incorrect communications – if information is incorrectly entered into the program, then it will produce incorrect data and statistics
- their expense – computer hardware and software can be expensive to buy and businesses often need to upgrade their computers and their programs to bigger, better and faster versions.

Using the figures in the margin, calculate:

- how much profit or loss the company has made each month
- how much profit or loss the company has made for the year.

Finally, save and print a copy of the spreadsheet to add to your portfolio of evidence.

Although most businesses nowadays use information technology to store and access information, there are advantages and disadvantages connected with relying on computers.

Activity

Identify three advantages of using computers to store and access financial information.

Some of the advantages you might have listed are:

- the quantity of information they can store – large amounts of data can be stored, sorted, calculated and accessed swiftly and efficiently
- that the information can be stored more securely than paper records – access to important data can be protected by special passwords, which means that only authorised people who have been given the passwords can access confidential information
- the speed with which they can provide information – calculations can be updated in seconds, which is extremely important for budget and business monitoring and stock control
- they enhance communications – facts, figures and even money can be swiftly and easily transferred between departments, companies and even countries
- their flexibility – laptop and notebook computers, which can be battery and mains powered, are lightweight, portable and can be used anywhere.

2.2,2.4 C Ⓒ
2.1, 2.2, 2.3 AN
2.4 IT

Assignment

This assignment has two parts.

1 **Find out from your work placement, school, college or other businesses with which you have contact (perhaps your bank, building society, optician, local supermarket) what types of software they use. Make a list of:**

- the names of the software
- what their applications are (whether they are database, spreadsheet, accounts, word processing or other programs)
- the suppliers and the costs of the software.

Gather together as much information and promotional material as you can about three types of IT-based programs, including:

- a word processing or desktop publishing program
- a spreadsheet or accounts program
- a database program.

Write a report and compare the functions and uses of these programs for producing and storing financial information.

2 **Work out what your income and expenses are likely to be over the next three months. The headings you choose will be personal to you, but you might want to include, for example:**

- travel (bus fares, etc.)
- books and magazines
- clothes
- entertainment
- savings.

Allocate to each of the headings the amount of money you intend to spend. Then keep a record of your income and each item of expenditure. At the end of each month, total the amounts and enter your expenditure in the appropriate column. You can now monitor your budget and check to see whether or not you are:

- overspending
- keeping to the allocations you have set yourself.

At the end of the three-month period, write a short report describing whether or not you stayed within your budget and, if not, the reasons for this.

3 Business documents

This section illustrates the range of routine business documents that all businesses regularly send and receive to:

- communicate externally:
  - with customers
  - with other businesses
- communicate internally:
  - with colleagues.

You will see what purposes a range of routine business documents serve, and the ways in which they can be processed. You will evaluate the quality of different business documents. You will also investigate systems that can be used for filing, storing and sending the various kinds of documents business generates.

The purposes of business documents

Creating a positive image

Businesses are keen to make sure that all the documents leaving their premises are correct and well presented. A poorly presented letter that is badly typed and contains spelling mistakes will give the impression that the company sending the letter is slapdash and disorganised. A carefully worded and presented document, however, looks professional and gives a good impression.

Because the appearance of business documentation is so important, many companies design their own letterhead. A company letterhead is pre-printed with the name, address, telephone, fax and VAT numbers. Most businesses tend to use the same logo, style of lettering and colours on all their business documents – letterheads, compliment slips, invoices, statements. This is called a house style. In addition, all the business documents may always follow a specific layout.

Activity

Working on your own, list at least two reasons for organisations choosing to produce their business documents on a word processor rather than a typewriter.

Examples of standard text that can be stored on disk and regularly inserted into documents are:

- legal text used by solicitors for insertion into contracts and similar documents
- text describing houses and other properties used by estate agents in their advertisements and brochures.

The main reasons businesses prefer to use word processors are:

- documentation produced on a word processor can be saved on disk for later reference or amendment whereas with a typewriter, it is usual to produce a top copy (the original) plus a carbon copy, so any further copies must be photocopied or typed again
- using a word processor, standard blocks of text can be stored on disk and quickly inserted into documents, which is particularly useful for form letters and for businesses that regularly use the same kind of wording again and again.

Types of business documents

In word processing software, typestyles are referred to as fonts. Here are some examples of different fonts in different sizes.

Century Schoolbook
Franklin Gothic
Garamond italic
Gill Sans
Baskerville
Optima
Zurich

Letters

Many companies, particularly large organisations, prefer to have their printed letters presented in what is known as 'fully blocked, open punctuation style'. With this style, no punctuation is used in the address, reference or date, and all the text is typed in blocks aligned with the left-hand margin.

Activity

You work as an administrative assistant for a company that sells children's clothing by mail order. One of your tasks every day is to make a list of all the incoming and outgoing mail. Think about the kinds of letters your company might send and receive (for example, it would be likely to send letters to customers informing them that certain items are out of stock and receive letters from customers complimenting or complaining about the company).

List up to four kinds of letters:

- your company might send to customers
- your company might receive from customers.

Your answers may have included any of the following. For letters sent out to customers you might have put:

- requests for and confirmation of payments
- apologies for delays or errors
- confirmation of orders received
- requests for further information required by the company
- giving information requested by customers
- details of times and dates when orders will be met.

For letters received from customers you might have written:

- complaints regarding quality of product or service, incorrect invoicing and so on

It is very important to keep copies of all written communications. All letters, memos, notices, invitations and so on must be properly filed so that when they are needed a business can swiftly and easily find the relevant document.

- confirmations of orders
- confirmations that payments have been made
- requests for refunds
- enquiries and requests for information.

Messages

Messages are often hand-written and can be:

- brief details added to a compliment slip or other document
- information to be passed on from one person to another in the same business (perhaps a record of a telephone conversation).

Even though business messages are not as formal as business letters, it is very important to write them clearly and legibly so that, for example, a telephone message can be acted on accurately.

Form letters

Businesses sometimes need to send out many copies of the same letter or very similar ones, and these are called **form letters**. Sometimes an identical form letter is sent to every recipient, and sometimes minor changes are necessary for each person.

Activity

You work in the offices of Katy's Kitchen, a firm that manufactures jams and pickles. Working in a small group, list at least three situations in which it would be appropriate to send exactly the same letter, and three situations in which it would be appropriate to send the same letter but with some minor changes to:

- 20 different customers
- 20 different colleagues who work with you.

You could have suggested the following. Sending the *same* form letter to customers to:

- invite them to the opening of a new shop
- notify them about changes to opening times
- confirm new procedures (delivery or payment, perhaps)
- confirm new prices.

Sending the same form letter to colleagues to:

- notify them of different working hours or holidays
- let them know about a Christmas party or other celebration
- tell them that a member of staff is leaving
- advise them about new working procedures.

Form letters are sometimes also referred to as macro letters or mail-merge letters.

The same form letter with minor changes could be sent to customers to:

- acknowledge receipt of payment
- notify them of unpaid invoices
- confirm that correspondence has been received
- confirm that an order has been received and let them know when it will be despatched.

Our ref: JHT/NB

Dear Sir/Madam

Thank you for your payment of   which
was received on   1995.
This amount has been credited to your account
and your outstanding balance
is now £   .

Yours faithfully,

J. Marshall
Credit Control

The same form letter with minor changes could be sent to colleagues to:

- confirm the dates of individually agreed annual holidays, work rotas or shifts
- let them know times for interviews or reviews
- acknowledge the number of customers contacted or sales made.

When large numbers of form letters are to be sent out, companies often use the mail-merge facility available in most word-processing programs. This facility allows the operator to add individual details, such as names, addresses and so on, to the various copies of a form letter.

Notices and invitations

If a large number of notices of forthcoming events or invitations to meetings are required, then these may be word processed. If a very large quantity of notices is required, they may be photocopied in house. If the event or meeting is particularly important, however, these notices may be produced by a commercial printer.

Memoranda

Memoranda, or memos, are most often used internally, and exchanged between departments or branches of the same company. Many companies will have a standard layout for their memos as part of their house style.

Memorandum

To: Sylvia Kemp, Training Department
From: Geetu Singh, Marketing Department
Date: 21 Spetember 1995
Re: Two-day workshop in Liverpool

Very many thanks for sending me the details of the training course.
I note that you will be arriving in Liverpool at lunchtime on the first day, and I would like the opportunity to meet with you to discuss further developments relating to the Hong Kong project.
Please call Joanne Winters, my secretary, to discuss how we might be able to arrange this during our time in Liverpool.

Activity

Working on your own, read through the list of situations described in the left-hand column below. Your task is to match each situation with the most appropriate document to use for it, listed in the right-hand column. For example, the first situation described is 'Inform staff of the date of the Christmas party' and it should be matched up with 'Memo' from the other column.

	Situations	*Documents*
1	Inform staff of the date of the Christmas party.	Letter
2	Inform a customer that they have not paid their invoice on time.	Printed or photocopied standard letter
3	Ask for a replacement pack of computer disks.	Memo
4	Invite customers to the opening of a new shop.	Compliment slip
5	Ask members of staff to attend a meeting.	
6	Make a complaint.	
7	Ask a supplier for a price list.	

The answers to this activity are at the end of this study unit.

2.2 C, 2.1, 2.2, 2.3 IT **C** **Activity**

You work in the Administration Department of Parkhurst & Wells, a large department store. Working on your own, use a word processor to prepare draft and final versions of two of the following documents:

- a memo to staff informing them that the Christmas party will be held on Tuesday 12 December 1995 in the Parkhurst & Wells restaurant
- a form letter to be sent to all customers when Parkhurst & Wells want to confirm that a cheque has been received
- a letter to D. J. Disks, returning a faulty pack of computer disks and asking for a replacement
- a letter of complaint to J. H. Shaw & Co. Limited regarding a faulty roll of curtain material delivered on 3 November 1995 costing £376.00.

Make sure you check the language, spelling, grammar and appearance of your documents carefully.

Comparing the different ways of processing business documents

Activity

You work in the Administration Department of Johnson & Company, Chartered Accountants. Your Manager has asked you to compare and evaluate the different methods of processing and producing:

- memos
- letters
- form letters
- reports and accounts for clients.

She asks you to think about producing them by:

- writing them by hand
- typing
- word processing
- printing
- photocopying

and to take into consideration:

- legibility – how easy this kind of document is to read
- the cost involved – how much this kind of document costs to produce
- the time taken to produce each document – how long it will take to produce this kind of document
- the ability to make changes – how easy it is to alter text and figures with this kind of document
- ease of storage – how this kind of document can be stored.

Using a word processor, prepare draft and final versions of a report to your Manager. In your report you should:

- recommend the method that you believe should be used to produce each of the documents listed above
- give the reasons for your choices.

Filing systems

Businesses send and receive large quantities of documentation. Every business must be able to store and find documents they have received and copies of documents they have sent out.

Activity

Working on your own, use a word processor to prepare draft and final versions of a memo to a fellow student describing the filing system you use to store the paperwork for this course.

Filing systems must allow staff to quickly find the document they need.

Documents of all kinds (letters, memos, reports, invoices, statements, purchase orders and so on) can be stored in:

- paper filing systems
- computerised filing systems.

Paper filing systems

A great deal of business information is still in the form of paperwork, so every company has to store a great deal of paper. This can take up a large amount of space.

Most companies keep their paperwork in three- or four-drawer filing cabinets. These contain individual suspension files and, usually, a separate suspension file is used to keep all the paperwork relating to each customer, supplier, type of document (such as memos), subject (say, sales figures or petty cash receipts) or other category as appropriate.

These are usually updated at regular intervals (say once every 12 months) when dead files are removed and, often, stored in clearly labelled cardboard boxes, sometimes called **archive files**. To store files securely, if required, cabinets or storage rooms are locked and keys only given to authorised people.

Information such as details about customers, suppliers, staff, students, products and so on may be kept in:

- a rotary index
- a strip index
- a box index.

These are good ways to store small amounts of information, but if there are lots of pieces of information, they may not always fit on to the strip or card. These kinds of storage systems, which are usually small and portable, can cause security problems because information can easily be removed.

The main systems used to classify information and documents are:

- alphabetical
- numerical
- subject.

The alphabetical system

This system is so-called because it uses the letters of the alphabet. When using this system, it is important to observe the following rules:

- always file under the first letter of the surname, so Mrs J. King would be filed under K, Masters, Woods & Associates would be filed under M, and Chemform Products Limited would be filed under C
- hyphenated surnames should be filed under the first letter, so Brown-Wilson should be filed under B
- where there are a number of items with the same surname, then the first name or initial should be taken into account, so Mrs A. Wilson would come before Mr H. Wilson, who, in turn, would come before S. Wilson & Partners
- company names that begin with a number should be filed alphabetically under the first letter of the word for that number, so 3J Systems would be filed under T for three and 9 Lives Cat Products would be filed under N for nine
- if a company name begins with The, this should be ignored and documents relating to them should be filed under the letter of the first word after this, so The Office Equipment Company would be filed under O.

Activity

You work in the Administration Department of Bargain Books. The company has just taken delivery of a new consignment of books. Your task, using a word processor, is to sort and file the books listed in the margin, applying the alphabetical system to the names of the authors:

W. McMahon, *The Longest Night*
Chloe Dennison and M. Shaw, *Springtime Gardening*
Deemar Ratanjali, *Team Working in Further and Higher Education*
Carol Smith, *New Book of Aromatherapy*
Melvin Shaw, *Advanced Chess Strategies*
The Writing Team, *Decision Making For Beginners*
K. Robson-Taylor, *Politics In Our Times*
Susan. B. Singh, *Cooking With Spices*
The Education Foundation, *Teaching Your Two-year-old*
P. K. Van Holden, *A Woman I Knew*
Alan Smith, *Song of Silence*.

The correct ordering of this list can be seen at the end of this study unit.

The numerical system

With the **numerical system**, each new item added to the filing cabinet is given a consecutive number. For instance, if the last suspension file in the cabinet held the paperwork for Mr J. Adams, number 326, then the next suspension file added would be number 327, no matter what the name. Because it would be impossible to find anything unless you could remember the number, numerical systems always have an alphabetical index as well.

This is how the numerical filing system works. When you add a new suspension file to the filing cabinet, you give it the next consecutive number, for example number 327. You also make out a record card with the number (327) and the name of the item (say, Brookleigh Electronics Limited). You file the record card alphabetically under B.

The main advantage of the numerical system is that it is very easy to add and remove items. The numerical system is also good for filing numbered documents, such as invoices and purchase orders.

The subject system

With this system, all the information relating to a given subject is filed together. So, a chef might file recipes under the headings:

- starters
- soups
- meat
- fish
- pasta and rice
- vegetables
- desserts.

Public libraries store information relating to their book stocks on microfilm. This is also a good way to protect old and valuable documents as they can still be read, but the originals do not need to be handled by the reader, thereby avoiding them being damaged.

Microfilm

Large amounts of information on paper can be stored on **microfilm, or microfiche**. Using this system, images of the documents are greatly reduced in size and stored on film, which can be viewed by placing the film sheets on a reading machine.

Computerised filing systems

All kinds of documents and information can be stored on floppy or hard disks, which can store large amounts of information. The main disadvantage is that data can be lost through hardware, software or human error.

All companies copy any information stored on the hard disk on to, generally, two sets of floppy disks. These disks are called 'back-up disks'. This is done so that if the computer crashes, then there is a back-up copy, which can be used to return any lost information to the system. The back-up copies are updated regularly, often once per day, so that as little information as possible is lost.

Many companies use a database to file and store information about customers, staff, stock and sales. Because, as we have seen, there is a possibility that computers can crash and data can be lost, some companies also keep what is known as a hard copy of the information. A hard copy is the paper printout of the information held on computer.

The database system

The term 'database' is also used to describe any bundle of information that is kept together in some kind of order and relates to similar topics. For instance, if you keep a file of recipes, that is a database. If you keep a list of manufacturers and suppliers of sportswear, that is a database.

You will know that there are many computer programs available that can be used to store and sort information. Using a **computer database**, it is possible find information in seconds.

This is how a computerised database works:

- the information (names, addresses, product types) is keyed in
- when a business wants to know how many customers they have in a particular location or what the sizes of orders are or what methods of delivery are used, the database could compile such a list.

Kumara works as a receptionist in a doctor's surgery. It is a busy practice, with over 12,000 patients to look after.

Kumara receives a telephone call from a patient who is extremely distressed and asking for an ambulance. In his confusion, the patient gives his name and date of birth, but not his address or telephone number.

Using the computerised database, Kumara is able to key in the patient's name and date of birth and search the computer files for the file that contains the matching details. Within two or three minutes, Kumara has, on the computer screen, the patient's details, including his address. She is then able to order an ambulance and also telephone the patient to check that he is all right until help arrives.

Activity

Contact the Manager of, or a senior person in, the Administration Department of a business you know. Find out:

- how business documents are stored – about their paper and computer systems
- what kinds of filing systems are used – alphabetical, numerical, subject or computer database
- how documents are processed – what kinds of documents are word processed, printed and photocopied
- how documents are most usually sent – which are sent by ordinary first- or second-class mail, special delivery, recorded delivery, registered post, fax and electronic mail.

When you have completed your research, use a word processor to write a short report on what you have found. Explain the advantages and disadvantages of the methods that this business (or your school or work placement) use to store, file, process and send documents.

Sending business documents

There are a number of ways in which a business can send documents to customers and other businesses. The method chosen will depend:

- on its urgency – whether or not speed is necessary
- if security is important or not – say, if the document is routine or valuable or highly confidential
- its bulk – whether or not the documents are very lengthy or heavy or if a number of documents are to be sent
- on cost – whether or not economy is important.

Businesses must take these factors into account when choosing how to send documents and select the method that most suits their needs. For example, if a company needed to send important papers quickly but also wanted to spend as little money as possible, it would have to decide:

- whether it was more important to send the documents quickly and safely or
- whether it was more important to use regular first-class post, which is cheaper than most other methods, but perhaps not as secure and does not guarantee next-day delivery.

Urgency

If a business needs to send a document fast, then the best methods to choose are either Royal Mail Special Delivery, a courier service, a facsimile machine or electronic mail

Businesses wishing to send information to organisations outside the UK can use facsimile machines, e-mail and, of course, Royal Mail. Post sent abroad can either travel by regular airmail or by Swiftair, which is an express airmail service.

Royal Mail Special Delivery

Special Delivery mail is guaranteed to arrive before 12.30 pm the next working day to all UK addresses, providing it has been posted before the latest acceptance time, which is usually about 30 minutes before post offices close in the afternoon. The item then receives priority over other mail and can be tracked by Royal Mail by means of the bar code on the label that is stuck to the envelope or parcel when it is posted. Special Delivery items must be signed for when they are received and senders can claim a refund of twice the Special Delivery fee if the item does not arrive on time.

Fax

Facsimile, fax, machines can be used to transfer written information, including graphs and pictures between one fax machine and another. The information is transferred through British Telecom telephone lines.

It is possible to fax information to any part of the world, and this is an ideal way to send printed information very quickly. However, very long documents (say, those over 20 pages), can take some time to send.

Electronic mail is often referred to as e-mail. Anyone using the e-mail facility must have a special e-mail address, which works in the same way as a telephone number. An example of an e-mail address is Susan Briers 27.18 @ Personnel Imperial. Org. Harlow. U.K.

Electronic mail, or e-mail

Computers can be used to send information and this is called **electronic mail, or e-mail**. To do this, the computer sending the message and the computer that is to receive the message must both be connected to the telephone network by a modem. The modem converts the message from the computer into signals, and sends the signals down the telephone line. This method is used by many companies to transfer large amounts of information, both figures and words, quickly and efficiently.

Security

Important documents, which may be valuable or highly confidential, can be sent by Recorded Delivery or Registered post (these are not guaranteed

to arrive the next day, but usually do). Documents sent either of these ways can be tracked by means of the bar code on the label attached to the envelope or parcel at the time of posting and must be signed for on delivery. There are also special courier services that collect items (anything from an envelope to a large parcel) and deliver them to their destination at an agreed time, say, the next day or within 24 hours.

Bulk

Businesses sometimes need to send heavy items or a number of similar items.

Datapost

PARCEL FORCE

This is a parcel service run by The Post Office that guarantees overnight delivery to most businesses in the UK.

Red Star

Red Star

This is a service available at certain train stations and uses the train system to transport bulky items.

Royal Mail Electronic Post

Sometimes businesses may need to send out thousands of similar letters to existing or potential customers. They may want to tell current customers about changes to prices or premises, or perhaps they want to advertise a new product or service. Businesses can supply Royal Mail with a disk containing the information, a supply of letterheads and a list of names and addresses. Royal Mail will print the information on the company's letterheads, organise the envelopes and make sure everything is delivered.

Cost

For many businesses, cost is a major factor when considering how to send information. This particularly applies if a business is not doing too well or if the business is overspending on the allocation set for postage.

The cheapest (and also the slowest) way to send information is to use Royal Mail second-class post or Parcelforce's parcel delivery service.

Activity

Working on your own, look at the following list of items that need to be sent and decide which of the methods given in the right-hand column would be the best to use. Explain the reasons for your choice.

Item	*Method of sending*
Urgent cheque for £2,000	Special Delivery, Registered, Registered Plus
Urgent quotation	Fax, Datapost, Recorded Delivery
Very urgent and important contract	Special Delviery, Recorded Delivery, Registered
£100 cash	Special Delivery, Registered, Registered Plus.

Compare your answers with those given at the end of this study unit.

2.2, 2.4 C ©
2.1, 2.2, 2.3, 2.4 IT

Assignment

Imagine that you work in the Administration Department of Now Music, a large company that sells records, cassettes and CDs by mail order.

Working on your own, complete this assignment, which is in two parts.

1 Use a word processor to prepare the following documents. You should make sure that you produce draft and final versions of each document. Keep a record of the things you changed between the draft and the final version and explain why you made the changes.

- A letter to Mr J. Hargreaves, Rose Cottage, Wood End, Brighton BN22 1TP, explaining that your company is out of stock of catalogue number BVY 765 102, Simply Red, *Stars*, on CD. Ask Mr Hargreaves if he wants to wait until this comes into stock, or if he would prefer a cassette, a refund or something else altogether.
- Invitation to all members of staff inviting them to attend a leaving party for Michael Baldwin, Catering Manager. The party is to be held in the staff canteen on Friday 15 September 1995 at 5.30 pm. Refreshments will be provided.
- A form letter your company could send to all customers, thanking them for their monthly payment and reminding them that all future payments will be due on the 10th of each month, not the 20th of each month as they have been up until now.
- A letter to M. Holland & Son, Printers, 9 Merriman Way, Dorset Road, Leeds LS8 7TD confirming her telephone order of 18 August 1995 and enclosing a note of the purchase order number that this order has been given – 27883.
- A letter to Mrs P. Lockwood, 29 Fairway Drive, Nottingham NG8 9UJ, returning her cheque for £17, dated 3 April 1995, explaining that the cheque has not been signed. Ask her to sign the cheque and return it to you.

- A memo to all managers in your company, reminding them that there will be a meeting in the boardroom on Monday 6 November 1995, starting at 10·00 am. The purpose of the meeting is to discuss the company budget for 1996.
- A memo to Gillian Morris who is taking over from you as Accounts Clerk when you go on holiday in the summer. Explain to Gillian why it is important that she makes sure that all financial transactions are accurately recorded. Also, explain to her why it is necessary that she keeps a record of every sale and every purchase in the form of a simple income and expenditure account.

2 Your next task is to assess each of the documents you have prepared and printed out. Write a short statement about each document and comment on the:

- spelling – if you are not sure of a word, use a dictionary or the spell-check facility on your word processor
- punctuation
- grammar
- appearance

and

- give a brief explanation of why you think the format (letter, memo, message, invitation) is appropriate.

Summary

You will now be familiar with the most common financial transactions that take place between businesses, their customers and their banks. You have looked at the importance of keeping accurate financial records, and you have seen the direct relationship between sales, purchases, budgets and annual accounts. You have also seen how businesses rely on everyone in the organisation making sure that financial documentation is carefully completed and thoroughly checked.

Information technology and computers can help businesses to communicate with one another, transfer messages and information, perform complicated calculations, store large amounts of information and produce professional-looking documents.

Finally, you have considered the many ways in which information can be filed, stored and accessed, and you have had the opportunity to compare how business documents can best be produced to meet the specific needs of a business, taking into account factors such as flexibility, and the cost and speed of production.

Review activity

You have now completed your work on this study unit and should spend some time reviewing what you have achieved.

1 Grading themes

For Intermediate GNVQs, you can achieve a higher grade depending on how much initiative and independent action you take in the areas of:

- planning
- information gathering
- evaluation
- quality of outcomes.

Action planning
Look over the assignments you worked on for this unit.

- Did you complete detailed action plans for each assignment?
- How much support did you need from your teacher/tutor to complete the plans?
- Did you regularly review and update your plans?
- How successful were you in achieving your plans and targets?
- What would you have done differently?

Information gathering
Look over all the assignments you worked on for this unit.

- Did you successfully identify the sorts of information you needed to complete activities and assignments?
- Did you succesfully gather the information you needed? How did you do this?
- How would you assess the quality of information you gathered? Was it:
  - useful and relevant
  - appropriate for your needs
  - accurate and complete?
- Were there any areas where you were not able to gather the information you needed?
- Why was this?
- What would you have done differently?

Evaluation
Evaluation is an important part of your GNVQ. It is one of the grading themes that will enable you to obtain a Merit or Distinction. As part of your evaluation, you should consider the following questions.

- Have I completed all the performance criteria for each element?
- What have I learned from this unit?
- How do my achievements compare with my Action Plan?
- What sources of information did I use and how did I access them?
- Is there anything I would do differently if I had to do it again?

Outcomes

- Did you present complete assignments that covered all of the areas mentioned in them?
- Did your assignment work show that you identified and selected only the appropriate parts from all the information you collected?
- Did you use business language and vocabulary accurately in your work to put information and points across clearly to your target audience?

2 Performance criteria and range

Look at the standards for this GNVQ unit. Work through the performance criteria for each element and check that you have done work to help you meet each one. Do this by noting down the relevant performance criteria number against the work.

Finally, check through the information given under the range.

3 Core skills

This unit has covered the following core skills:

- Communication level 2: 2.1, 2.2, 2.3, 2.4
- Information technology level 2: 2.1, 2.2, 2.3, 2.4
- Application of number level 2: 2.1, 2.2, 2.3.

Answers to activities

page 152

You will have spotted a number of mistakes on the invoice from Rowley Foods. These are:

Invoice from Rowley Foods	*Purchase order* placed by Save & Spend
1 Your order no.: 98100217	Order no.: 98000217
2 Date of your order: 4 March 1994	Date of order: 4 March 1995
3 48 Black Forest gâteaux at £1.20 each = £77.70 (overcharged by £20.10)	48 Black Forest gâteaux at £1.20 each = £57.60
4 72 Fudge Delight at 78p each = £54.72	72 Fudge Delight at 76p each = £54.72
(the unit price is *incorrect*, but the total price is *correct*)	
5 130 Toffee Crunch at £1.12 each = £143.00	130 Toffee Crunch at £1.10 each = £143.00
(the unit price is *incorrect*, but the total price is *correct*)	
6 125 Raspberry Pavlova at £1.08 each = £135.00	25 Raspberry Pavlova at £1.08 each = £27.00
(the unit price is *correct*, but the quantity is *incorrect*)	

7 The total amount due column has been incorrectly added up as the total amount due, using the figures shown, should be £453.62, not £435.62. The total amount of the goods ordered comes to £325.52. If the invoice had been paid without checking the figures, Save & Spend would have overpaid £110.10.

It is rare for firms to send out invoices containing as many mistakes as our example. Even so, incorrect invoices are sent out from time to time, which is why it is so important for the purchaser to check the figures.

page 158

This is how the receipts match up to the transactions.
1 deposit of £3,200 in cash and cheques
2 purchase of items costing £5
3 purchase of a car costing £8,200
4 purchase of goods by telephone
5 purchase of parts costing £620 from Midvale Engineering Co.

page 163

The cheque for Swift Supplies should be made out for the amount of £673.48 because:

- in Document 1, the invoice dated 21 September, the sum of 21 diaries at 5.99 = £147.00, *not* £157.00, so the total amount due for this invoice is £427.55, not £437.55
- in Document 4, the statement dated 23 September, because of the error made regarding the total for the diaries, the total of invoice 78511290 should be £427.55, plus VAT, *not* £437.55, plus VAT, and, further, the statement does not show a credit of £350.00 for the Lotus fax machine (this is shown in Document 3, the goods received note) that was returned to the supplier (there is also a credit note for this amount from the supplier).

page 168

1 £42,000, sales
2 £28,720
3 £1,780, profit

page 179

Situations	*Documents*
1	Memo
2	Letter or form letter
3	Letter
4	Printed or photocopied form letter
5	Memo
6	Letter
7	Letter

page 182

Chloe Dennison and M. Shaw, *Springtime Gardening*
The Education Foundation, *Teaching Your Two-year-old*
P. K. Van Holden, *A Woman I Knew*
W. McMahon, *The Longest Night*
Deemar Ratanjali, *Team Working in Further and Higher Education*
K. Robson-Taylor, *Politics In Our Times*
Melvin Shaw, *Advanced Chess Strategies*

PURCHASE ORDER No. 32666					
From: Superfit Gym and Health Centre Market Road Manchester M22 5YG			**To:** Prestige Office Stationery 14 Holly Court Manchester M26 3ED		
Deliver to: Above address			**Special instructions:** None		
Reference	**Quantity**	**Details**	**Price**	**VAT @ 17.5%**	**Total price**
	20 reams	Copier paper @ £2.20 per ream	£44.00	£7.70	£51.70
	1	Angled desklamp	£32.00	£5.60	£37.60
	12	Roller-ball pens @ 65p each	£7.80	£1.37	£9.17
	2 rolls	Sticky tape @ 70p each	£1.40	£0.25	£1.65
	24	Telephone message pads @ 60p each	£14.40	£2.52	£16.92
		Totals:	£99.60	£17.44	£117.04
Authorised by: Tina King					

page 187 Susan. B. Singh, *Cooking With Spices*
Alan Smith, *Song of Silence*
Carol Smith, *New Book of Aromatherapy*
The Writing Team, *Decision Making For Beginners.*

Item	*The best method to use for sending this item would be*
Urgent cheque for £2,000	Special Delivery (next-day delivery, priority treatment)
Urgent quotation	Fax (immediate delivery)
Very important contract	Recorded (priority treatment)
£100 cash	Registered (very secure and covers cash and valuables up to £500)

Invoice

Superfit Gym and Health Centre
Market Road, Manchester M22 5YG

Mr J. Johnstone
Kimberley, Clark & Wilson
West House
87 West Road
Manchester M34 8HN

Deliver to: Kimberley, Clark & Wilson, Sycamore House, Colne Avenue, Manchester M27 10NN

Date: 17 July 1995

Invoice No.	Your Account No.	Your Order No.	Date of Your Order	
27756	880026	45661	10 July 1995	
Quantity	**Description**	**Unit price**	**VAT**	**Total price**
	company club membership for 1 year	£592.00	£103.60	£695.60
12 pairs	Running shoes @ £7 each	£84.00		£84.00
12	Tracksuits @ £22.50 each	£270.00		£270.00
		Total price	£946.00	
		VAT at 17.5%	£103.00	
		Total amount due	£1,049.60	

E & O E Terms: 30 days VAT registration no. 901 657 223

Invoice

Superfit Gym and Health Centre
Market Road, Manchester M22 5YG

Mrs J. Bennett
238 Alderson Avenue
Manchester M33 8BG

Date: 17 July 1995

Invoice No.	Your Account No.	Your Order No.	Date of Your Order	
27755	879931			
Quantity	**Description**	**Unit price**	**VAT**	**Total price**
	Club membership for 3 months	£48.00	£8.40	£56.40
2	Suncradle sessions @ £7 each	£14.00	£2.45	£16.45
		Total amount	£62.00	
		VAT at 17.5%	£10.85	
		Total amount due	£72.85	

E & O E Terms: 30 days VAT registration no. 901 657 223

Glossary

annual accounts information that shows how much the business has earned and how much the business has spent over a 12-month period

APR (annual percentage rate) the amount of interest charged on loans made by banks, building societies and other lending organisations

archive file dead file that is stored in a separate filing cabinet or archive box

assets the property of an individual or company, including money, buildings, furniture etc.

authorised cheque signatory the person (or people) authorised by a business to sign cheques on behalf of the business

BACS (bureau automated clearing system) computerised system used to transfer money between bank accounts in the UK

balance sheet document that shows the money owed by the business and the money and goods owned by the business and the difference between these

bank sort code a reference number which identifies the bank, printed on cheques and paying-in slips

budget a plan for expenditure that lays down the amount of money available to be spent on specific things, such as staff pay, petrol, petty cash and so on

cash discount offered by the seller to the purchaser to encourage the purchaser to settle invoices quickly. Same as prompt payment discount

cheque counterfoil the part of the cheque that remains in the chequebook

cheque guarantee card a card that guarantees that the bank will honour the cheque. There is usually a £50 or £100 limit on the card

crash computer failure caused by errors in the hardware (equipment), software (programs), power failures, power surges, human error or a combination of these

credit card can be used to pay for goods and services, it is swiped through an electronic funds transfer at point of sale machine (EFTPOS). This system automatically adds the cost of the item(s) to the cardholder's account and the owner of the card is given both a till receipt and a receipt with the full details of the card transaction

credit note if a customer has overpaid, returned goods or not received goods, a business will issue a credit note for the sum of money involved

database any bundle of stored data that relates to one or similar topics, such as recipes, addresses, football scores

debit cards widely accepted plastic cards that are 'swiped' through an EFTPOS machine. The EFTPOS system automatically transfers the money from the purchaser's account to the seller's account. With debit cards there is no bill to pay at the end of the month as the money has already been paid out of the cardholder's account

delivery note document that is given to the customer when the goods are delivered

direct debit payment made out of the customer's account at the request of the supplier. The amount may vary from month to month but is usually made on the same date

drawings money or goods taken out of a business for personal use by the owner of the business

EDI (electronic data interchange) electronic means of transferring information and money between accounts

electronic mail, or e-mail system that uses telephone lines to transfer information between computers

facsimile, or fax, machines they use telephone lines to transfer written information

financial transaction a sale, purchase or transfer of funds

form letter a standard letter with spaces for individual details

goods received note a document that is completed when goods are delivered

inward transaction a financial transaction that brings money into the business

liability money or anything that is owed by a business

memoranda, or memos used internally to exchange information between colleagues

microfilm, or microfiche system for keeping images of paper documents on film

monitoring the process of carefully observing what is happening in a business, particularly with regard to the money coming in and the money going out

numerical filing system items are filed by consecutive numbers, but each also has a record card that is filed alphabetically

outward transaction a financial transaction is a payment of money out of the business

petty cash cash made available for small purchases, such as coffee, small packets of envelopes, taxi fares and so on

petty cash voucher document that must be completed when a petty cash purchase is made

profit and loss account a master document that shows all the expenditure and all the sales a company has made over a 12-month period, and whether it has made a profit or loss

prompt payment discount this is offered by the seller to the purchaser to encourage the purchaser to settle invoices quickly. Same as cash discount

purchase invoice the bill the customer receives listing the goods purchased and their prices

purchase order sometimes called order forms, these documents give the details of the service or product the customer wants to buy

receipt any document which proves that money has been paid, e.g. a till roll, cheque counterfoil, bank statement

sales invoice the bill the supplier sends listing the goods supplied and their prices

spreadsheet computer software used for performing calculations

standing order prearranged payment from the customer's bank account to the supplier's bank account for the same amount of money on the same date every month

statement of account a printed statement listing purchases, payments and credits

SWIFT (Society of Worldwide Interbank Telecommunications) computerised system used to transfer money and messages between accounts in different countries

trade discount sometimes offered by the seller to the purchaser to encourage the purchaser to place a large order or to buy regularly

turnover figures all of the income generated by a business. This includes core business (such as sales of a product), plus any other service(s) the business might provide as a means of generating income

Index

accounts 167
accounts departments 166
Acts of Parliament 70, 98
administration 147–95
administration function 60
advertising
  consumer targets 104–5
  objectives 106
  point-of-sale 113
  promotion function 112–16
Advertising Standards Authority (ASA) 119, 120
advice notes 153
Advisory, Conciliation and Arbitration Service (ACAS) 69, 98
age
  consumer demand factor 106
  consumers 103
alphabetical filing systems 181–2
annual accounts 161, 167, 194
annual percentage rate (APR) 157, 194
APR *see* annual percentage rate
archive files 181, 194
assets 168, 194
authorised cheque signatories 159, 194

BACS *see* bureau automated clearing system
balance sheets 167, 168, 194
bank sort code 156, 194
board of directors 52, 55
budgets 161, 169–71, 194
bulk delivery 184, 186
bureau automated clearing system (BACS) 157, 194
business documents 175–88
business environment 18–20, 21–34
business links 18–20
business organisations 146
  business environment 18–27
  customer-led 138–9
  employment 35–46
  industrial sectors 6–11
  job roles 79–85
  markets 28–32
  mission statement 5
  ownership, types of 11–17
  people in 51–98
  products 33–4
  promotion, purpose of 116–19
  purposes 3–5
  small businesses 5–6
  structures and functions 52–65

capital goods 49
career opportunities 40
careers 91–4
cash discounts 164, 194
CB Security case study 13
change and structure 64–5
Chantel Cooke case study 38–9
charge cards 155
charities 5
cheque counterfoils 156, 194
cheque guarantee cards 194
cheques 155–6
cinema 112
closed shops 69, 98
co-operatives 15, 49
comlaints 131, 132–3
commercial radio 112
commercial television 112
common law 71, 98
communications 126–9
  non-verbal 128
  oral 127–9
  telephones 128–9
  written 129
community work 90
competitions 113
competitive environment 26, 64
computer databases 172, 183–4
computer (IT) services 61, 171–4, 175–6, 183–4
computerised filing systems 183–4
conditions of employment 76–8
consumables 49
consumer law 133–5
consumer market 30–1, 33
consumer protection 131–4
consumers 146
  characteristics 102–6
  demand trends 106–10
  importance 101–10
  supply needs 102
contract work 63, 64
contracts 98
  employment 76–7
core workers 49
costs, delivery 186
crashes 183, 194
credit cards 155, 156, 194
credit notes 154, 163, 194
customer services 61–2, 125–36
  communication 126–9
  improving 137–42
customers 62–3, 64, 146
  care of 126
  communications with 126–9
  expectations 64
  importance 101–10
  market research 108–9
  needs 125–6
  protection 131–4
  satisfaction 139–42
  types 130–1

databases 172, 183–4, 194
Datapost 186
debit cards 155, 156, 194
delegates 98
delivery 184–6
delivery notes 154, 194
demand 146
  consumer confidence 107
  consumer trends 106–10
demand satisfaction 32
demography, consumers 103
departments 58–63
development areas 23
direct debits 157, 194
direct marketing 114–15
direct response advertising 114, 146
directors 80, 98
Disabled Persons (Employment) Acts (1944 and 1958) 74
disagreements 67–70
disciplinary procedure 67–8, 98
discounts 164
discrimination 74–6, 98
distribution 60–1
drawings 194
durable goods 49

e-mail 185, 194
economies of scale 49
EDI *see* electronic data interchange
EFTPOS *see* electronic funds transfer at point of sale
electronic data interchange (EDI) 155, 157, 194
electronic funds transfer at point of sale (EFTPOS) 156, 157
electronic mail 185, 194
employees
  health and safety 73
  rights and responsibilities 66–78
employers, rights and responsibilities 66–78
employment 35–46, 49
  career choice 91–4
  consumer categories 103
  contracts of 76–7
  financial rewards 38–9
  legislation 70–8
  opportunities of 88–90
  patterns of 36–7, 43–6
  regional differences 42–4
  terms and conditions 76–8
  types 35–6, 86–8
  UK 35–44
Employment Acts (1980, 1982, 1990) 70
employment package 38–41
equal opportunities 74–6, 98
Equal Pay Acts (1970 and 1983) 74
essential services 4
ethical environment 27, 49
Europe, employment patterns 44–6
European Union 70–2
executive directors 80, 98
expenditure 169–70
external accounts 167

Factories Act (1961) 72
family businesses 87
fax (facsimile) communications 129, 185, 194
filing systems 180–4
finance 147–95
finance departments 59
financial, promotion planning 122
financial transactions 149–50, 194
  completing documents 161–74
  monitoring information 168–73
  purchases 150–3
  records of 149–50
  sales 153–4
fixed costs 171
flat structures 56, 82
flexitime 40, 49, 63, 64
flow production 49
form letters 177–8, 194
four Ps 111
franchises 15–16, 49, 87, 98
full-time employment 35, 88–9
functional managers 57
functions 52–3, 58–63, 85, 98

gender
  consumer demand factor 106
  consumers 103
glossaries
  business organisations 49
  consumers and customers 146
  financial/administrative 194–5
  people in business 98
goods 102, 146
goods received notes 151–2, 194
government assistance
  employment 44–5
  location of businesses 23–4
government market 30, 31
grievance procedure 67, 98
Gross Domestic Product (GDP) 9, 10, 49

hand-written receipts 166
HASAW *see* Health and Safety at Work Act
health and safety 131–2
Health and Safety at Work Act (1974) (HASAW) 72–3
health and safety policies 73–4
helping others purpose 5
hierarchies 54–6, 98
hire purchase 155, 156–7
homeworking 63, 64
hours of work 39–40
house style 175

image purpose 116
incorporated businesses 14, 49
industrial action 69
industrial market 6, 31
industrial sectors 6–11
industrial tribunals 68, 98
information
  careers 91–2
  consumer demand 107
  customer needs 125–6
  customer trends 108–9
  financial 168–73
information flow 55
information technology (IT) 61, 171–4, 175–6, 183–4
internal accounts 167
invitations 178
invoices 152–3, 154, 163, 165
inward transactions 150, 194

JCT Ltd case study 25
job market 88–90
job production 49
job roles 79–85
job security 40
job sharing 63, 64
jobs, *see also* employment
junior managers 83

Leather World case study 5–6
legal environment 26–7
legislation, workplace 70–8
letterheads 175
letters 176–7
liabilities 168, 194
lifestyle
  consumer demand factor 106
  consumers 103, 105
limited company 14, 49
listener profile 146
Livewire 88
local authority undertakings 11, 17
local business environment 19–20
local businesses 53
local environment 27
location of businesses 21–5
logistics 60–1
Lucozade case study 116

magazines 112–13
mailing lists 114
management structures 52–7

managers 80–1, 83, 98
managing director 98
market 146
market research 146
  customer monitoring 140–1
  customers 108–9
market share 4, 29–30, 49
marketing 32, 49, 59–60, 146
  promotion objectives 111
markets and products 28–34, 49
matrix structure 57, 98
medium, promotion 118
memoranda 178, 194
memos 178, 194
merit goods 49
message, promotions 118
messages 177
microfiche 183, 194
microfilm 183, 194
middle managers 83
mission statement 5, 49
monitoring 161, 168–9, 194
motivation 66–7
multinational businesses 53

national businesses 53
National Insurance contributions 77
nationalised industries 11, 17
natural environment 27
needs 125–6, 146
newspapers 112–13
non-paid work 90
non-profit making organisations 5
notices 178
numerical filing systems 182, 194

objectives 49
  marketing 111
Offices Shops and Railway Premises Act (1963) 72
operatives 81
opportunities, employment 88–90
oral communications 127–9
organisation charts 52–7, 98
organisations 52–65
  departments 58–63
  hierarchical structures 55–6
  matrix structure 57
outward transactions 150, 194
ownership 11–17

paper filing systems 181
part-time employment 35, 63, 89
partnerships 11, 12–13, 49, 87, 98
Pay-As-You-Earn (PAYE) 77, 98
payment documents 165
payment methods 155–8
payslips 165
performance-related pay 98
peripheral workers 49
permanent employment 35–6
personal qualities 93
personnel
  departments 58–9
  rights 66–78
  roles 79–85
petty cash 151, 195
petty cash vouchers 158, 165, 195
planning, promotional materials 120–2
point-of-sale advertising 113
policies 73–4, 75
presentation 175–6
press release 146
primary sector 6, 7–8, 49
Prince's Youth Business Trust 88, 91–2
printed receipts 166
private sector 11–17, 49
product life cycle (PLC) 33–4, 49
production 59, 81
production operatives 81
productivity payments 98
products 146
  categories 28–9
  consumer characteristics 103–6
  marketing activities 32
  new products 33–4
profit 49
  business purpose 3
profit and loss account 167, 195
project managers 57
promotion 146
  constraints 119–20
  cost factor 117
  elements 118–19
  integration of methods 116–17
  legislation on 119–20
  types 112–16
promotional materials 111–24
  evaluating 122–3
  planning 120–2
  purpose 116–19
prompt payment discount 164, 195
proprietors 98

protection of customers 131–3
public corporations 11, 17, 49
public library case study 101
public limited company (plc) 14–15
public relations 115, 146
public sector 11, 17–18, 49
public sector businesses 17–18
public services 49
purchase documents 150–3, 161–3
purchase invoices 152–3, 163, 195
purchase orders 148, 151, 153, 162, 195
purchases 150–1
purchasing department 61
pyramid structures 55–6, 82

quality assurance 64–5

Race Relations Act (1976) 74
receipt documents 165
receipts 157–8, 166, 195
records 149–50, 166
  security 159
Red Star delivery 186
refunds 126
regional policy 49
Registrar of Companies 14
replacements 126
research and development 59
responsibilities
  people in business 66–78
  tasks 79, 85
rewards, employees 66–7
rights, people in business 66–78
Roddick, Anita 15
roles, workplace 79–85
Royal Mail Electronic Post 186
Royal Mail Special Delivery 185
Running Free case study 19

safety at work 40, 71–4
sales
  codes of practice 119
  documents 153–4, 161, 163, 164
  invoices 154, 163, 164, 195
  performance monitoring 139
  promotions support 113
  transactions 149, 153–4

sales and marketing 59–60
sales revenue 49
Savoy Videos case study 107
secondary sector 6, 8–9, 49
security 159, 185–6
self-employment 36, 86–8
sending business documents 184–6
senior managers 83
services 102, 146
services assistance 49
Sex Discrimination Acts (1975 and 1986) 74
shift work 40, 63
skills identification 79, 85, 92–3
small businesses 5–6
small organisations 53–4
social costs 49
social environment 27
Society of Worldwide Interbank Telecommunications (SWIFT) 157, 195
sole traders 11–12, 49, 53–4, 98
span of control 98
sponsorship 115, 146
spreadsheets 172–3, 195
staff
  levels of 82–3
  roles 79–85
standing orders 157, 195
state-owned businesses 17–18
statement of account 154, 158, 166, 195
statute law 71, 98
strengths and weaknesses 92–4
strikes 69
structures, organisational 52–65, 64–5, 98
subject filing systems 183
supervisors 81, 98
suppliers 62–3
support staff 81
SWIFT *see* Society of Worldwide Interbank Telecommunications

targets, promotional 116
tasks, responsibilities 79, 85
team members 81
teamwork 64, 83–4
technology, consumer demand factor 106
technology advances 64
TECs *see* Training and Enterprise Councils
telephones 128–9
temporary employment 36
terms of employment 76–8
tertiary sector 9–11, 49
trade discount 164, 195
Trade Union Act (1984) 70
trade union membership 68–70
training 40–1
Training and Enterprise Councils (TECs) 49, 88–9, 91
travel to work 39
trends 146
turnover figures 149, 195

UK employment 35–44
unemployment rates 43
unlimited liability 12, 49
unsocial hours 40
urgency, business documents 184–5

value added tax (VAT) 161–2, 164
value of market 29
VAT *see* value added tax
VDU equipment 72
voluntary work 90

wants 146
wealth status 103
word processors 175–6
working conditions 38
working patterns 63
workplace legislation 70–8
written communications 129

Acknowledgements

We are grateful to the following for permission to reproduce copyright material:

Unit 1: Business Link magazines for an extract from the article 'The Team that Can' from *Business Link* magazine, June 1992; Central Statistical Office for the Controller of Her Majesty's Stationery Office for extracts from Tables 4.12, 4.19 & 4.21 from *Social Trends* 1994; Neilson for data from a table which appeared in *Financial Times*, 19.1.95

Unit 2: Central Statistical Office for the Controller of Her Majesty's Stationery Office for a table from *Social Trends* 24, 1994; Guardian Newspapers Ltd for an extract from an article in *The Guardian* © 21.1.95; LiveWIRE for an extract from *The Link* newspaper, Summer 1994[1].

[1]The extract is from an article in *The Link* newspaper for the youth enterprise network, Summer 1994 issue. *The Link* is published by LiveWIRE, the national scheme to help young people start up and develop their own businesses, supported by Shell UK Limited.

Unit 3: Economist Newspapers Ltd for the Table 'Multimediators' in *The Economist* 17.9.94, © The Economist

We are grateful to the following for permission to reproduce photos and other illustrative copyright material:
Mercury Communications and British Telecommunications Plc, page 4; Leslie Garland Picture Library, page 7; Ace Photo Agency (Gabe Palmer), page 8; Allen and Harris, page 9; David Hoffman, page 11; J. Allen Cash Photolibrary, page 16; Department of Trade and Industry, page 23; Trevor Clifford, page 33. Leo Cullum, page 51; Robert Harding Picture Library (Adam Woolfitt), page 54; Tony Stone Worldwide (Tim Brown), page 61; Popperfoto/Reuter, page 70; The Telegraph Colour Library, page 72; Sally and Richard Greenhill, page 74; Impact Photos, page 75; Royal Mail, page 76; Photofusion (Sarah Wyld) and John Birdsall, page 84; Prince's Youth Trust, page 88; The Telegraph Colour Library (L Lawry), Trevor Clifford, *The Nursing Times*, *The Bookseller* and *The Caterer and Hotelkeeper*, page 91.
We are unable to trace the copyright holders of 'Love conquered fear', page 86 and would be grateful for any information that would enable us to do so. Life File, page 102; Robert Harding Picture Library (Gary White), page 103; The Controller of HMSO and the Central Statistical Office, page 108; Trevor Clifford, page 113; Eye Ubiquitous (Sean Aidan), page 115; Encyclopaedia Brittanica International Ltd, pages 113 & 117; Homepride, page 116; Barclaycard, page 118; The Advertising Standards Authority Ltd, page 119; British Telecommunications Plc, page 129; Tesco, page 138; McDonald's page 141; Banking Information Service, pages 155 & 166; Anglian Water, Mercury Communications, MFI, page 175; Trevor Clifford, pages 181 & 182; Parcelforce, Red Star (British Rail); page 186.

Introduction to GNVQ: Advanced
Business: Advanced Level
Business in the economy
GNVQ
Financial forecasting and monitoring

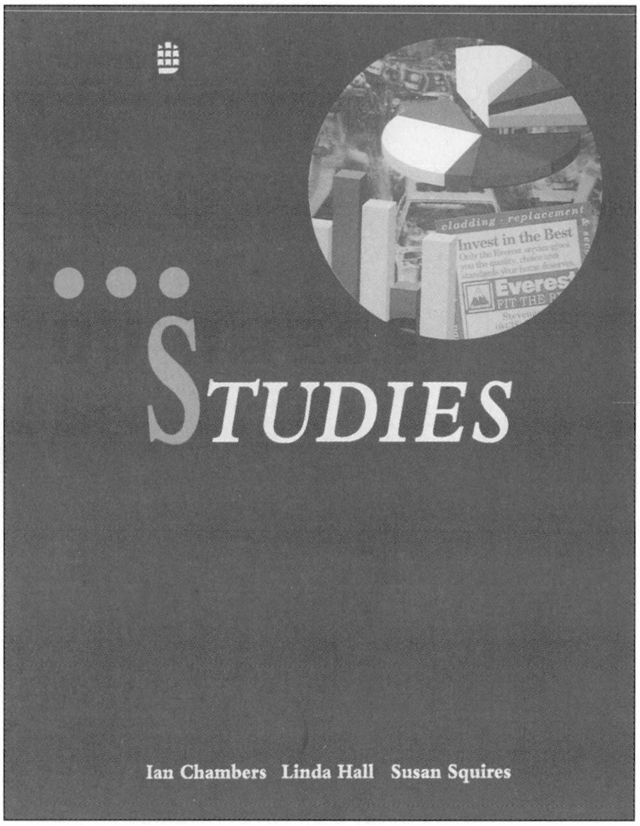

Business Studies contains a wide variety of activities which give students opportunities to check their understanding, interpret data and practise their IT skills. Case studies and questions at the end of each theme, and a glossary of terms at the end of each unit help students to make effective use of business terminology and concepts.

This lively and accessible full colour text is clearly structured and is ideal for GCSE Business Studies or used to support Intermediate GNVQ Business.

Students Book	0 582 24483 8
Teacher's Guide	0 582 24482 XA

For more information ring the Longman Customer Information Centre on 01279 633921